BOUNDARY LAB

ADVANCE PRAISE FOR THE BOOK

'With every passing year, competitive sport looms larger in the economy and popular culture of India and the world. Inevitably, sportswriting is flourishing too, with a steady stream of books celebrating great players, famous teams and thrilling contests. Yet, for all their material and symbolic significance in the life of humans, the institutions that regulate competitive sport have largely escaped the critical attention of writers and scholars. This lacuna is comprehensively filled by Nandan Kamath's superb new book. Using an array of examples from across different sporting domains, he examines such vitally important subjects as conflict of interest, the structure of sport governing bodies, the galloping rise of sponsorship and commercialization, the role of the law and the significance of the state. Kamath engages the reader with his crisp prose, using his carefully chosen case studies to illustrate themes of wider social and economic importance. His book is wholly original in conception and impressively thorough in its execution. It deserves, and shall surely command, a wide and enduring readership'—Ramachandra Guha, historian and writer

'Multilayered, articulate, objective, affectionate, a deeply thoughtful book about sport and its many engagements with society and life that have never been so thoroughly examined'—Sharda Ugra, sportswriter

'*Boundary Lab* takes you on an enlightening journey that will forever change the way you look at competitive sport. If, like me, you are curious about the intricate and multifaceted world of Indian sports, this book is a great read'—Rahul Dravid, former Indian cricket team captain and national coach

'Every chapter in *Boundary Lab* starts with an intriguing question, and in getting to the bottom of that issue, takes you on a journey through one specific facet of the unique and distinctive world of Indian sport. From betting in sport to the power of national sports federations, each chapter is carefully detailed and thought-provoking. This is an important book, one that anyone with an interest in Indian sport should read'—Joy Bhattacharjya, sports administrator and analyst

BOUNDARY LAB

Inside the Global Experiment Called Sport

NANDAN KAMATH

PENGUIN
VIKING
An imprint of Penguin Random House

VIKING

USA | Canada | UK | Ireland | Australia
New Zealand | India | South Africa | China | Singapore

Viking is part of the Penguin Random House group of companies
whose addresses can be found at global.penguinrandomhouse.com

Published by Penguin Random House India Pvt. Ltd
4th Floor, Capital Tower 1, MG Road,
Gurugram 122 002, Haryana, India

First published in Viking by Penguin Random House India 2024

Illustrations by Kruthika N.S.
Research support from R. Seshank Shekar and Shubham Jain

10 9 8 7 6 5 4 3 2 1

The views and opinions expressed in this book are the author's own and the facts are as reported by him which have been verified to the extent possible, and the publishers are not in any way liable for the same.

ISBN 9780670097951

Typeset in Goudy Old Style by MAP Systems, Bengaluru, India
Printed at Replika Press Pvt. Ltd, India

www.penguin.co.in

To my parents, coaches and teachers.
You're all responsible for the errors in this book.

Contents

List of Abbreviations and Glossary

AFI:	Athletics Federation of India
AICF:	All India Chess Federation
AIFF:	All India Football Federation
ASCI Code:	Advertising Standards Council of India Code for Self-Regulation of Advertising Content in India
BCCI:	Board of Control for Cricket in India
BRICS:	Brazil, Russia, India, China and South Africa
CAS:	Court of Arbitration for Sport
CBA:	Collective Bargaining Agreement
CBI:	Central Bureau of Investigation
CCI:	Competition Commission of India
CEO:	Chief Executive Officer
CoA:	Committee of Administrators
Code:	World Anti-Doping Code
COMPAT:	Competition Appellate Tribunal
Contract Act:	Indian Contract Act, 1872
CSR:	Corporate Social Responsibility
ECtHR:	European Court of Human Rights
EU:	European Union
FIA:	Fédération Internationale de l'Automobile
FIDE:	Fédération Internationale des Échecs
FIFA:	Fédération Internationale de Football Association

FINA:	Fédération Internationale de Natation (now World Aquatics)
FIH:	Fédération Internationale de Hockey
GAISF:	General Association of International Sports Federations
Gambling Act:	Public Gambling Act, 1867
GDPR:	General Data Protection Regulation
IAAF:	International Amateur Athletic Federation (now World Athletics)
ICA:	Indian Cricketers' Association
ICAS:	International Council of Arbitration for Sport
ICC:	International Cricket Council
ICL:	Indian Cricket League
IOA:	Indian Olympic Association
IOC:	International Olympic Committee
IPC:	Indian Penal Code, 1860
IPL:	Indian Premier League
Lodha Committee:	Justice R.M. Lodha Committee
MCOCA:	Maharashtra Control of Organised Crime Act, 1999
MLB:	Major League Baseball
NADA:	National Anti Doping Agency
NBA:	National Basketball Association
NCAA:	National Collegiate Athletic Association
NFL:	National Football League
NFT:	Non-Fungible Token
NOC:	National Olympic Committee
NSF:	National Sports Federation
PCR:	Polymerase Chain Reaction
PGA:	Professional Golfers' Association of America

PPP:	Public-Private Partnership
Rs:	Indian Rupees
RTI Act:	Right to Information Act, 2005
SGB:	Sport Governing Body
SJN:	Social Justice and Nation Building
Sports Code:	National Sports Development Code of India, 2011
Sports Ministry:	Ministry of Youth Affairs and Sports, Government of India
Supreme Court:	The Hon'ble Supreme Court of India
TNCA:	Tamil Nadu Cricket Association
TRAI:	Telecom Regulatory Authority of India
UCI:	Union Cycliste Internationale
UEFA:	Union of European Football Associations
UK:	United Kingdom
US:	United States of America
USOPC:	United States Olympic & Paralympic Committee
WADA:	World Anti-Doping Agency
WSH:	World Series Hockey

Before the Toss

'*Cometh the hour, Kamath the man!*' read the headline in the University of Oxford's student newspaper. Despite a bad back and a torn hamstring, I had led my college cricket team to a famous win. As a national-level junior cricketer back home in India, I had grown accustomed to seeing my name in print—but this headline was an unexpected turning point.

My pride at snagging a sports page mention was overshadowed by envy. *How had I not thought of that line before?* Scoring puns had overtaken scoring runs as a measure of my self-worth. I knew my time as an aspiring professional athlete was up. Perhaps I was meant to be a man of letters instead?

My sporting dreams had seen better times.

The long summer school breaks were carefree days when bats, balls and racquets took over from textbooks and the boundaries of cramped spaces were stretched by a little boy's imagination. For endless hours, I role-played my way through Wimbledon, the Olympic Games and 'World Cups' in cricket, football and hockey. I have been Stefan Edberg. Carl Lewis. Sunil Gavaskar. Diego Maradona. Floris Jan Bovelander. Sometimes, I have been all of them on the same day.

Sport brought the universe into my backyard. I was bitten early by the sports bug, and I have never recovered.

I have no memory of the first time I played sport—it's a bit like my birth. But I do know that at some point I was hooked, and that my life has never been the same again. It took me on a journey of examination, exploration and experimentation until the thrill of competition took over. A starting position on the school hockey and cricket teams was a daydream come true. The visceral emotions of my first competitive match are still etched vividly in my memory. It was a moment of 'ignition'.

I spent hours in front of the mirror trying to perfect my technique. Every patch of open space was an invitation to practise a full bowling run-up. An outsize poster of a beaming Kapil Dev loomed over me as I fell asleep each night, still holding my cricket bat.

My schoolteachers remember me as the boy with his eyes not on the blackboard but on the playfield visible from the classroom window. Class notes were copied on weekends, homework assignments were completed in the autorickshaw on the way home from sports practice. Exam preparations were a bit like the last two overs of an IPL match—whatever the result, a close finish was more or less guaranteed. I did well on the inter-school cricket circuit and went on to captain the junior state cricket side. These experiences enveloped—and defined—my teenage years.

In retrospect, I had heroes whom I wanted to emulate, but sport was mainly about evolving *my* relationship with *myself*.

Who am I? What am I capable of?

Sport helped me navigate this big, bewildering world I was expected to make sense of. Can I do that again? Exploring meant extending. Why didn't it work? Extending meant failure. Failure meant exploring again. For a young introvert, sport was a solution to boredom and loneliness, a balm to hurt, an avenue for new experiences and a source of invaluable friendships.

Those who play sport know this: it always has something for you, a little gift around every corner. A newspaper mention here, a thoughtful compliment from a senior coach there. The feeling of leather hitting the willow's sweet spot, the sound of a penalty corner shot clattering into the goal boards. And we know this too: that the more sport gives, the more it teases and tantalizes with the promise of even more to come, until the seductive high of achievement begins to trump the simple joy of giving the ball an almighty thump.

And then one day you face the reckoning; you realize that the Peter Pan years have to end.

Difficult choices confronted me. Throughout school—and despite all the sport—I had excelled academically. Indian sport was underdeveloped, with meaningful careers in sport a rarity unless you were a Sachin Tendulkar, which—unfortunately for everyone, but most of all for me—I wasn't. Other life choices began competing with the chance to progress in sport. At my law school interview, I was told I would have to leave my sporting aspirations behind if I wanted to make it through the five-year course, let alone succeed in the profession.

Giving up something I loved was a strangely empowering experience. I enjoyed reading about the rule of law and the role of law, and threw myself into my studies. New doors opened, bringing me academic opportunities that had, once, seemed even more unlikely than my sporting dreams.

My cupboard was now full of black suits. The cricket whites were not discarded, but they had to be mothballed. The mirror I had shadow-practised in front of was now used to ensure that my ties were knotted just right.

But sport—once it is in your blood—can surprise you in unexpected ways. I started my career as a technology and corporate lawyer in faraway California, but life came full circle to bring me back to Indian sport.

Having cut my teeth in the legal profession in Silicon Valley, I felt the urge to return home to Bangalore and engage entrepreneurially with Indian sport. Living in the US, I had seen what a professional sports ecosystem looked and felt like. I found it difficult to accept that we couldn't do better in India. At the time, Indian sport was steeped in cynicism and a systemic lack of self-belief. Along with a couple of friends, I established the organization that evolved into the GoSports Foundation, to support the journeys of Indian athletes, to create champions—even role models—from among us. This gave me a vantage point to observe the athlete journey at close quarters. The ecosystem in which Indian athletes develop has evolved significantly and GoSports Foundation has played its part.

I also found myself answering a steady stream of legal questions from friends and former teammates. When the IPL launched in 2008, I was in the right place at the right time as Indian sport began to professionalize. Over the years, I have had a chance to work with athletes, governing bodies, franchise teams, businesses and governments. I also helped establish the Sports and Society Accelerator, a non-profit with a mission to universalize sports and physical activity in India.

All this has kept me engaged and even excited, but there have been moments of reckoning and introspection. Are my contributions meaningful? Why have I given sports an oversized role in my life? These became critical personal questions. The search for answers has led to my own evolution, from being a sports enthusiast to sports explorer, and then on to sports evangelist.

The second-century Roman poet Juvenal referred to sport as the second part of the 'bread and circuses' ploy that governments use to satiate their people and divert their attention from the other goings-on of the day. Similarly, numerous Marxist scholars have compared sport to religion, calling it an 'opiate of the masses' that distracts the working class from the real economic issues that affect their lives.

George Orwell suggested that serious sport has nothing to do with fair play. 'It is bound up with hatred, jealousy, boastfulness, disregard for all rules and sadistic pleasure in witnessing violence: in other words, it is war minus the shooting,' he famously wrote. And C.L.R. James, commenting on sport's place in the larger social and cultural context, asked, 'What do they know of cricket who only cricket know?' Sport has also been characterized as a set of meaningless challenges and goals, pursued for their own sake, with no intrinsic purpose.

While it remains valid and important to question the role of sport in these ways, my experiences have provoked a different type of inquiry. What does sport contribute to our world and to our understanding of it? How do we give it the best chance to play this role? I found myself occupied—often, even consumed—with such questions; this book is written as an outcome of that inquiry, and it is designed to provoke more of these conversations.

Sport has helped me understand myself better, build an identity and find direction when I faced ambiguity. It has changed the way I engage with others. The central question I asked myself while planning this book is, does sport also have the power to do all of this for society at large?

A polarized world provides opportunities to both divide and unite, to 'otherize' and to empathize; it allows for acts of extreme selfishness and for abundant generosity. What role does sport have here?

As I thought more about it, I began to make connections between different aspects of my work. Patterns began to emerge in my mind. This led me to bring together my understanding of legal concepts, my knowledge of Indian sport and interesting case studies in this book.

Sport helps us explore the many mysteries of being human. It feeds our quest to experiment, understand and find meaning.

It tends to confront the most challenging social and political issues well before these pop up in our societies. It calls upon us to find universal answers and commonality in ways few other pursuits do.

In the galis, on the maidans, in boardrooms, legislatures and law courts, in the great arenas of the world or in our homes—wherever we find ourselves, we can all get behind this power of sport. For that, we must understand what it does for us, the rules we must play by, those we must break, and the unique gifts that lie beyond these boundaries.

Chapter 1

On Meaning

Is Mr India a sportsperson or a contestant in a beauty pageant?

Bodybuilder Amit Chaudhary had been crowned 'Mr India'—and he was distraught.

The Uttar Pradesh state government had opened up recruitment for the post of sub-inspector in the police force and had reserved 2 per cent of the openings for those who had excelled in sports. Chaudhary applied under this quota and was rejected on the grounds that bodybuilding was not a 'sport' and, therefore, he was technically not a 'sportsman'.

He petitioned the police department first and then the Governor of Uttar Pradesh. The Bodybuilders Association also protested, arguing that the government's stance would bring down the morale of their members and mar their prospects. None of these efforts bore fruit.

For context, keep in mind that professional bodybuilders eat about six meals a day. Their high protein diet involves a daily intake of at least half a dozen eggs, half a kilogram or more of chicken, multiple shakes, supplements and more. They target gym work to achieve specific goals based on what will be assessed in competition. This diet and training regimen makes bodybuilding an expensive pursuit. In competition, judges evaluate the contestant's symmetry and muscularity across a number of poses and postures.

A police job for Amit Chaudhary would give him a secure livelihood. As a last resort, he approached the Allahabad High Court to claim eligibility for the post. The State maintained that bodybuilding was not a sport. Participants came on stage 'as a show piece flexing and moving their muscles all over the body, particularly the thighs, stomach, chest and biceps', the State said. Any person could exhibit his body, and while the show may receive admiration, it 'cannot be a source of enjoyment or entertainment', the State countered.[1]

In summary, its stance was that the title of Mr India was akin to a female in a beauty contest winning the 'Miss India' or 'Miss Universe' crown. Such contests required no coordination, agility or body control and lacked clear judging standards, the State suggested.

Questions remain: Is this a sport or a beauty pageant for men? Who decides? Which standards do they use to arrive at a decision? At stake is a job and a secure future for Mr India and the self-worth of the community of bodybuilders he represents.

Body of evidence

At some point in its past, every sport was just an activity or a pastime. A few pioneers found or created implements and experimented with them. The way these people interacted with their own bodies, with their implements and with others perhaps amused them, challenged them or simply brought them together.

Then word spreads and more people want to test their prowess against the original creators. Sometimes, it ends there; at other times, such activities catch the fancy of gradually growing groups of people. As participants increase, various individuals experiment, and these experiments expand the possibilities. Sometimes, individuals and groups pull in different directions, modifying the original activity to suit their own needs.

Once the participant base attains critical mass, a set of common rules and metrics are formulated in order for competitions to be possible, for comparisons to be made. A tipping point is reached when interest grows and participation scales. There is now social acceptance, leading to shared purpose and meaning in the activity. From then on, the status of a sport and its future are more or less self-sustaining.

A good example of this evolution is Pickleball, a sport that evolved from combining aspects of a few other sports.[2] Pickleball is currently one of the world's fastest-growing sports. It is not of recent vintage. One weekend in 1965, a United States (US) Congressman returned to his home near Seattle after a round of golf with his businessman friend. The two of them found their families sitting around, bored and at a loose end. The grounds had a badminton court but lacked a full set of badminton rackets. The friends improvised, playing instead with table tennis paddles and a perforated plastic ball.

At first, the net was at the badminton height of 60 inches and they only volleyed the ball over the net. Once they found that the ball bounced well on the court's asphalt surface, they lowered the net to 36 inches, adding new dimensions to the game. The following weekend, another friend came over to play and the three men made up rules and a scoring system for the game. But it was not until 1984 that an association was formed and the first rulebook was published. More than fifty years after its invention, this hybrid of badminton, table tennis and tennis has begun to explode in popularity.*

* 'Pickleball' does not involve any pickles. There are different accounts of how it got its name. The first suggests that the name is a hat-tip to the combination of different sports, reminiscent of the pickle boat in

It is instructive to deconstruct popular sports and understand their origin stories. Many sporting disciplines are an expression of military combat pursuits—fencing, archery, shooting, boxing and equestrianism come to mind. A messenger racing to carry the news of victory in war led to the emergence of the marathon. Some other sports, such as football, cricket, badminton—and Pickleball—are concoctions born out of the human impulse to create, innovate and amuse, using implements and locations that are handy.

The word 'sport' itself comes from the French word '*desporter*'—a pleasurable pastime or activity. That original meaning has evolved; while watching a movie or reading a book would fall under the definition of *desporter*, they are not considered to be sport, whereas pursuits such as running, throwing, swimming, gymnastics, football and cricket are. And somewhere in this grey area lies the answer to the question of what defines sport, and how and when an activity becomes a sport in the legal sense of the word.

Weights and measures

Three major considerations are involved in evaluating whether an activity qualifies as a sport: the type of activity, clear principles and rules, and a competitive structure. Given the role sport plays in society, these need to be unpacked and assessed to see how they make sense.

Most conventional definitions see a 'sport' as involving physical activity or exertion—but how much physical exertion is enough to qualify? After all, sport comes in many types: physical sports (such as rugby and athletics), mind sports (such as chess and bridge), motorized sports (such as Formula One

---

rowing where oarsmen were chosen from the leftovers of the other boats. The other says the sport was named after the US Congressman's dog Pickles, who would chase the ball and run away with it.

and powerboating), coordination sports (such as billiards and snooker) and animal-supported sports (such as horse racing and equestrianism).

Activities such as boxing, weightlifting and running have obvious physical components. Archery, shooting or cue sports require less physical exertion and more complex physical coordination skills. In equestrian sports, most of the physical exertion is done by the horse, with the rider's primary task being to harness and control its prowess. Chess requires just enough physical exertion to move a piece a centimetre or three at a time (as an aside, recent research suggests that the mental exertion required of chess can be so intense that players can burn up to 6000 calories a day in top-flight competition).[3]

Clearly, therefore, a sport cannot be defined purely on the metric of the physical exertion involved. Influential organizations such as the International Olympic Committee (IOC) and SportAccord—formerly known as the General Association of International Sports Federations (GAISF)—have assumed the authority to recognize 'sports' federations and determine which of them make the Olympic programme. None of these organizations has a test for the degree of physicality needed (or, for that matter, the number of calories to be burned) for an activity to qualify as a sport. But, still, physicality remains a popular condition to designate an activity as 'sport'.

A second requirement for a sport to be recognized as such is that a 'sport' has to be played according to well-defined principles and rules. These may be universal or they could have regional or local variations—for example, the sport we call 'rugby' has at least three formal variations, applicable in different parts of the world.

In formal settings, such as in regulated competition, rules may be defined and implemented by independent organizers. In an informal setting, such as in a game among friends, participants may make up, adapt, modify or relax these rules. Either way, defined rules are essential as they help participants understand the demands of the game, how to play and the metrics of success. Rules help frame any competition involving the activity and provide a skeleton for the flow of the game.

The third key metric of a 'sport' is the existence of organized competition. The underlying question is whether there is some motivation for an individual or team to demonstrate superior skill against other participants. Regular comparisons are an important aspect of demonstrating aptitude, refining technique, improving performance and thereby enhancing the sport. Recreational sports participants may, of course, have different objectives such as health, fitness, social status or amusement. Whatever the motivation, it is enabled by some form of measurement and scoring system and structured competition, either with the self or against an opponent. While not a sufficient element in itself, competition remains another necessary condition for an activity to qualify as a sport.

In addition to these three filters, the GAISF (now SportAccord) has historically required that a 'sport' should not be harmful to any living creature, that it generally should not rely on equipment provided by a single supplier, and it should not have any element of 'luck' specifically designed into it.[4]

There are many activities that require an element of physical or mental skill (e.g., circus acrobatics, crossword puzzles), have established game rules (e.g., ludo, bingo) or have a competitive element (e.g., academic examinations, singing competitions). However, none of these is conventionally considered a sport. Thus, the definition of 'sport' requires an indeterminate, yet contextual, combination of features.

To understand why a single objective test is not feasible, consider the case of competitive video gaming or esports. As with chess, learnt skills and strategy are essential to succeeding at it. Physical movements might include clicking buttons on a controller or otherwise relaying information to a computer with coordination and timing. Typically, the aim is to control the actions of virtual players or figures in a parallel digital domain. The rules are coded into the games and the level of competition is intense, having reached a point where cases of doping are increasingly common in esports.

In the current scenario, all this plays out in a finite world created by a private publisher. The parameters of this world are written in code, and the digital architecture determines what is possible and what is not. This is quite different from the physical world and the human body, the features, limits and boundaries of which our species is still exploring and understanding.

Esports has not yet been formally recognized as a sport. However, it has been designated as a medal event in the Asian Games and as a pilot event at the Commonwealth Games. Given the wide interest, esports also attracted the attention of the IOC, which launched an Olympic Virtual Series in 2021. The inaugural series attracted over 2,50,000 participants representing over 100 countries. This evolved into the Olympic Esports Week, first held in Singapore in 2023.

While all of this indicates that esports is moving towards formal recognition as a sport, it will have to first overcome concerns relating to in-game violence and abuse, the private ownership and closed structure of game platforms, integrity concerns and issues with existing governance structures.

Ultimately, what we see as 'sport' is the product of a broad, often global, social consensus that evolves—and can intensify—over time. This involves intrinsic social adoption, acceptance and systematization that cannot be forced or precisely measured. While any attempt to find an objective test or tests is likely to fail, when a combination of the three factors is present, a 'sport' is recognizable.

Gaining mass

Why does any of this matter? Why do we need to find a definition? These are not merely theoretical questions. They have social, political, economic and legal consequences. Recognition as 'sport' makes an activity eligible to be included in the framework of organized competitions. This could be across amateur and professional levels, starting from the grassroots and going all the way to professional leagues and mega sporting events such as the Olympic Games and the World Cups. And this, in turn, has repercussions–including the financial well-being of both sport and sportspersons, as the example of bodybuilder Amit Chaudhary shows.

There are hundreds of sports played around the world. Some, like Australian Rules Football and American Football, are played primarily in certain countries or regions. Others, like Association Football (popularly known as soccer), enjoy worldwide popularity.

Regardless of their recognition status, not all 'sports' make it to major events such as the Olympic Games. Formal recognition as a sport and the presence of an umbrella international federation are preconditions to being considered for inclusion by the IOC.

The IOC uses thirty-five different criteria to determine which disciplines and events make it to the Olympic Games programme for each edition of the Games.[5] Those disciplines that make the cut feature in the Olympic programme and gain prominence and global salience. Others that don't may gradually fall into disuse and face adverse economic and social consequences.

It is difficult to believe, for instance, that tug-of-war was a sport at five successive Summer Olympic Games held between 1900 and 1920. These days, it might make it to the odd birthday party or feature in a school's sports day. A century away from the Olympic Games can do that to a sport.

Squash—which is a legitimate sport by any definition, and played around the world—has only recently made it to the Olympic Games programme. It will be a medal sport for the first time at the Los Angeles 2028 Olympic Games.

Not all sports need inclusion in the Olympic Games to prosper. Cricket—with its thriving commerce—is a prominent example. It was played just once at the Olympics—in 1900 as a single match between Great Britain and a French team that, oddly, included at least eleven British nationals. Cricket's popularity and commerce have grown outside the Olympic movement. At the 2028 Olympics, cricket will join squash and three other new sports as medal events. It is debatable whether cricket will gain more from the Olympics or vice versa. This is a testament to the sport's independent stature and following.

Inclusion in the Olympic Games doesn't itself guarantee widespread popularity, participation and prosperity. The modern pentathlon comes to mind.

Despite that, many make the effort to create an international federation for their sport. International federations for mixed martial arts and cheerleading have been formally recognized. That the Indian government has made a strong push for recognition of yoga as a sport shows how much this classification means.

This is because once an activity is seen as a sport, it signals to society that it is something worth focusing on and investing in. It is a call to people and businesses to congregate around it, commit to it, and enable it to grow. Investments of time and money are made. This increases participation and exposure, and attracts talent and interest. Local events, private capital and sponsorships follow, coaching academies spring up, equipment is manufactured, kids are coached, clubs and schools field teams and nurture talent. In short, the sport grows, and the growth of this interdependent ecosystem supports the social prominence, economic viability and sustainability of the activity.

Recognition as a sport, and more so, inclusion in the Olympic Games programme, can also commandeer public resources to be invested in the sport's development and growth. Governments might also create legal and policy structures that facilitate its promotion and expansion. This could take the shape of land, government funding, subsidies, tax exemptions and eligibility for recognition as a charity.

In India, the Ministry of Youth Affairs and Sports, Government of India (Sports Ministry) recognizes national sports federations (NSFs) in disciplines that are broadly recognized as sports, making them eligible for financial grants for infrastructure, coaching and development programmes, and for hosting domestic and international competitions. This can help the sport grow across the country and at various levels. An ecosystem vital for sustainability can emerge. NSFs can also field national teams in international competitions using national names and insignia that are otherwise unavailable for private use. Similarly, private funding, investments and sponsorships will naturally be directed to recognized sports and their competitions.

Flexing it

What makes a sport endure over generations? Some sports, like athletics and archery, have lasted for centuries while others have fizzled out or disappeared altogether. How do some sports deliver value to a large number of participants, while others, like tug-of-war, are unable to sustain their social salience?

At least part of the answer lies in the fact that the skills that some sports require have inherent value. They can be useful outside sport. Running fast or far, and throwing or directing items accurately, can be useful in many different contexts to lead a more effective and efficient life. For instance, a quick-paced Supreme Court lawyer can make haste between two courtrooms and appear in multiple cases around the same time. A sprightly commuter might win the battle to alight a departing Mumbai local train. With some practice and experience, the newspaper vendor in Chennai can consistently toss the daily right into the second-floor balcony every morning. Sports present the laboratory environments in which these techniques can be worked on, perfected and then passed on for everyday use.

The long-term benefit of playing, or even watching, sport may not always be immediately apparent. Certain sports involve primary skills with no immediate or obvious social value. Think of badminton, tennis, volleyball or basketball, for instance. There is no apparent societal need for masses of people who are capable of smashing round objects across nets or dunking them into baskets. But sports such as these provide certain derivative physical—and even social—value. Playing them enhances fitness, reduces illness, teaches teamwork and discipline, improves hand-eye coordination, inculcates strategic thinking and concentration and provides a safe space to process failure and build resilience. These faculties enhance the primary skills of hitting a shuttlecock or hitting, lobbing or throwing a ball—but they also come in handy when transitioning out of amateur or even competitive sport into life outside the arena.

Besides such direct benefits, the aesthetic appeal of sport provides its own unquantifiable, but very real, benefits. Watching an artistic gymnast or a stylish batter provides pure pleasure; it pushes aside the cares of the workaday world and thus serves as a safety valve; and it creates a store of memories that can, when relived, lift the spirits. Think, for instance, of how many times you have waxed eloquent about a Sachin Tendulkar straight drive, or a Lionel Messi dribble, and the joy that reliving those moments brings you and your friends. Observing, enjoying and internalizing excellence in any realm can be uplifting, even if there is no direct correlation between one's personal aptitudes and the skills being observed.

Sports such as billiards and snooker may have fewer of these intrinsic benefits, but they—like most sports—are still fun to play and are entertaining and engaging for audiences. Many sports may seem trivial and meaningless, but they bring people together in a common pursuit. Clubs and societies are formed, people congregate, participate, follow others and interact. Fan clubs and common interest groups grow around the activity. Family bonds and friendships are strengthened around shared experiences. Parents play with their kids or take them to events. Adults volunteer as community coaches. All this feeds into a basic human desire to interact, to belong, to be part of a tribe. Sport is a gateway to this tribalism.

Sport can also be a powerful tool for secondary and extrinsic public goals, such as fitness and public health, social cohesion and transformation, perceptions about self and community, and the demonstration of local, regional, national and international prowess and pride. An active and interactive population not only leads a physically and mentally healthier life but also has a social glue that keeps it together, despite differences. The sense of achievement and confidence that participants derive from sport will inevitably spill over into the community.

All of this speaks to why a proper definition of 'sport' is important. The recognition of an activity as a sport is a form of social contract. It is an acknowledgement of its public value as a common pursuit with a known objective, and a sign of the community's willingness to support, celebrate and derive benefit from the quest, the experimentation, the exploration and the outcome.

Activity, competition and rules—the three main criteria for recognizing a 'sport'—together act as a qualitative barometer of how society views a pursuit. They provide a measure of how useful the common skill can be for all of us, whether enough people have tested it and found it meaningful to participate in, and whether there is a structure in place that encourages its adoption and growth.

These criteria look at what the activity already is. They also consider what it can potentially be, what it can offer to the individual and the collective. This social contract is an intermediate reward. While it is an endorsement, it is also an encouragement and a provocation to do more with ourselves, to explore our capabilities as a species, even sometimes to lead change in society. It does so by encouraging us to keep pushing boundaries—physical, social, political and more. Have we already seen the fastest and strongest possible male and female? How much better can humans get?

While entertainment and engagement might be obvious social expectations, we also expect sport to act as a laboratory in which we can collectively experiment and compete—to help us understand ourselves and our species.

Mind over muscle

When we met him at the start of this chapter, Mr India Amit Chaudhary was running from pillar to post trying to convince the powers that be that bodybuilding was, in fact, a sport.

He succeeded. In 1999, in *Amit Chaudhary v. State of Uttar Pradesh,*[6] the Allahabad High Court held that bodybuilding was an 'integral and inseparable part' of the sport of gymnastics, one of the sports covered in the government's recruitment advertisement.

Looking at bodybuilding's objectives closely, the court recognized it as a practice of strengthening the body, especially shaping and enlarging the muscles by exercise. It held that success in the activity can only come from the consistent endeavour to grow and develop one's body in a coordinated manner so 'the natural growth and movements of the muscles of the different parts of the body take place in a graceful sequence'. It recognized the existence of regular competitions involving bodybuilders, which spectators found 'thrilling, exciting and entertaining'.

Finding a place for bodybuilding in the genus of gymnastics, the court recognized that all gymnastics involves a form of physical conditioning, and that competitive gymnastics performances, like bodybuilding poses, are merely the display and end result of such preparation, conditioning and exercise.

The court objected to the State's attempt to equate bodybuilding to beauty contests, which it felt were held for altogether different purposes of exhibiting contestants' beauty and other talents that had nothing to do with gymnastic activity. It accepted Chaudhary's plea and held that he had a right to be considered for an interview or a trial for the post under the 'sports' quota.

The fact that a Mr India approached the court, seeking the right to apply for a police post, speaks of the challenges he and his peers face when attempting to independently sustain their careers. Chaudhary was fortunate to find a sensitive judge, who construed the letter and spirit of the police 'sports quota' openly and liberally, perhaps understanding the importance of this question to Chaudhary's, and his peers', livelihoods and sense of self-worth. Of course, you don't need to be a High Court judge to recognize that recruiting a professional bodybuilder to the police department isn't the worst idea in the world.

What this case demonstrates is that the criteria to determine whether an activity is a sport can appear ambiguous and self-referential, setting up a chicken-and-egg situation. The best way for an activity to become a sport is to find wide social consensus, and the best chance for an activity to be adopted by a large number of people is through recognition as a sport. All said and done, the broad criteria for what is 'sport' and what is not have been in place for centuries, dynamically guiding people and societies on what is worth aspiring for.

At a time when global consensus on anything is rare, sport helps us build connections, find purpose and expand our world. Clear definition or not, sport always finds its meaning.

Chapter 2

On Change

Why did Ultimate introduce referees?

With its origins in American counter-culture, Ultimate began as a sport with no referees. Played with a frisbee, this mixed-gender team sport relied entirely on the principle of the 'Spirit of the Game'. Designed with self-regulation as a core principle, it left adjudication to the players, expecting them to call their own fouls.

Can a sport work without independent adjudicators? It can, but not for everyone and not in every situation. While the norm in Ultimate remains self-refereeing, club competitions have introduced different types of quasi-referees in the form of Observers and Game Advisors.

Observers do not make active in-game calls but act as mediators when players can't achieve consensus and request a decision. Game Advisors interpret the rules and provide suggestions when requested, with players still having to take the final call. Televised professional leagues have gone a step further and employed a full-blown empowered referee model.

Is Ultimate, then, a failed experiment in self-moderation and self-regulation? Was the move to independent referees inevitable for professional competition? Let's take a shot at finding out.

Regulating in a crosswind

As human beings, our behaviour is influenced by many factors. These include the built world we live in, the laws of physics, our perceptions of rationality and self-interest, our self-image, our physical capacity and capabilities, the costs and benefits of our actions, our notions of right and wrong, and the rules we are subject to. Though we may think that we are making a decision for one specific reason, we are subliminally influenced by many of these different forces acting together—and often, we do not even realize the existence of these influences.

In the hands of those seeking to control or shape behaviour, these influences can become levers of regulation and moderation. A handy framework to understand these levers is provided by Lawrence Lessig in his seminal work on Internet regulation, *Code*.[1] In a chapter titled 'What things regulate?', Lessig writes of the forces that constrain liberty and regulate human conduct.

Lessig identifies four forces: laws, norms, markets and architecture. These act through constraints, signals and nudges, incentives and disincentives. Certain behaviours are prevented or discouraged. Others are facilitated and encouraged.

Let's say you are hungry and walking down a street full of restaurants. Which one will you choose to eat at? Your decision will be driven by a combination of the cuisine, the brand, the cost of the food, your budget, the other people eating there, your friends' recommendations, the restaurant's ratings, its décor, your state of health—one could go on.

Lessig explains that we must recognize the interplay between and among these four forces; rather than seeing them as discrete forces acting by themselves, he calls for them to be integrated into a single comprehensive account. You don't just walk into the pizzeria because you like pizza. You are influenced, constrained and nudged in many ways to make that decision, and if any one of the factors were different, you might act differently.

This framework has since been broadened as a socioeconomic theory of regulation, popularized as the 'pathetic dot theory' or the New Chicago School theory, to discuss how the lives of individuals (the pathetic dots in question) are regulated by the four forces.[2] It can help us think about sport, just as it helped Lessig think about the Internet.*

Let's look at each of the four forces in the context of sport.

A sport governing body (SGB) issues rules and regulations that specify how a sport is to be played and governed—laws, so

* There are many parallels between sport regulation and Internet regulation. Sport and the Internet institutions both claim a self-professedly autonomous and global character. They seek the right to self-govern, lest their essential value to humanity be lost. They are both embroiled in ongoing—and possibly defining—tussles with governments and State institutions that seek control over them.

to speak. There are consequences for breaching these rules, and these can be considered as constraints. A footballer deliberately taking down an attacker in the box gets a red card, and the opponents get a penalty kick. A long-jumper who oversteps the line has their jump disallowed. For sports competition to work, the rules must have sharp edges and be applied objectively, uniformly and without favour.

Equally, there is a spirit and an essence of sport that is beyond these rules, often flowing from the origins of where and how the sport was first played. The Australian Open, the French Open, Wimbledon and the US Open are the four Grand Slams of tennis. They are played on different surfaces—hardcourt, clay and grass—which means player techniques and tactics vary, too. The differences do not end here. Each has a unique sub-culture with local codes on clothing—players must wear only white at Wimbledon—and expectations from crowd behaviour—in New York, catcalls from spectators while the point is on are not uncommon.

Similarly, when Ultimate expects a player to call their own fouls, it is appealing to their conscience, which is itself rooted in cultural norms. Gaining the respect of one's peers and a reputation for fairness are elevated in the hierarchy of norms, and the fear of losing them is enhanced. Codes of ethics and industry practices establish and enforce values and principles, though the notion of the 'spirit of the sport' can go beyond these. SGBs may also reward participants for 'fair play' and 'upholding the spirit', reinforcing the importance of these. At their core, both laws and norms seek to incentivize certain behaviours and disincentivize others.

The third regulator is the market, since modern professional and globalized sport is largely driven by commerce. The nature of sports business models, market signals and nudges, and the cost and ease of access and participation can each act as constraints on decision-making and human conduct. In 2008, the Indian Premier League (IPL) was launched and fifteen years later came the Women's Premier League (WPL). The unprecedented commercial value these leagues have generated, including for male and female players, has changed cricket fundamentally, including the aspirations of players, the infrastructure available, the outlets for talent identification and development, the participation rates and even the global governance of the sport and its multiple formats.

And finally, the characteristics and features of the natural world and of the physical and virtual worlds we build (architecture) constrain and shape our capability, capacity, flexibility and interaction. These may include the realities and limitations of the human body and of technology, the shape of sports equipment and the nature of materials used in making them, the flooring of a court surface, the size of a field, the state of a cricket pitch, the weather, the range of possibilities in an esports world and so on. The enhanced quality of willow available, new technologies used to shape it into cricket bats, matches played at night when the leather ball gets wet and slippery, and smaller boundaries—together, these changes rearchitect the balance between batters and bowlers, provoking both to innovate for survival and success.

At various points in this book, we will explore each of these forces as they play out in different sporting contexts. For now, keep this framework in mind as a device to help you spot one or more of the four levers in action.

Lessig also reminds us that a change in one force might have an impact on another, and affect the regulation of the whole. There is rarely a single steady state. He explains that 'some constraints will support each other' and 'others may undermine others', with all of them being in a dynamic, interdependent balance with each other. So, he suggests, a complete view must consider the four forces together.

Followers of football will be familiar with the various styles associated with different national teams. The archetypes include the Brazilian '*jogo bonito*' samba style, the creative short passes of Spanish '*tiki-taka*', the clinical and structured play of the Germans, Dutch 'total football', the British 'long ball', and the organized '*catenaccio*' defence of the Italians.[3]

Much has been written on how each of these is a product of the particular region's geography, history, tradition, culture, values and priorities, and this is a fascinating rabbit hole to go down into. For instance, was the Italians' transition from the attacking style of the 1930s and 1940s to the 'door-bolt' defence a product of the prevailing insecurity in post-World War II Europe? Did economic recovery and growing prosperity prompt the 'total football' revolution in the 1970s?

Does the interplay among the four forces of regulation explain why Ultimate's professional leagues introduced referees? Before we find out, let's dig deeper into one of the four forces—the law.

Ruled out

Intrinsically, law is the least elegant and sophisticated of the four forces. It can be somewhat like a blunt hammer, often imposing broad curbs on freedom and liberty across the population when sharper alternatives might have been available. This leaves limited room for nuance and context.

Laws can involve principles, prohibitions and punishments, but they rarely leave space for discussion, negotiation and evolution. To a hammer, everything looks like a nail. When the law tries to intervene, some of the consequences could be those that were intended, but there could also be others that were not. For instance, if crimes against women go up, a law that prohibits employers from staffing women workers on the night shift is unlikely to solve the issue but is certain to impact women's livelihoods and rights.

Yet, the law is often the default tool regulators use to try and shepherd change. A law can be drafted, its passage can symbolize action and strong feelings can be assuaged quickly. Laws can direct, they can dissuade, and they can establish incentives and disincentives for certain types of human conduct.

Law may also act indirectly by influencing the other three forces. For instance, a law could be passed that requires every sports academy to have an accessible ramp and signage in Braille. Here, the law is impacting physical architecture with a view to making sports more inclusive.

Similarly, league rules might impose a 'cap' or upper limit on player salaries for each participating team. In this case, the law is regulating the market for talent, with a view to promoting balance among teams to keep the competition interesting. In the absence of a salary cap, think of what a team owner with deep pockets—for instance, the Mumbai Indians in Indian cricket's IPL—could do. With no financial constraints, they could assemble a large squad of the world's best players, some of whom would play while others would warm the bench, inaccessible to opponents. Such a team could become unbeatable, and this would erode the thrill and uncertainty of sport for participants and spectators alike.

Norms, markets and architecture are constantly changing, interacting with the other three forces, influencing and being influenced. This produces a constant state of multifactorial dynamism.

A delicate balance

Sport can be played for leisure and recreation or as a competitive activity in pursuit of performance and outcomes. Regardless of the motivation, sport's universality is at the heart of its purpose. It does not need translation across different nationalities, languages or cultures. It can be both the medium and the message.

Within sport, organized sport receives prime focus and attention. The core purpose of all sport, and organized sport in particular, involves the collective exploration and celebration of human capabilities. The achievement of one of us resonates with all of us. It shows us what our bodies, our species, all of us as humans, are capable of. It is no accident that the Olympic motto is *Citius, Altius, Fortius—Communiter*, i.e., Faster, Higher, Stronger—Together. Elite athletes play for themselves, their teams and their countries but also—we hope—for humanity. Their achievements give us materials for our conversations—those we have with others and also those we have with ourselves.

The public purpose and role of sport encourages governments to fund sporting activity, host public sports events and invite recreational and elite sport into the public sphere. It enables business models to be built to connect athletes to spectators, viewers and fans. These audiences want to be encouraged, inspired or simply entertained. All this creates the right incentives for athletes to pursue excellence.

Given the potential social role of sport, which principles can we use to build frameworks for it to deliver on its promise?

Economic theory classifies goods and services into private goods, public goods, club goods and common resources.[4] Private goods, such as food and petrol, can only be enjoyed to the exclusion of others. When someone consumes private goods, no one else can use them. They can also be protected from use by others with control, possession and ownership.

Public goods, such as national defence services and the air we breathe, are non-rivalrous and non-excludable. This means that one person's use does not deplete the supply or availability of the goods for everyone else. Public goods are incapable of being cordoned off. We can all use them simultaneously without needing anyone else's permission.

There are also hybrid goods, having partial characteristics of both private and public goods. Think of public parks or beaches—you cannot exclude anyone from using them but, at peak usage times, the excess demand for limited space can make them incapable of being used simultaneously by everyone who wants to.

Organized sport has the character of a hybrid good. For practical purposes, a universal competition structure requires artificial scarcity; opportunities for participation and progression must be limited and exclusionary.

At the same time, organized sport has another interesting feature—no one can be excluded from enjoying the secondary value of a sport. This includes watching it, making meaning with it, imitating players in recreational play and allowing it to serve a personal need such as entertainment, inspiration or education.

Public goods—and hybrid goods such as sport—require careful management and protection. There is an optimal way in which they can be used for social well-being. Leaving them unregulated is rarely the best option. They are naturally vulnerable to depletion and wastage. Anyone can use them without paying a personal price: the 'free rider' problem. Left unchecked, these goods can be privately stripped of their value and depleted to the extent that no one can then benefit from them. This is known as the 'tragedy of the commons'.

Sport regulation, therefore, has a challenge on its hands. It must enable exploration and excellence by creating safe spaces and protections that enable athletes to extend themselves, and incentivize achievement by rewarding success. Simultaneously, it must also reflect on sport's nature by examining whether it provides fair competition and a level playing field, while ensuring that participants act responsibly. The search for this delicate balance will come up often in this book.

Ultimately

Not only do laws, rules, institutions and tools have to live up to these standards, but they also must remain dynamic and responsive. Organized sport, as we know it today, changed massively over the course of the twentieth century, and the pace of change has only picked up in the twenty-first century.

Commercialization, professionalization, globalization, medicalization and the entry of science and technology have fundamentally altered the markets, the norms and the architecture of sport. This has changed the way sport is played, watched and engaged with, and has forced legal and policy responses.

As organized sport got commercialized, its governance had to evolve from a mere event-hosting mode to a wider role in managing a complex multistakeholder ecosystem. New participants, like media rights holders and sponsors, were invited into the system. Their expectations and demands had to be satisfied and managed.

Conflict is inevitable in such an environment, and when the commercial stakes are raised, dispute resolution takes on even greater importance.

Amateurism also gave way to professionalism. As sport went from avocation to vocation, athletes went from playing for intrinsic rewards to seeking external incentives and compensation. Driven by outcome orientation and hyper-competitiveness, new moral codes have taken shape.

All this has happened alongside major developments in medicine, science and technology, which have altered sport in many ways. Enhancements in the understanding of food science, exercise physiology and coaching techniques have paved the way for fitter, stronger and more skilled athletes. New performance-enhancing substances and methods have challenged notions of fair play. Advances in equipment, playing surfaces and stadium design have brought new dimensions to the game.

While these changes have taken place on the playing side, there has also been a tectonic shift on the consumer side of sport. Broadcast technologies have enabled sport to be watched anywhere in the world with just a phone and a data connection. Digital technologies have created virtual worlds in which sport can be played. Human data of all sorts is collected and processed at an unprecedented scale and pace. Today, a match played in one country could have a broadcaster located in a second country relaying the content to an audience in a third country with sponsors from a fourth and athletes from a fifth country.

These developments have transformed the way we live, the way we play and the way we engage with sport. Changes in the markets, in morals and in architecture are happening all the time. The law is not immune to such change. The dynamics of sport today are different from both a century ago and even a decade ago. The next ten years will likely bring even more change.

Speaking of change, let's look again at what transpired in Ultimate. American Ultimate Disc League and Major League Ultimate are two professional leagues that are televised. Many things need to fall into place for televised sport to succeed commercially. Both leagues brought in referees to make the game more appealing to spectators and fans. Why did they do this?

Self-refereeing in Ultimate was leading to stalemates and time delays while players discussed, exchanged their points of view and tried to fairly apply the rules of the game as well as the 'Spirit'. Broadcast audiences have many choices these days and can be fickle. Give them the slightest reason and they will change the channel or stream. The leagues felt it was necessary to keep the game moving and audiences continuously engaged.

Hence the advent of the independent referee, who is able to cut to the chase by issuing a decision, thus reducing the ebbs and maintaining the flow and tempo of the game. Audiences also tend to perceive referees as a source of stability, authority and consistency in the application of rules. Incidentally, the referees also took the pressure off elite players, who could focus entirely on playing rather than having to keep up with policing rules and monitoring fouls. As the commercial stakes grow, every little play and advantage matters. Despite the 'Spirit' being embedded in the culture of Ultimate, self-officiating can come under pressure when matches are competitive.

Keep in mind that Ultimate was a sport that had 'no referees' as part of its core ethic. The moral framework of the sport hasn't changed much on the ground, and this unique feature continues to attract players and audiences. Yet, its professional organizers chose to alter its core, influenced by the need to broadcast free-flowing, engaging and monetizable content for television and online streaming audiences.

We live in complex societies. Each has a unique mix of Lessig's four forces and none is in a permanently stable state. Knowing this, sport provides us with a unique opportunity. It imposes a universal set of rules on a set of commonly accepted and structured human activities. The rules and architecture are the same—or at least similar—anywhere in the world and for everyone who competes. This takes two of the four forces out of the state of dynamism, providing us with a chance to isolate and closely observe the interplay between the other two—morals and markets.

Sport often finds itself on the frontlines of many significant social and cultural battles before they emerge across our societies. Many of these are provoked by changes brought about by commercialization or the reordering of values in society. If sport is to find universal resolution to these conflicts—as it must—it has to approach the task with fairness as its sole guide. This imbues sport with the character of a sandbox and an experimental lab—politically neutral ground to test human boundaries, understand the essence of competing values and find common ground.

There is one final twist to the refereeing rules of professional Ultimate. Players can invoke an 'integrity rule' and overrule a referee's call. However, they are only allowed to do this when the overruling would go against their own team. Referees don't always get things right, and putting the moral onus back on players—who know exactly how the play went—keeps the 'Spirit' alive.

You could see a frisbee as just another 'pathetic dot'. But, carried by the prevailing winds, it reveals to us the crosswinds and counter-currents we must all navigate.

Chapter 3

On Autonomy

Why was the garbage not cleared after the IPL match?

In April 2012, the Royal Challengers Bangalore (RCB) played the Delhi Daredevils (DD) in an Indian Premier League (IPL) day-night cricket match before a capacity crowd in Bangalore.

An IPL match produces approximately 18 tonnes of garbage and waste, including water bottles, uneaten food, posters and placards. The RCB-DD game was no exception. The morning after, the M. Chinnaswamy Stadium was a mess; the Bangalore City Corporation had not cleared the mountainous piles of garbage.[1]

The Karnataka State Cricket Association, which hosted the game, was at the time led by two former national players of repute: Anil Kumble was President and Javagal Srinath was Secretary. They had made one costly error—they had refused to accede to the city corporation's demand for 450 free VIP passes for each RCB home match, instead offering them only 250 regular tickets.

Corporation officials did not take kindly to this. They promised payback—and here it was. Things got dirty.

Organizing a sports event is no simple task. It needs coordination with multiple government departments for access, permissions, licences and support. These can involve police deployments for crowd management, security cover for teams, officials and the public, or more mundane aspects like being allowed to play music at night or display advertising at the venue. Post-match garbage clearance is part of that checklist. Each such task comes wrapped in bureaucratic red tape.

The case of the uncleared garbage is emblematic of the challenges sports organizers face. It explains why our sport governing bodies (SGBs) enthusiastically welcome politicians and government officials to occupy powerful positions in their organizations. A politician has the unparalleled ability to open doors and negotiate knotty bureaucratic and administrative issues. Difficult tasks can be made easy.

Worldwide, there is a long history of sports relying on patronage, and India is no exception. Before Independence, rulers of various princely states were sport's principal benefactors. For many decades leading into the 1940s, the maharajas of Patiala, Holkar, Baroda and Nawanagar, among others, built cricket stadiums, funded teams of illustrious players on international tours and hosted matches in the country. After Independence, power shifted to democratic institutions and the royals' spheres of influence diminished. They could no longer patronize sport, and this created a vacuum. Indian sport needed new sources of support, and the politician stepped into this breach.

Through the early decades of independent India, sports remained low on the list of national priorities, and understandably so, with other critical aspects of life, livelihoods and nation-building needing resources and attention. In such an environment, politicians held the keys to scarce public funds and controlled the governmental machinery. Organizations gratefully accepted whatever funds and opportunities they could unlock; after all, it was a matter of survival.

As the Indian polity and economy developed, opportunities grew. Yet, the level of political involvement in most of India's

SGBs—and their dependence on public funds—has not diminished. Proximity to political power has become embedded in these bodies to a degree that is unique among democratic countries.[2]

What explains this? Is it inevitable? Should we be concerned? These questions deserve closer scrutiny.

Pyramid scheme

When kids play, making up the rules is half the fun. Hit the cricket ball into the unfriendly neighbour's house and you are out. The two coconut trees are the goalposts. Improvisation responds to local context and is an outlet for creativity.

Once sport moves to its more organized version, uniform rules and regulations become the norm. They apply similarly to everyone, everywhere. Neutrality becomes as important as uniformity. Rather than the participants, independent sports organizations—with no skin in the actual game—make the official rules.

Around the world, each discipline—be it football, cricket, athletics, or any other sport—is generally organized on a single, common platform of governance. This platform takes the form of a pyramid. It provides one formal, official, global structure for the sport. The pyramid involves international, regional, national, state and local governing bodies, typically set up as non-governmental non-profits.*

Each tier of the pyramid claims the exclusive authority to govern and administer the sport within its territory. This authority stems from a system of hierarchical and peer recognition. Each body is recognized by its superior body, and also by its peers at the same level of the pyramid. There is only one body at each level within any jurisdiction. Each subordinate federation becomes a member of the body immediately above it in the pyramid.

For example, in India, cricket players register with clubs and play in local leagues. These clubs are governed by the respective district associations. These associations, in turn, are governed by the respective state cricket association, which is a member of the Board of Control for Cricket in India (BCCI). The BCCI is itself a member of the International Cricket Council (ICC).

In this structure, official recognition works top-down. The ICC recognizes the BCCI as a member. The BCCI recognizes each state association. Each state association recognizes its district associations, which in turn recognize the clubs, and these clubs admit players into the fold. When playing against their national teams, the BCCI effectively recognizes Cricket Australia, Sri Lanka Cricket, etc., as peers, while itself receiving

* Private leagues like the NBA, NFL and the NHL in the US do not operate within the sports pyramid, but they do share players and many common rules with international federations and members that are part of the pyramid.

peer recognition from them. This model exists across the spectrum of organized sports.

This pyramidal structure connects players, clubs, teams and governing bodies across the world. It brings them all under the same umbrella. Everyone can then be part of the same competition and play by the same rules. Through this tiered system, the best can be identified at each level and allowed to progress to higher tiers of competition. This creates a defined pathway for athletes and teams. They can begin at the lowest rung and potentially progress through the pyramid all the way up to elite international competition.

Advancing the principle of 'solidarity' within the pyramid, the single structure also enables revenue to be distributed to all levels of the sport from top to bottom. Sponsorship and media rights revenues that international federations earn at major events like World Cups can be funnelled to national boards, from there to the state associations, then to the districts, and finally to the clubs and players. In this way, income from the sport can be reinvested into developing it from the lower tiers upward. This keeps the pyramid replenished and healthy while bringing singularity, uniformity and universality to its governance.

SGBs play important roles including enforcing rules, developing the sport, entering teams into competitions and hosting competitions. As there is only one SGB per geography at any level, they become the only seller and only buyer within their spheres of control. The degree of control SGBs wield can be significant and pervasive.

For example, the National Sports Federation (NSF) for swimming enjoys certain monopolistic powers to sanction and hold competitive national swimming events and provide swimmers with opportunities to participate. It is also a monopsony because it is the only buyer of the swimming talent produced in the region. Nobody else can form or select a national swimming team or select participants and enter them into international swimming competitions. It is also the sole purchaser of products and services to be used in official sport, and it sets the technical and other standards for these products and services. This gives it considerable economic and political power over the swimming ecosystem.

Autonomous vehicles

SGBs' powers over an entire aspect of human endeavour are not the product of an international agreement or mandate by states. They are best described as self-proclaimed and peer-recognized.

International federations claim their authority by requiring their national-level members to comply with their rules and decisions. Those members are then asked to impose these rules and decisions on their own members. The rules thus become a condition of every person's participation in organized sport. For instance, footballers everywhere in the world follow the rules and regulations issued by the Fédération Internationale de Football Association (FIFA), football's international federation.

In turn, NSFs derive their authority from the recognition of the international federation, peer recognition and the resulting recognition by national governments. Their legitimacy can also come from having a diverse and adequately representative member base, a democratic structure and regular elections. All these bodies also claim to be 'autonomous' institutions, entitled to function without undue external influence from state machinery and public authorities.

The concept of autonomy was first introduced into the Olympic Charter in 1949. Here, the International Olympic Committee (IOC) specified that its constituent-member National Olympic Committees (NOCs) should be politically and legally autonomous in relation to governments, and also in relation to economic or religious authorities. The autonomy is both horizontal and vertical, i.e., in respect of the state and public authorities, and also superior bodies in the sports pyramid.

Autonomy is asserted in the name of safeguarding sport from political, legal and commercial influence. The IOC describes it as a necessity for the Olympic and sports movement, to preserve the values of sport, the integrity of competitions, their credibility and legitimacy. It suggests that without autonomy, the primacy and uniqueness of sport cannot be protected.

Along these lines, the Olympic Charter requires states to respect the autonomy of the SGBs within their territory. Failure to do so leads to suspension or de-recognition of the SGBs by the IOC and other international bodies. This limits the ability of the country to field national teams and enter participants in the Olympic Games and other international competitions. Ultimately, this impacts all the athletes from the affected segment of the pyramid.

How much of state involvement constitutes 'undue interference' is a contested and controversial question. Most states exercise varying degrees of regulatory oversight over SGBs. Some legal systems regulate sport and oversee SGBs through their governments, tasking separate ministries or departments with the role. This is the model followed in India, where the Ministry of Youth Affairs and Sports (Sports Ministry) oversees the recognition of SGBs.

A few nations have established independent statutory bodies to regulate and oversee SGBs within their territories. For instance, the Australian Sports Commission is a statutory agency responsible for granting recognition, distributing funds and providing strategic guidance and leadership for sporting activity in Australia. Similarly, the United States Olympic and Paralympic Committee (USOPC) is a creation of the Ted Stevens

Olympic and Amateur Sports Act, which extends the reach of its provisions to the USOPC's members, the country's NSFs.

Many other jurisdictions have a laissez-faire approach, implicitly granting SGBs recognition by not objecting to their assertion and exercise of powers. They do not have statutory agencies or separate government departments or ministries, merely requiring the bodies to comply with federal, state and local laws that they encounter in the normal course.

International federations prefer to operate with as much autonomy and as little oversight as possible. Several of them, including the IOC and FIFA, are headquartered in Switzerland, which provides a legal framework that is flexible–some might argue too flexible–for their activities.

Autonomy is critical to protect sport from undue influences. However, autonomy mixed with pervasive and exclusive control can make for a heady cocktail. Power corrupts; absolute power corrupts absolutely. This begs the question: which legitimate safeguards can governments put in place to ensure that SGBs perform their functions and duties in a fair and transparent manner? Are there safeguards to protect national interest and the interests of the public?

Recycling autonomy

SGBs claim they are private bodies managing the sports pyramid under their self-styled model of 'sports democracy'. However, the effects of decisions within the pyramid are felt well beyond the walls of the pyramid. They impact potential future participants, members of the public, businesses and other stakeholders.

In the interest of neutrality, SGBs are populated by those not playing the sport. They assume the power to establish rules and organize and govern not only the bodies themselves but also wider competitions and processes. This means that rule-makers do not suffer the consequences of their decisions, while those affected by them might have no say at all.

Sports governors can schedule a match in peak summer conditions and watch it from the air-conditioned comfort of a hospitality box. If they fail to implement a concussion policy, they risk no injury. They might overprice match tickets and undersupply them to the public, but they and their families will get free passes. Seen through this lens, the need for wider accountability of these bodies, their people and their processes is evident.

Repeated corruption scandals involving sport's most prominent governors brought the pyramid structure into the global legal spotlight. Governments stopped taking the claim of autonomy at face value and started asking tougher questions, subjecting the bodies to closer scrutiny. They demanded responsibility and accountability. Sensing the threat, the Olympic movement responded by calling SGBs to demonstrate responsible 'good governance' and 'unity'[3] in a bid to effectively shield the sports movement from attempts at government control and external regulation.

The 'Basic universal principles of good governance of the Olympic and Sports Movement', first issued by the IOC in 2008, were born of these responsive discussions and efforts. Interestingly, these principles were formulated as ethical standards rather than legal requirements, as acts of self-restraint rather than obligations. All organizations within the Olympic Movement were required to accept and comply with the principles.

Transparency, responsibility and accountability were emphasized as mandatory values for Olympic constituents. They were expected to self-monitor these. In making its case for balance, the IOC suggested that national legislation must be general and should not impinge on or substitute for the ability of sports organizations to make their own rules and govern themselves. It also stated that any public funding of these bodies must not give rise to 'disproportionate obligations' that could lead to unwarranted interference or pressure.

By putting into play extensive principles of self-governance, the IOC shifted the narrative from an absolutist notion of autonomy to one that was to be accompanied by responsible actions. Under this model of responsible autonomy, while autonomy still did not have to be earned—after all, it was inherent and self-proclaimed—it was important to show that it was not being misused. Good governance became a shield but was also entrenched as an essential normative element of SGBs' conduct.

Coding Indian sport

There have been many attempts to build a governance framework for Indian sport. The first governmental guidelines for NSFs were introduced in 1975, and these were reissued in 1988, 1997 and 2001. A National Sports Policy was issued in 1984 and again in 2001, and another attempt was made at a national-level framework for sports governance and administration through the draft Comprehensive National Sports Policy 2007—which, however, was never issued.

In 2011, a couple of drafts of the National Sports Development Bill were formulated. It proposed hard coding into legislation certain standards of good governance for NSFs. The Bill was placed before the Cabinet of ministers, which included a number of people who concurrently held leadership positions in sport. The draft was rejected by the Cabinet and was then revised based on the Cabinet's feedback and concerns.

The updated version of the Bill in 2013 did not find too many takers within the government, either. Perhaps unsurprisingly, the lingering objections were not as much on the expected standards of institutional accountability as they were on the retirement age, term limits and tenure limits the Bill proposed for office bearers of NSFs.

In India, to operate as an NSF and enjoy all the powers and privileges that come with that status, an SGB must first be endorsed by the relevant international federation, admitted to membership by the Indian Olympic Association (IOA), where relevant, and also be recognized by the Sports Ministry. The standards and procedures for the Sports Ministry's recognition process—required to be undertaken annually—are laid out in a series of administrative decisions issued over four decades that were eventually compiled and published as the National Sports Development Code of India, 2011 (Sports Code).

The Sports Code recognizes NSFs as the custodians and guardians of their sport. It calls upon them to act with legal, operational and financial integrity and transparency, and provides for suspension or withdrawal of NSF status where the standards are not met.

There have been multiple attempts to revise the Sports Code to bring it in line with contemporary standards, but none of these has progressed very far. Multiple committees have been created, and reports and new draft codes submitted. These have all reached dead ends. The government even withdrew a revised draft Sports Code it had submitted to the Delhi High Court.

Without judicial intervention, even the existing Sports Code—with all its warts—wouldn't have had teeth. In the 2009 case of *Narinder Batra v. Union of India*,[4] the Delhi High Court recognized the Sports Ministry's administrative directions as a legitimate exercise of the government's authority in the absence of legislation on the topic.

In the subsequent case of *Rahul Mehra v. Union of India*,[5] the Delhi High Court ruled that—claims of autonomy notwithstanding—the Sports Ministry not only can but also must, hold NSFs to prudential norms outlined in the Sports

Code in the public interest. Yet, for more than a decade, the Sports Code has not been applied by the government in a uniform and systematic manner, leading to uneven governance (and performance) across the country's NSFs.

Despite the yawning gap between sporting potential and sporting reality in India, most attempts at bringing public accountability into sports governance have been effectively stymied by those in power. Legislative and policy reforms have been blocked. The principle of autonomy has been used as both sword and shield.

When challenged or questioned, the typical defence of an SGB is that it is a private body. Any proposed governance measure is interpreted by SGBs as government interference, a violation of their autonomy and a risk to the future of Indian sport. When under this type of pressure, it is not uncommon for an NSF to request its international federation to threaten it with de-recognition, knowing that such a measure would result in the loss of participating rights for athletes from the country. Over the years, such tactics have been used as bargaining chips with the government.

When the Sports Bill was being mooted in 2011, for instance, the Indian Olympic Association (IOA) wrote to the IOC, which then threatened 'appropriate measures' against India if the Sports Ministry proceeded with the Bill. As we saw before, the Sports Bill did not pass for various other reasons. In 2012, the IOC went ahead and suspended the IOA on grounds of failure to follow IOC guidelines and as a protective measure against government interference.[6] The IOA had followed the election guidelines of the Sports Code instead of the Olympic Charter, which the IOC classified as being a product of undue government interference.

Because of the suspension, the three Indian competitors at the 2014 Winter Olympic Games could not compete under the Indian flag. The stand-off was finally resolved when Indian government officials and the IOA reached an agreement with the IOC and the suspension was revoked.[7]

The scenario was repeated with the All India Football Federation (AIFF) in 2022, when the court-monitored reforms in the body were allegedly stalled at the urging of its incumbent president, the former central minister and parliamentarian Praful Patel.[8] By this time, Patel had overstayed the tenure limits of the Sports Code in his post. However, he remained a member of the FIFA Council. In August 2022, FIFA suspended the AIFF on grounds of undue third-party interference.[9] Among other things, India's hosting rights to the FIFA Under 17 Women's World Cup were put in jeopardy. The suspension was subsequently withdrawn thanks to the active intervention of the Indian government and the World Cup was successfully hosted later in the year.[10]

Again, the disconnects between governance failures and the sites of their consequences are stark. The adverse effects of de-recognition of NSFs or other SGBs are felt most acutely by participating athletes and teams, who are neither culpable nor have any power to remedy the situation. Indian athletes have had to play under the Olympic flag when the IOA and other NSFs were de-recognized, losing the privilege of representing their country. When FIFA derecognized the AIFF in 2022, Gokulam Kerala FC, a club team from the Indian Women's League, was disqualified from participating in the Asian Women's Club Championship 2022; having already travelled to Uzbekistan, the team was given forty-eight hours to return home.[11]

When they are pushed into a corner, NSFs use the pain of the athlete to frame an emotive appeal to the government to step back. Negotiations and the accountability-interference tug-of-war take place. This game is played ad infinitum between nominally autonomous SGBs and those who seek accountability from them, be they athletes, members of the public, the courts or—when it chooses to act—the government. During the periods of suspension of SGBs, sports governors carry on with their lives and livelihoods largely unscathed, at most a little irritated with their inability to wield power over their domains.

Of course, there are legitimate, important and enduring reasons to protect the autonomy of institutions from government capture, and particularly from the sway of the politics of popularity. However, when the governors' primary interests are their own entrenchment, the nuance between external interference and public accountability is bound to be lost.

Calling interference

Sports events garner publicity, media coverage and interest. They attract powerful figures who are eager to build a personal profile and find fame. These platforms also provide opportunities to create a positive image by demonstrating and projecting public-oriented volunteer service.

Benefits to 'honorary' office-bearers include access to events like the Olympic Games and World Cups, official international travel and hefty daily allowances. Add to all of this the ability to exercise control and discretion over the careers and lives of famous and influential athletes. The keys to the resources and decisions of the SGB are more than just the cherry on this cake. Controlling the supply of match tickets, making hiring calls and participating in lucrative commercial negotiations all present opportunities for favour-giving and, sometimes, for rent-seeking. All in all, the leadership of an SGB can be very useful, and most valuable in the hands of someone who knows how to use it for personal benefit.[12]

With all the manoeuvring behind the scenes in Indian sport, there is limited opportunity for internal accountability mechanisms to play out within SGBs. Having politically powerful people in the boardroom can dilute the willingness and ability of alternative voices to be heard, and for red flags to be raised in cases of maladministration. Structurally, these organizations dilute their already tenuous relationship with democratic representation.

When the control of theoretically autonomous institutions is in the hands of political—albeit democratically elected—representatives, public accountability has few remaining outlets. This state of play in India eats at the very core of the justifications advanced for protecting the SGBs' autonomy.

This played out most starkly in the early months of 2023 when multiple elite and emerging Indian wrestlers—including Olympic and Commonwealth Games medallists—took to the streets to protest. They felt their allegations of sexual harassment and intimidation against Brij Bhushan Sharan Singh, the President of the Wrestling Federation of India and a sitting member of Parliament from the ruling party, were not fairly and adequately addressed. The protests garnered significant public support and put the government in a tight spot. For once, a political party might have regretted having its member heading an SGB, even if that feeling was only fleeting.[13]

The principles of autonomy and accountability are often presented as being opposing forces. Let's be clear that the end goal of both is to protect and promote the public interest and fairness, not the institutions—and certainly not the people who populate them as governors. Fail to recognize this and the mechanisms meant to protect sport become virtually meaningless.

Perversely, there is little incentive for political actors to focus on the broader issues of improving the ease of living and doing business, which impact the organization of civic activities such as sports events. The resulting friction that SGBs continue to face when dealing with governmental bodies in India—as in the case of the Bangalore City Corporation and the uncleared garbage at the M. Chinnaswamy Stadium—further embeds the role of political favour and clout.

Indian sport is thus caught in a double bind of power play and regulatory capture. When public officials care more about their VIP passes than the health and sanitation needs of the city they are meant to serve, the routes out of this mess seem narrow and challenging to traverse.

Despite all this, it is amazing to see how hope springs eternal within Indian sport. That hope is precious, and the fount of that hope is all of us.

Chapter 4

On Balance

Should popular choice determine World Cup structure?

There are matchups, and then there are matchups. An Argentina v. Brazil football match, a New Zealand v. Australia tie in rugby or an India v. Pakistan encounter in cricket would be the highlight clashes of the respective World Cups.

There is background, competitiveness and context to these rivalries. The contending teams have outsized fan followings and the matches are guaranteed high TV viewership. This makes them prized events for the broadcaster that owns the media rights to the tournament. It is in the broadcaster's commercial interest that such matchups occur in the course of a tournament, and also that such games are scheduled at a time tailored to maximize viewership.

There are various factors that impact whether—and when—such a matchup will take place. These include the qualifying criteria, the grouping of teams, the progression structure, the schedule, and the location, timing and sequence of the event.

Let's say a sport governing body (SGB) receives a firm request from its official broadcaster to engineer the tournament's design to guarantee at least one match between such arch-rivals in the course of the tournament. The broadcaster may also request that such matches, wherever in the world they are held, be scheduled at prime time on a holiday or a weekend, in Latin America, Down Under or in the Indian subcontinent, respectively.

How should the SGB respond? Is all fair in love, war and tournament scheduling?

Interested and motivated

Organized sport is simultaneously a social, cultural and commercial activity. It brings a diverse set of participants into one ecosystem. Each person, group or organization comes to sport to take away something uniquely valuable to them. Most give something back to sport along the way: money, time, interest, emotion. A chart at the end of this chapter lists the various participants in the sports universe, their roles and their motivations.

Private participants are expected to act in self-interest. Those playing a public role must consider wider societal interests when they make decisions. In some cases, private persons might participate in the activities of public bodies, for example, by sitting on the board. In other cases, public functionaries might play roles in private bodies, as we have seen is the case with our SGBs in India.

Participants could have many different interests, objectives and duties at the same time. Some of these might be private in nature, and others public. They will each advocate and pursue these interests and try to exert their influence on the outcome. Roles may also overlap. A coach might simultaneously be a talent scout and a team manager, or an SGB might be an event organizer, run an academy and also own or control the stadium in which an event is held. Not everyone in the same role will have the same priorities, and they might respond differently to the same situations and stimuli.

When participants understand their own and others' interests and motivations, it throws light on their relative roles and interdependence. Convergent interests can enable coordination, cooperation, collaboration and partnerships. When interests are divergent, it can foster respect, in the best-case scenario. Either way, this exercise of understanding the ecosystem can help define boundaries, establish priorities, facilitate dispute resolution and help us design regulations and institutional structures.

Welcome to the multistakeholder model of sport, one that is always in a dynamic state where one participant's action is likely to echo throughout the system and impact many others.

Parks and recreation

Governance plays a vital role in sport. It involves the balancing of various stakeholders' interests with give and take, concessions and compromises, ideally all determined through fair process. As discussed in a previous chapter, organized sport is a quasi-public good that needs careful management and care to avoid the 'tragedy of the commons'. Access and use must be regulated. If all of its users act individually and in self-interest, the good will be depleted, and could even be destroyed by excessive use.

The sports pyramid needs to be tended like a public park. It must be open to all, to be enjoyed without overexploitation. Come and take photos of the flowers, but don't pluck them. Swim in the lake, but don't pollute it. Sometimes the park must be closed for maintenance. At other times, entry must be regulated to avoid overcrowding. A park needs security guards, maintenance staff, gardeners and gatekeepers. This way the park can be kept replenished, safe and healthy for everyone to enjoy. Sports administrators must play a similar role.

In the case of the hypothetical demand from broadcasters for the most popular World Cup matchups, the final decision has to consider both short- and long-term impacts on the sport. Would deliberately engineering a particular matchup into a tournament schedule further the values of sport? Will scheduling a particularly juicy matchup for maximum viewership impact other participating teams and even the natural progression of the tournament? These are complex decisions with many types of consequences. Governance involves deciding which of these is 'fair game' and which is not. This begs the question of what good governance is and how it can be encouraged through institutional design and protocols.

Governance architecture, ethics frameworks, incentive structures and legal consequences can jointly contribute. Remember the four forces of regulation? Checks and balances are vital, particularly in autonomous bodies. They can bring normative focus, fairness and responsibility to institutional decision-making. Although no structure can guarantee balance and fairness, there are ways to reduce the risks of misuse of power.

Maintaining formation

Poor administration will invariably bring about poor results on the field. Although good governance does not guarantee good results, it does give players and teams a better chance at success, and other stakeholders a fair opportunity to contribute and participate.

There is an underlying dichotomy that is important to recognize. Organized sport can be intense and competitive; thus, only the best players meet qualifying standards and have the opportunity to participate in major events. On the other hand, those who govern sport have no skill-based constraints or requirements. The ability to win elections within closed—and carefully controlled—membership bodies is the primary determinant of who exercises power and control over sport. Unlike the players, who face the pressure of performance and results all the time, sports administrators aren't used to appraisals or performance reviews. They have no skin in the game and face no real consequences for sub-par governance.

In recognition of the limitations of member-elected boards, there have been calls for more independent directors, public representatives and athlete representatives to be inducted to the boards of SGBs. This is intended to bring different perspectives, wider representation of interests, new talent pools and more voices and balance to the organization. It can disrupt 'group think' and bring issues on to the board agenda that might otherwise not have been discussed. When it comes to force-fitting a high-viewership matchup into a tournament, for instance, an independent director or former player on the board might point out the importance of a random draw if the tournament is to maintain its stature, integrity and public respect.

Age is a related issue. Most elite sportspersons are in their twenties or thirties. However, the members of administrative bodies tend to be much older. The Sports Code, for instance, requires office-bearers of national sports federations (NSFs) to retire at age seventy—more than twice the age of the sportspersons they manage. This creates a disconnect between the governors, who are often ill-informed about the demands modern sport places on a player, and the governed. For instance, it can be challenging for senior administrators to understand issues like gender fluidity and athlete mental health—matters that were not mainstream public conversations when they were younger and developing their world views.

On the flip side, governance is a job that requires experience and a cool head, and sport should not miss out on administrators who have these qualities simply because of generic age cut-offs.

As the Olympic Charter does for IOC members, the Sports Code establishes term and tenure restrictions on office-bearers of NSFs. They can generally serve two successive terms of up to four years each, after which a minimum 'cooling-off' period of four years is prescribed before they can seek re-election.[1] The constitutional documents of the Indian Olympic Association (IOA), as amended in 2022 under the Supreme Court's supervision, went a step further and placed an overall cap of three terms—of up to four years each—on its office-bearers.[2] Term limits ensure that elections are held periodically, and tenure restrictions allow for new people and fresh approaches. Age and term limits are supported by the belief that power is best exercised when it is not permanent, and that prolonged incumbency can entrench power to an institution's detriment.

That said, organizations also need stability and continuity, and the balance between experience and novelty needs to be maintained. Some of FIFA's most powerful presidents, Jules Rimet, Joao Havelange and Sepp Blatter, held power for thirty-three, twenty-four and seventeen years, respectively.

Along similar lines of thinking, the constitutions of many SGBs carefully allocate decision-making powers between the board and the general body (also known as the general assembly). The general body includes representatives of all members (i.e., constituent clubs, district or state or national associations), and the body's constitution can determine which decisions require their active endorsement and to which extent, e.g., 50 per cent majority or 75 per cent supermajority.

Requiring general body approval puts decisions up for member scrutiny and requires those in power to work on achieving a wider consensus. Changing the SGB's statutory auditors or passing accounts, for instance, might need a majority vote of the general body. This is not left to the board, which might have perverse incentives to unseat honest professionals who are unwilling to bend rules at their instance. Changing the name of the organization or moving its headquarters might require a general body supermajority vote given the long-term impact such a decision might have. More routine items, like approving a sponsorship contract or appointing a CEO, might be left to the board to steer.

These architectural safeguards recognize that structural checks and balances can add value to governance. They cannot guarantee that qualified and public-spirited people will be elected to SGBs, but they can encourage diverse views and limit the concentration and entrenchment of power. To supplement these measures, SGBs also lean on cultural and normative frameworks that promote ethical conduct by administrators and participants.

Conductors' conduct

Despite their wider implications, many significant decisions in sport are made in private. When processes are kept away from public scrutiny, guardrails become important. These typically come in the form of codes of conduct and ethics. These codes are written standards of expected behaviour that reflect desired values and principles, and can go beyond basic legal responsibilities in scope and sweep.

A code of ethics guides and prods people within an organization to put the institution's interests before—and above—their own. It recognizes the economic, political and social influences that decision-makers encounter when exercising their powers and undertaking their functions.

With numerous corruption scandals rocking SGBs, written codes of conduct and ethics have become the norm. These codes are wide-ranging and cover SGB officials; they may also include subordinate bodies, members, officials, players and those indirectly involved such as vendors, service providers, related parties, etc. They also require their institutional members to implement the same standards within their organizations so that these flow through the system.

The codes will usually include rules relating to conflict of interest, a gift and commissions policy, and an anti-corruption policy that prohibits activities relating to betting, gaming, gambling, impropriety, match-fixing, etc. In some cases, SGBs will establish formal ethics panels and procedures to investigate breaches and recommend sanctions. These reinforce the desired moral standards of the institution.

Through such codes, an ethics framework can be established. Expectations can then be communicated across the organization. The codes encourage participants to examine their own conduct and nudge them to give primacy to the interests of sport at all times.

Hattricks

Conflicts of interest can arise in a variety of situations, and managing them is a central aspect of good governance. For example, an SGB may award a stadium construction contract to a company or an entity that is co-owned by its secretary. It may change its regulations in a manner that favours a particular manufacturer of shoes or equipment that has the president of the SGB as brand ambassador. Such conflicts of interest can give rise to bias and corruption, actual or perceived. They can also result in decisions that are not grounded in democratic processes, leading to sub-optimal choices and negative perceptions.

Not all conflicts need a remedy, but most of them need understanding, acknowledgement, disclosure and management. They become problematic when a person's public responsibilities collide with their private or personal interests, or when multiple public responsibilities clash with each other. There can be conflicts in private settings but these can be overcome with consent. This is not the case with a public or quasi-public office. In such roles and positions, there is an expectation of independence and neutrality.

When there is a conflict, a person might exploit their official position and make decisions for the wrong reasons. Outcomes get skewed if public officials put their own private interests first. Even where the person acts completely impartially, the mere existence of the conflict can create an appearance of bias and result in a loss of trust and public confidence in the institution or process.

This is why a judge holding shares in a company should never decide cases involving that company or others in the same sector, and a selector must never participate in selecting a team when their son or daughter is a potential candidate. In such cases, it is impossible to obtain consent from everyone who could be affected by the conflict. While rules can, sometimes, prevent a conflict of interest from arising—for instance, the Indian Constitution's bar on members of Parliament holding an 'office of profit'—most cases involve managing conflicts. This can be done by implementing measures such as disclosure and registration of the interests, recusal of the conflicted person from certain decisions and, in extreme cases, elimination of the conflict through resignation from the position.

Conflicts of interest can be commercial or non-commercial, direct or indirect, and can be real, potential or perceived. A real conflict of interest is a situation where the interest is already present in a manner that interferes with a public or quasi-public decision. The SGB's allotment of a construction contract to its secretary's firm is an example. A potential conflict of interest is one that is foreseeable but has not yet become real—for example, the selector with a son or daughter playing the sport at a high level. A perceived conflict of interest is where there is a reasonable apprehension that a conflict of interest exists, making decisions open to question. The change of equipment regulations, even if made for legitimate technical reasons, comes into question when the president is a brand ambassador of a company that would stand to benefit.

A person embroiled in a controversy relating to their alleged conflict of interest can tend to be confused about what the fuss is all about. They can feel like it is all a storm in a teacup while asserting their own fairness, innocence and integrity. Just because the bias may be neither intentional nor *mala fide*, however, does not mean that it is non-existent. In public office, it isn't enough that justice is done, it must also be perceived to be done.

Conflict of interest can be poorly understood. People—especially experienced ones called upon to govern public institutions—are bound to have picked up many interests and played many roles in their careers. Every dual involvement is not inherently problematic. For instance, a retired athlete who qualifies as a referee can legitimately officiate a match involving some of their former teammates. The head of a sports university can be an office-bearer of an SGB. Taking an extreme approach to conflict of interest can sometimes be counterproductive.

On the flip side, many conflicts of interest that should concern the public tend to be ignored. For instance, motivated research that does not disclose sources of funding, or an office-bearer endorsing a competitor of the SGB's official sponsor or broadcaster, should invite scrutiny.

In the multistakeholder scheme of sports governance, conflicts of interest must be understood and managed with nuance and care. This will help align the interests of sport, the organizations that administer it, and the people who serve within them.

On the fence

The relationship between sport and global politics is complicated. There have been instances of governments forcing athletes to stay away from competitions hosted in specific countries, visas being refused to athletes from certain countries during international competitions, and resistance by organizers to raising particular national flags and to playing national anthems. All of these consequences were faced by various athletes following the Russian invasion of Ukraine in 2022. Politics casting a shadow over international sport is not new—it harks back to the Western bloc's boycott of the 1980 Moscow Olympic Games and the Soviet bloc's boycott of the

1984 Los Angeles Olympic Games that followed. SGBs try to avoid wading into these complexities, but it is not easy for them to entirely ignore significant global issues.

According to their own constitutions and statutes, SGBs are expected to remain politically neutral and not make decisions in a manner influenced by politics or governmental prerogatives. The sports movement sees this as an essential orientation to deliver on the moral force and universality of sport. It wants sporting decisions to be made for sporting reasons alone, free from non-sporting influence. After all, this is the ideal that the principle of autonomy tries to protect.

Every SGB will encounter politics from external sources and also from within. In response, it is standard practice for it to choose to be apathetic, disinterested and detached. It may sit on the fence or even actively refuse to take a position. This can be challenging in politically charged situations and environments, but a focus on the universality of sport can also help build bridges in the most difficult of situations. At the 2018 Winter Olympic Games, for example, North and South Korea entered a unified team into the women's ice hockey competition.

By keeping politics at an arm's length, sport can also prevent majoritarianism and prevailing political sentiments from trumping sporting values, and can also avoid its platforms being instrumentalized for political point-scoring.

While sport cannot by itself prevent wars or resolve conflicts, it can provide a platform for dialogue and friendship that resonate beyond sport. Scholars have pointed to the central role of sport, especially the Rugby World Cup, in nation-building and social cohesion in South Africa's post-apartheid era. To achieve such goals, sport needs to stay true to its core objective. Remaining politically neutral is a challenging and controversial—but important—tool in sport's arsenal.

Out of bounds

Corruption is a form of decay, rooted in dishonest and fraudulent conduct. Historically, sport has seen instances of corruption at every level. It often emerges from conflicts of interest, existing or created. Typically, it involves bribery or other inappropriate means of exerting influence. It brings these influences into the decision-making process and skews governance away from balance and fair play. A typical example is the grant of inflated contracts by administrators in exchange for kickbacks or bribes.

The extent and scale of corruption can be driven by environmental changes and factors. These include greater commercialization and politicization of sport, and the hyper-competitive and result-driven environment it is played in. Imagine an office-bearer of an SGB who is paid off by the broadcaster to manipulate the World Cup schedule to include that lucrative matchup. The broadcaster stands to make much more advertising revenue and wouldn't mind sharing some of it with 'facilitators' along the way.

Corruption has generally been understood as inappropriate conduct by a person in a public position. The inappropriateness comes from putting private interests above public duties. Such corruption is extractive and depletive of value. However, sometimes corruption can also further a public cause. A good example is of the bribery of officials who vote on which city or country gets to host the Olympic Games or FIFA World Cup. This results in a successful bid and not merely personal gain or benefit to the bribe-giver.

Anti-corruption laws recognize the need for specific laws to address misuse of office where general criminal laws may be inadequate. Different legal instruments, including some national laws with extra-territorial jurisdiction, deal with acts of corruption involving public officials. FIFA officials from different jurisdictions have been prosecuted in the United States of America (US) under such laws, for instance, in cases related to illegal payments, kickbacks and bribes given in exchange for votes that would decide the hosting rights to the FIFA World Cup.[3]

In India, there is the case of *K. Balaji Iyengar v. State of Kerala*[4] involving a young cricketer levelling corruption and misappropriation allegations against the President and Secretary of the Kerala Cricket Association. The Kerala High Court held that officials of the state cricket association perform public duties and are 'public servants' for the purposes of the Prevention of Corruption Act, 1988. The pervasive powers exercised by SGBs and their governors found mention in the court's reasoning. When officials in SGBs are recognized as holding quasi-public office, this obliges them to carry out their functions with probity. Failure to do so makes them eligible for criminal prosecution.

This characterization of sports officials as public servants broadly aligns with the understanding that SGBs are quasi-public institutions and are thus accountable to the public. Identifying and prosecuting corruption helps promote institutional integrity by punishing and deterring deviant self-dealing. Where internal architectural guardrails, ethics codes and conflict of interest policies are ineffective, the law can act as a safety valve and provide remedies to members of the public.

Balance beam

The wide range of stakeholders involved makes effective governance of sport a complex pursuit. Players and clubs, local, national and international organizations, spectators, the media, commercial and non-commercial partners, educational and training bodies, even the government and members of the public, are participants in this ecosystem. Each of them has different priorities. Some of them will be at odds with each other, others will find alignments.

All of them want something from sport: money, brand, experiences, power. How much should they be given? What is claimed from them in return? Recognizing, regulating and balancing interests requires carefully designed and consistently implemented policies, protocols, practices and dispute-resolution mechanisms. Remember, sport governors must act as security guards, maintenance staff, gardeners and gatekeepers all at once.

Circling back to our case study of tournament schedules, a broadcaster might request that an India v. Pakistan cricket match—that is legitimately part of the draw—be scheduled on the tournament's first Sunday afternoon (Indian subcontinent time). Accommodating such a request is likely to have little negative impact on the integrity and fairness of the event, while it will add significant commercial and social value to many stakeholders. Such tailoring of schedules regularly happens in England's domestic football competitions, such as the Premier League and FA Cup, with the organizers working openly with broadcasters to prioritize high viewership matches.

How about manufacturing a popular contest that might otherwise not have been? FIFA and World Rugby conduct tournament draws by picking lots to group teams that have qualified for the tournament. Would it be acceptable if they instead designed the qualification and scheduling process to ensure that teams from Argentina and Brazil, or New Zealand and Australia, were either in the same group or inevitably met in the knockout stage? Despite the potential commercial upside for their broadcaster, this would likely backfire. Fair play is one of those principles that you cannot put a price on.

Many juicy apples grow in the garden of sport. Some will be poisoned. Bite carefully.

Stakeholders, their activities, their interests and motivations

Who?	What?	Why?
Athletes	Training, competition, endorsements, retirement, giving back to sport and society, charity work	Sporting progression, personal growth, financial reward, sporting compensation, social and peer recognition, public profile, awards, brand value, post-retirement security, livelihood, legacy
Sports agents	Talent recruitment, team signings, transfers, marketing	Livelihood, reputation, profit
Talent scouts	Talent spotting and identification, talent assessment, recommendations to teams and talent recruitment	Livelihood, reputation, profit
Coaches	Talent progression, coaching, technical management of athlete or team	Livelihood, reputation
Managers	Team management, talent recruitment, talent management	Livelihood, reputation
Academies	Athlete recruitment, coach recruitment, talent development, team partnerships	Sustainability, legacy, profit

Who?	What?	Why?
Clubs/teams	Athlete recruitment, coach recruitment, tournament entry and participation, marketing, sponsorships, partnerships, content development, fan engagement, brand value	Sporting success, sustainability, brand value, legacy, profit
Stadium owners/ operators	Stadium construction, stadium maintenance and management, ticketing, security and safety, concessions, entertainment, spectator engagement	Utilization, sustainability, profit
Event organizers/ owners	Event bidding and acquisition, entry management, event operations and management, marketing, sponsorships, partnerships	Participation, profile, profit
Broadcasters	Rights acquisition, content carriage and distribution, advertising sales and display, subscriber acquisition	Return on investment, brand value, profit

Who?	**What?**	**Why?**
Sponsors	Partner acquisition, brand integration, brand exposure, consumer engagement, consumer research	Return on investment, brand value, profit
Advertisers	Brand exposure, consumer engagement	Return on investment, brand value, profit
Spectators	Stadium attendance (bums on seats), match consumption, in-stadium concession consumption, second-screen consumption	In-stadium experience, engagement, entertainment
Viewers	Match viewership, second-screen consumption	Television experience, engagement, entertainment
Fans	Brand consumption and engagement	Engagement, identification, inspiration, emulation
Non-rights holder media	Event attendance, coverage, content distribution and marketing, advertising sales	Profit
Sports businesses	Service delivery, product development and marketing, brand development, sales	Brand value, scale, return on investment, profit
Sports-allied businesses	Brand development, fan engagement, sales	Brand value, scale, return on investment, profit

Who?	**What?**	**Why?**
Non-profit organizations	Programme development, programme monitoring and evaluation, fundraising	Developmental goals, return on investment, human development indicators
Sports federations/ governors	Stakeholder management, rule-making, sanctioning, governance, dispute resolution, government relations	Fair play, balance of interests, power, legacy
Governments	Regulatory oversight, funding, prioritization of resource application, permissions and event support	International positioning, health, fitness, human development indicators, social and cultural development indicators, economic growth, tourism, jobs, identity, nationalism
International non-governmental organizations	Programme development, programme monitoring and evaluation, fundraising, grant making, government relations	International comity, peace, human development indicators

Chapter 5

On Reform

Does Virat Kohli not play for the 'Indian team'?

'This is not a national side in the sense of having the sanction of the Government, but a side picked by the BCCI amongst Indian players': this was the argument made by the Board of Control for Cricket in India (BCCI) in the Delhi High Court in 2004.

The BCCI contended that it was a private body, performed no public duties and owed no obligations to the public. If we take this argument forward, it means that Virat Kohli and his teammates would be playing for 'a BCCI-selected team of Indian players' and not the 'Indian team'. This would be quite a mouthful for commentators and spectators alike. Thankfully for all concerned, the Delhi High Court termed this contention 'inexplicable', and in its order in the case of *Rahul Mehra v. Union of India*,[1] said: 'The teeming millions regard it as the national team, the players feel that they are playing for India and the oppo(sing) teams, be they from Australia or Pakistan, all know that they are playing against India.'

This case would not be the last time the legal status of the BCCI was questioned before the constitutional courts.[2] Registered as a society in 1940 under the Madras Societies Registration Act of 1860, the BCCI has always maintained that it is a private members' body. It takes no government grants, generates its own funds and claims it is accountable solely to its members and not to the public.

Despite having supported its activities and tacitly recognized its authority to select national teams, the Government of India and the Sports Ministry have never formally recognized the BCCI as a national sports federation (NSF). As a result, the governance standards in the Sports Code have not applied to the BCCI.

The BCCI and its member association boards have historically housed state and national politicians, including multiple chief ministers, a future finance minister, a future sports minister, a future home minister and even a future prime minister. Sharad Pawar, Lalu Prasad Yadav, Arun Jaitley, Anurag Thakur, Amit Shah and Narendra Modi have all led various cricket bodies. The corridors of cricket are as good a place as any to cut one's teeth in the world of politics. The Government of India's attempts at passing a sports governance law—one that would have also applied to the BCCI—were rebuffed thanks to objections from the Cabinet, populated as it was by serving and former BCCI officials.[3]

Thus, the BCCI has enjoyed an unparalleled degree of autonomy—some would even call it immunity—from two branches of the government, i.e., the executive and the legislature. This is the story of the BCCI's tryst with the third branch of government—the Indian judiciary. It was a battle that played out over an entire decade, leaving both the BCCI and the higher judiciary bruised. It is a tale of how difficult reform can be, even for the highest court in the land, when law is the only tool available.

Finding the gaps

The 2013 edition of the Indian Premier League (IPL), India's most prominent professional cricket league, put in motion a chain of events that would lead to the most significant judicial intervention in Indian cricket.

The police arrested and then charged three IPL players—S. Sreesanth (a member of India's World Cup-winning squad), Ajit Chandila and Ankeet Chavan—with 'spot-fixing', a form of match manipulation orchestrated by players paid by bookies.[4] The police also alleged that two people associated with participating IPL teams—Gurunath Meiyappan[5] (the son-in-law of N. Srinivasan, the president of the BCCI at the time) and Raj Kundra[6] (co-owner of the Rajasthan Royals franchise)—had placed illegal bets on IPL matches.

As the news broke, the BCCI moved quickly into action mode. It banned the three players for life along with another teammate of theirs, Amit Singh[7] (the terms of some of these bans have since been reduced by the Supreme Court of India[8] and the BCCI Ombudsman[9]). It also summarily assembled an ad hoc committee including two retired judges, who speedily absolved Gurunath Meiyappan and Raj Kundra of any culpability, citing a lack of evidence against them or the two teams they were related to.[10]

Soon after, a petition was filed in the Bombay High Court questioning this committee's constitution and processes, and the court agreed that the proceedings were suspect.[11] The matter then went to the Supreme Court, which appointed an independent external panel—the Justice Mudgal Probe Panel—to investigate and provide findings and recommendations.

The Supreme Court also struck down a controversial amendment that had been made to the BCCI's regulations.[12] Sharad Pawar, then president of the BCCI, had permitted N. Srinivasan, then treasurer of the BCCI, to bid for, own and operate an IPL team. Realizing that this would go against clause 6.2.4 of the BCCI regulations—which stated that no administrator of BCCI could have, directly or indirectly, any commercial interest in the matches or events conducted by the BCCI—a post-facto amendment was made that exempted the IPL from this clause.

The Supreme Court frowned on this sequence of events, and this disapproval became an important frame of reference for the court's approach in the case. The Supreme Court found itself unable to turn a blind eye to what it considered to be institutionalized conflicts of interest within the BCCI. Thus began the *Board of Control for Cricket in India v. Cricket Association of Bihar*[13] saga in the Supreme Court.

The Justice Mudgal Probe Panel found enough evidence against Gurunath Meiyappan and Raj Kundra on the charge of illegal betting.[14] Next, the Supreme Court constituted the Justice R.M. Lodha Committee (Lodha Committee) comprising former Chief Justice of India Mr Justice (retd.) R.M. Lodha and former Supreme Court judges Mr Justice (retd.) Ashok Bhan and Mr Justice (retd.) R.V. Raveendran.[15]

The Supreme Court noted the sequence of events that had allowed the treasurer of the BCCI to own an IPL team, the misaligned incentives this created and the impact on procedural fairness. It expressed a need to protect the integrity of India's national passion.

The Lodha Committee was tasked with recommending action to be taken against the two persons found to have indulged in illegal betting, and against their associated franchises. The Supreme Court also requested the panel to provide recommendations on preventing sporting frauds and conflicts of interest within the BCCI, improving player welfare, streamlining the functioning of the BCCI and making it more responsive and accountable to the public at large.[16] The Lodha Committee recommended, and the Supreme Court endorsed, life bans from involvement in cricket for both individuals, and a two-year suspension from the IPL for the two franchises.[17]

In response to questionnaires[18] and requests for feedback sent by the Lodha Committee, the BCCI and its state associations responded summarily, refusing to engage substantively or substantially. Their main contention was that they were private bodies enjoying autonomy and freedom of association, and that the constitutional courts lacked jurisdiction over them. This resulted in the Lodha Committee not receiving feedback from the BCCI and its dozens of member associations–arguably the primary stakeholders in the BCCI's functioning.

Umpire's call

On 4 January 2016, the Lodha Committee presented its 'Report of the Supreme Court Committee on Reforms in Cricket' to the apex court. It recommended a substantial governance overhaul of the BCCI and its member associations. Its detailed suggestions were largely structural and architectural, oriented towards establishing internal and external checks and balances for the institution.

Recommendations included a nationally representative membership structure for the BCCI (also commonly known as 'One State One Vote'),* with clarity on voting and playing rights and on the grant of disbursements to members. The Lodha Committee recommended measures to reduce concentration and misuse of power, and to provide representation to former

* Owing to its inception in British times, the BCCI's structure reflected the political realities of those times. In more than one instance, a state had more than one cricket association, each of which had a vote. For instance, Gujarat had three associations–Baroda, Saurashtra and Gujarat, each of them fielding a separate team in the Ranji Trophy. Similarly, Maharashtra had three–Mumbai, Maharashtra and Vidarbha. United Andhra Pradesh had two–Hyderabad and Andhra Pradesh. These were the anomalies that 'One State One Vote' sought to rectify.

players (both male and female) in decision-making through the creation of an Apex Council for the BCCI.

It also recommended period limits on the terms and tenures of office bearers and officials, and a retirement age of seventy for anyone serving in the BCCI. Another of its suggestions was that ministers, government servants and any persons occupying a post in any other SGB in the country should be disqualified from holding office. It also proposed the separation of governance and management, involving a corporate structure in which the BCCI was to be managed by 'professionals with established skill-sets'. This was to include an experienced chief executive officer (CEO) assisted by a team of six managers to handle non-cricketing affairs, and through defined committees, many of which were to be comprised of former players only.

Recognizing the importance of the IPL as a revenue generator for the BCCI, it suggested a separate Governing Council for the IPL. To protect player welfare, it proposed a fifteen-day break for national players before and after the IPL season. The Lodha Committee also suggested the establishment of a Cricket Players' Association, an association of ex-cricketers to be funded and financed by the BCCI. This was to look after and advocate the interests of current and former professionals. It also suggested the introduction of a compulsory registration process for player agents, seeing rogue agents as a risk to the integrity of cricket.

Observing that there was a lack of awareness in relation to the issue of conflict of interest within the BCCI set-up, the Lodha Committee proposed a policy that explained the concept, provided illustrations and proposed solutions and sanctions. This was intended to apply to everyone who was part of the BCCI structure, whether as a player, an official or in any other capacity.

The recommendations also included the creation of three new authorities to provide external supervision and oversight of the BCCI's functions. This first was an ombudsman (a retired

Supreme Court judge or a former Chief Justice of a high court) to resolve any internal disputes or grievances or complaints made by members of the public in respect of ticketing, access and facilities at stadia and lack of transparency in the award of contracts for goods and services. Next, an ethics officer (a former judge of a High Court) to institute and decide on matters of ethics, including conflicts of interest. Finally, an electoral officer (a former Election Commissioner of India) to oversee and administer the BCCI's elections.

For additional transparency and oversight, the Lodha Committee also suggested bringing the BCCI within the purview of the Right to Information Act, 2005 (RTI Act), the establishment of fair and transparent criteria for awarding contracts and appointing professionals and contractors, full transparency of all tenders floated and bids invited, display on the BCCI website and at the BCCI office of all rules and regulations as well as financial and other reports.

In relation to integrity, the Lodha Committee sought due consideration on whether match-fixing should be criminalized, and whether betting on cricket should be legalized with proper safeguards (including prohibition of betting by all administrators, players, owners and officials in rules and regulations). It also suggested the establishment of a disciplinary committee (consisting of the ombudsman, the ethics officer and the BCCI CEO) to address match-fixing cases, measures to educate and sensitize cricketers about game ethics, and better coordination with the government on investigations, record maintenance and due diligence.

Holistically, the Lodha Committee recognized the need for uniformity in the constitution, structure and functioning of member associations for proper governance of the game. It recommended that all member associations must reflect similar provisions, policies and structures in their constitutions.

This was proposed to be made a pre-condition for them to exercise voting rights in the BCCI, and to avail of other member benefits like distribution of their annual subsidy.

The Lodha Committee also recommended that the BCCI appoint an independent auditor to conduct a member audit, verifying their use of BCCI grants, recording their targets and milestones, and submitting these in a compliance report to the BCCI. In addition, they would be obliged to grant membership and voting rights to former international players hailing from their state.

In the interests of the viewing public, the Lodha Committee also made certain recommendations in relation to appropriate forms of advertising during the broadcast of cricket matches. It proposed that the entire space of the screen during the broadcast be dedicated to the display of the game, save for a small sponsor logo or sign. It also suggested that, during Test matches, advertisements be allowed only in breaks taken by both teams for drinks, lunch and tea, so as not to deprive the viewers of on-field activity between and during overs. As is apparent, some of these recommendations were quite granular and specific, trying to address known frustrations.

Follow-on

The recommendations of the Lodha Committee Report faced strong resistance from the BCCI and its members. Expectedly, they moved the Supreme Court against the implementation of the report.[19]

On the proposed membership structure, the BCCI argued that restricting full membership status (and therefore voting rights) only to state associations would be unfair to certain non-state associations such as Saurashtra, Vidarbha and Mumbai that have historically made significant contributions to the development and growth of cricket in the country.

The BCCI opposed the proposed age cap of seventy years on office-bearers, the limitation on terms for office-bearers and the cooling-off period between terms. It also argued that the ban on ministers, government servants and persons holding honorary posts in another SGB from being part of the BCCI violated the constitutional freedom of association under Article 19(1)(c), and was 'patently unreasonable'. It argued that it would be unjust to deny an individual the full right to freedom of association and the necessary core right to be part of the management of the affairs of such association and have a say in its functioning. Such a restriction, the BCCI stated, would also hamper the continuity of meritorious and deserving administrators and impact the development of cricket.

After much back and forth, on 18 July 2016, a two-judge bench of the Supreme Court, comprising Chief Justice T.S. Thakur and Justice Ibrahim Kalifulla, accepted a majority of the key recommendations made by the Lodha Committee. It ordered that amendments be carried out to the BCCI's constitution and that other actions be taken to implement the recommendations it had endorsed.[20]

The Supreme Court did not agree with the Lodha Committee's suggestion on limiting the airing of advertisements during matches and on inducting two franchisee representatives into the IPL Governing Council, explaining the negative financial consequences and conflict of interest these would result in, respectively. The Supreme Court also refused to impose a monetary value on the recommended funds for the establishment of the Cricket Players' Association, leaving it to the discretion of the BCCI.

The court recognized that the recommendations to bring the BCCI under the scope of the RTI Act and to legalize betting in India were the mandate of the legislature and did not impose any related obligations on the BCCI. The Supreme Court placed the onus on the Law Commission of India to examine the viability of implementing these two particular matters and recommending a suitable course of action to the Central government.

The Supreme Court also requested the Lodha Committee to oversee the BCCI reform process. The Lodha Committee submitted status reports to the Supreme Court describing the challenges it faced with implementing the reforms in the face of the BCCI's resistance.[21] The BCCI filed a review petition in the Supreme Court. This was dismissed. The BCCI then filed a curative petition. This was also dismissed. Faced with continued resistance to reform, the Supreme Court removed the incumbent office-bearers of the BCCI,[22] appointed a Committee of Administrators (CoA), and requested the CoA to take up the reins of the BCCI and implement the judicial reforms.[23]

Under the supervision of the CoA, the BCCI registered a new constitution that reflected the Supreme Court-mandated structure. Over time, there were a few relaxations allowed by the Supreme Court, including an exception to the 'One State One Vote' mandate, with legacy state associations being given full membership based on their cricketing history and on the interpretation of the tenure and cooling-off provisions.

The Supreme Court also held that the Lodha Committee's requirements were to be implemented by the BCCI member associations as well, and the CoA was tasked with overseeing the amendment to their constitutions in line with the BCCI-level reforms.

The CoA remained in place for far longer than the few months in which it was meant to complete the transition. By the time the BCCI elections were held in October 2019, the constitutions of the BCCI and of most of its member associations had been overhauled.

At this point, the BCCI had gone from enjoying absolute immunity from the law and the state to becoming the most regulated SGB in India.

Between 1877 and 1939, there were ninety-nine 'timeless' Test matches played—these would go on until a result was achieved, even if it took longer than five days of play. The last timeless Test was played in 1939. It was the final Test of a five-match series between England and South Africa in Durban. This is the longest Test match on record, but even that did not enable a result. The match was abandoned as a draw after nine days of play spread over twelve days. The English team's ship home was departing and they couldn't afford to miss it. It should surprise no one that the timeless format was never tried again.

Not unlike the match in Durban, the BCCI's encounter with the Supreme Court had already become a long-drawn-out affair. It was a timeless test for both, and it was far from over.

Through the defence

In authoring its orders enforcing reform, the Supreme Court was not unaware of the principle of autonomy within the sports movement. In fact, it dealt with it explicitly in the course of the proceedings. A letter written by the President of BCCI Anurag Thakur to the ICC, of which the BCCI is a prominent member, was brought to the court's attention.

In this letter, Thakur had allegedly requested the President of the ICC to state that the recommendation of appointing a nominee of the government auditor's office to the BCCI Apex Council and the IPL Governing Council would constitute a violation of the Memorandum and Articles of Association of the ICC, which prohibited 'government interference' in the working or functioning of its members, grounds for immediate suspension of the member.[24]

The Supreme Court did not take kindly to what it saw as an attempt to derail the reforms. It commented that a measure undertaken in an attempt to increase financial transparency and accountability in the BCCI would be appreciated—rather than objected to—by the ICC. The move to give the government auditor's nominee a seat at the governance table is unparalleled in Indian sport. This moved the needle on public accountability, going far beyond the Sports Ministry's binary recognition process for NSFs contemplated in the Sports Code. The limits on autonomy had been expanded.

Interestingly, the Supreme Court did not express a view on the extent of an SGB's autonomy from judicial process, and the appropriateness of its own intervention in the context of the principle of autonomy. In some ways, the exceptional treatment the BCCI had thus far obtained, including its steadfast refusal to be recognized as an NSF, opened the door for pointed and exceptional treatment by the judiciary. The ICC took no action against the BCCI, tacitly acquiescing to the judicially mandated reforms in its member body.

On the other hand, the Supreme Court took firm steps to separate the BCCI from state functionaries and from state executive and legislative power. The Lodha Committee recommended, and the Supreme Court upheld, the bar on ministers, government servants and those holding public office from taking posts within the BCCI. The institutional depoliticization the Supreme Court attempted through this move has no known precedent in global sports governance. The Court was perhaps aware of its own unique position, from among the three branches of government, to free the BCCI from political control.

In doing as it did, the Supreme Court postulated a version of autonomy that was to be earned and supervised, rather than one that was inherent or self-regulated.

Boundaries

In the course of the proceedings, the BCCI had asserted that it was a private, non-statutory membership body with no declared monopoly. In response, the Supreme Court further crystallized the concept and consequences of the BCCI's 'public function', which the judiciary had previously recognized.

The Supreme Court did not decide whether or not the BCCI was to be classified as 'State', a requirement for the Supreme Court to intervene and provide judicial remedies under Article 32 of the Constitution of India (for violation of fundamental rights). However, reasserting its holding in *Zee Telefilms Ltd. and Anr. v. Union Of India and Ors.*,[25] it definitively held that the BCCI was not immune from judicial questioning under Article 226 of the Constitution (for violation of fundamental as well as legal rights), and was subject to requirements of public law in respect of a number of its functions.

Even though it was a private body in structure, the Supreme Court recognized that the BCCI exerted exclusive and pervasive control over selecting Indian teams, the activities of players and officials and the broader cricket ecosystem which potentially includes every Indian citizen. Thus, it performed a public function of grave importance and needed to be responsible and accountable in its functioning, the Supreme Court held.

The absence of financial, functional or administrative control by the government was deemed irrelevant to the analysis, given that the government had, *de facto*, allowed the BCCI to exercise its powers without demur or protest. On these grounds, the Supreme Court exercised its powers to bring the Lodha Committee reforms to life. It also firmly placed the public, the fan and the non-members of BCCI as legally recognized stakeholders in cricket administration.

The recognition that many of the BCCI's functions are 'public' in nature also helps put the reforms in context. The new and inclusive membership structure, with at least one member association in each state and union territory, ensured national-level coverage of the BCCI. This finally brought every Indian, regardless of birthplace or location, into the BCCI's fold as a potential state and national representative cricketer.

The rationalization of the membership structure and removal of the zonal representation in the selection committee also reduced the concentration of power and the creation of regional blocs. The Apex Council's mix of councillors elected by members and those nominated by the Cricket Players' Association (one male and one female) and by the government auditor recognized the importance of accountability not only to members but also to the player community and the public at large. It also brought diverse voices to decision-making.

The separation between governance and executive management—through the creation of a CEO and senior managerial posts and executive committees—promoted professionalization and internal checks and balances between those setting the vision and policy and those implementing them. The separation of functions also sought to reduce the extent of discretion vested in one or a handful of individuals.

Transparency was promoted by obliging the BCCI to publish information on rules, decisions, accounts and annual reports on its website and to keep them available for public inspection. Requiring tender processes to be followed for the grant of material contracts and clear criteria for vendor selection aimed for greater neutrality, prevention of conflicts of interest and the removal of personal favours.

The insertion of a conflict of interest policy put the focus on ethical conduct by decision-makers in quasi-public positions across the board, emphasizing the importance of preventing the privatization of benefits. The introduction of senior external officials of standing in the posts of ombudsman, ethics officer and electoral officer brought a new degree of independence to dispute resolution and created fora for players, officials and fans to have grievances addressed and for elections to be conducted freely and fairly.

The Supreme Court also suggested that the government give due consideration to bringing the BCCI under the purview of the RTI Act, making it amenable and subject to information-sharing requests from the public.

Together, these are architectural measures to increase the flow of information, enforce documentation, dissipate powers and responsibilities, bring in multiple layers of decision review, align personal and institutional interests, have more voices represented and insert independence in dispute resolution and grievance redressal. This brought into play a widened notion of who the BCCI was representing through the institutionalization of its public functions.

As mentioned above, the Supreme Court was able to enforce the reforms not only in the BCCI but also in its member associations, and amendments to the constitutions and governance structures of these bodies were also carried out. At the time, such a degree of systemic reform—at multiple levels of the sports pyramid at once—had been outside the powers of either the executive or the legislature.

Sport's position in the state list of the Indian Constitution has limited the legislative powers of Parliament, as only the states are empowered by the Constitution to regulate sports activities. The union government's administrative powers under the Sports Code extended only to NSFs and not to state sports associations. The principle of vertical autonomy—which protects bodies from excessive interference by the superior bodies they are affiliated with—has also insulated these state associations from accountability, oversight and supervision.

Unconstrained by the Constitution's legislative scheme or concepts of autonomy, the Supreme Court went deeper down the sports pyramid, making its judgment and associated reforms binding not only on the BCCI but also on all of its member associations at the state level. In addition to the structural changes it enforced in each member association's constitution, the Supreme Court required the BCCI's auditor to carry out a periodic performance audit of each member association to determine whether and how it had utilized BCCI-disbursed funds to develop cricket in its region. The distribution of future funding from BCCI was to be dependent on the results of such audits. This meant that the BCCI could not deliberately look the other way or put its head in the sand once it had disbursed grants to its members.

The state associations pushed back strongly, asserting their constitutional rights to freedom of association. In the final reckoning, the Supreme Court and the CoA were able to require a majority of the state associations to update their constitutions and also admit former international cricketers as members.[26] The Supreme Court and the CoA went deeper than any previous effort at sports regulation in the country. They faced great resistance from the BCCI member associations.

Yet, despite knowing how many of the member associations were structured to support the entrenchment of power, they did not closely examine, verify and reconstitute the existing membership structures of the member associations.

Some member associations are deliberately stuffed with dozens of members of the same family, their employees and even domestic staff. Others are constituted by member clubs, all of which are controlled by a handful of people who each own multiple clubs. Others allowed voting by proxy, where large numbers of member votes could be aggregated by a few constituents. It is practically impossible to break into the membership of these bodies without the blessings of the people in power.

The CoA did add a few former international cricketers as voting members to these bodies. However, this was largely anecdotal and, by not taking on the challenging task of examining the legitimacy of existing voting members, the CoA naturally limited the impact of the reforms. At the end of the process, votes were in the same hands and the existing power structures remained undisturbed.[27]

The tail wags

Was the judicial intervention in cricket administration necessary or over-intrusive? Was it going to kill the goose that was laying so many golden eggs? Or was it needed to keep the goose healthy and protect the supply of these eggs? Why attack cricket—unambiguously India's best run and most successfully commercialized sport? The greater the power, the greater the responsibility? Did the court have jurisdiction? Can governance of a national asset like cricket be left to the discretion of a few people? Would this weaken India's position in the global governance of the game? Were the judges acting with judicial hats on or were they, like almost everyone else in the country, just cricket fans wanting to have their say? One's stand on these matters is likely to be a factor of where one sits.

Despite reflecting contemporary governance principles in most aspects, the reforms were characterized as 'revolutionary' for Indian sport. This laid bare the historical gaps in sports governance practice. Some argue that the Supreme Court went too far. Others posit that it didn't go far enough. Many of the structural changes were addressed at the top of the pyramid, focusing on who could (and couldn't) stand for elections. By not addressing the very bottom of the pyramid and reconstituting the voting membership of the state associations, it left incumbent power structures untouched. In the first elections held under the new BCCI constitution in 2019, all posts were uncontested, with exactly one nominee for each post.[28]

The officials of the BCCI and its member associations did not give up the fight; rather, they consistently pushed back against the Supreme Court's efforts. The reforms were antithetical to the freedom and flexibility these people had enjoyed. Once the CoA demitted office and the new office-bearers were installed, the BCCI got down to work[29] and filed petitions in the Supreme Court in December 2019 and April 2020.[30] These petitions requested the Supreme Court to reverse most of the changes it had made in the BCCI, and sought to reclaim the board's right to amend its own constitution without the Supreme Court's consent.

A new season

The case went into cold storage while multiple office-bearers overstayed their permitted terms of office. It sprang back to life just in time for the next BCCI election in 2022.

In a major about-turn, a division bench led by Justice D.Y. Chandrachud walked back many of the material reforms originally undertaken, based on the Supreme Court's own order from a bench that had included Justice D.Y. Chandrachud himself.[31]

The Supreme Court blessed multiple amendments to the BCCI constitution. These included extensions to the possible terms and tenures of officials and the relaxation of the cooling-off requirements, which had originally been put in place with the stated intent of 'preventing the concentration of power in a few hands, dispersing authority and preventing cricketing oligopolies from forming'.

As a result of the amendment, the incumbent president and secretary of the BCCI, Sourav Ganguly and Jay Shah, regained eligibility for re-election even though they had already served two consecutive terms between the BCCI and its member bodies. While the bench did not accept the BCCI's plea to lift the bar on those above seventy years of age from holding posts, it removed holding 'public office' and 'serving in another sporting body' as disqualifications for officials.[32]

It also allowed those who had been charged with a criminal offence to stand for office so long as they had not been convicted and sentenced to imprisonment for at least three years, opening the door for undertrials to serve in the BCCI structure. The court explained that this was necessary to prevent frivolous prosecutions leading to 'unfair' disqualifications. This change enabled P. Sarath Chandra Reddy to be re-elected to the post of president of the Andhra Cricket Association, one of the BCCI's member state associations. In November 2022, he contested—and won—the election from his jail cell in Delhi, where he was detained as an accused in a money laundering case.[33]

The Supreme Court also fortified the role of the secretary of the BCCI, giving the functionary wide-ranging power over all management personnel and the operations of the Apex Council, including supervision of the CEO's functioning. However, the bench did not accept the BCCI's plea to dispense with the

Supreme Court's prior consent to make further amendments to its constitution.

After nine years of back and forth in the courts, the involvement of multiple Chief Justices of India, former Chief Justices of India and a future Chief Justice of India, hundreds of hours of court time and hundreds of crores of rupees spent on legal fees, things more or less returned to square one. Following in the footsteps of 2019, the 2022 BCCI election was also completed with every post uncontested. Jay Shah was re-elected as secretary, and Sourav Ganguly did not contest the election.

Expressing his disappointment on the progressive chipping away at the key reforms by successive Supreme Court benches in 2016, 2018 and 2022, Justice Lodha described the reforms as a 'snow mountain' that BCCI officials found very difficult to navigate, which is why they preferred to wait for the 'weather to change'.[34] In other words, they played for 'no result', knowing that in a timeless Test, they could outlast the challenging spell from combative judges and wait for a more amenable bench or a change of heart.

Overall, the Supreme Court seemed to come out the worse for wear with subsequent judges seemingly regretting the hard stance their predecessors had taken against the politically mighty BCCI. In many reckonings, both institutions have suffered damage to their independence and autonomy as a result of the proceedings. It seems unlikely that the Supreme Court will engage again with the subject of BCCI governance in a hurry.

When understood in the context of where Indian sports governance stood at the time, the principles laid down by the Lodha Committee and the Supreme Court, and the structures they employed, were path-breaking. Even though many of the changes have been ignored, diluted and eventually reversed in the case of the BCCI, a new vocabulary and new standards for Indian sports governance emerged. These have already formed the basis for judicially overseen changes in multiple other SGBs where reform was overdue, including the Indian Olympic Association (IOA) and the NSFs for football, hockey, chess, judo, table tennis and equestrian.

However well-intentioned reforms might be, wholesale institutional change is challenging at the best of times. Trying to impose it against the will of those in power can be exhausting and unproductive. They will push back, hard, as they did in this case. Adopting the tactics one might in a timeless Test, the Supreme Court's attack was worn down, session by session and hearing by hearing.

What the prolonged battle between the Supreme Court and the BCCI teaches us is this: the law as an instrument of change must factor in existing architectures, morals and markets. Unless it is going to do the hard work of breaking these down completely before reshaping them, inertia will likely have the upper hand. Otherwise, it is the slow, incremental—often unnoticed—legal reforms that have the best chance at influencing these other levers and eventually effecting change.

The weather will turn again, and other ships will have to depart their ports. Change is a given, but one thing's for certain: Kohli plays for 'India', and not even the BCCI's lawyers will dispute that again.

Chapter 6

On Difference

Should we hold separate women's chess events?

Forty-two pairs of female and male chess players, matched for ability, were pitted against each other in a series of contests over the Internet as part of a research study.[1] Though all the line-ups had female players playing against male opponents, in some cases the female players were misled into believing that they were playing female opponents.

The study found that female chess players showed a 50 per cent performance decline when they (rightly) knew they were playing a male opponent. This 'disadvantage' disappeared when they (mistakenly) thought they were playing against female opponents. These results are significant and impact the way sports competitions are designed.

The most obvious physiological differences between male and female competitors—such as aerobic capacity and muscular structure—do not make one gender intrinsically more likely to outperform the other at chess. Why, then, would women perform better when they 'think' they are playing against women than they do when they 'know' they are playing against men?

Square off

Competition is an essential element of organized sport. It is the path to finding the best performers. In the pyramid structure, winners will progress until there is only one left at the top, as the overall champion. Club champion, district champion, state champion, national champion, continental champion, world champion. Getting to the top of any sport is gruelling.

While sports events can have many different objectives and formats, they invariably involve winning and losing. An event's design provides context, relevance and salience. Events with large fan followings are set up to be challenging for participants and engaging for spectators and viewers.

In their design, events will generally fall into one of these categories across various criteria:

Geography: International/world (e.g., FIFA World Cup), regional/divisional (e.g., Asian Games), national/domestic (e.g., Ranji Trophy), zonal/state (e.g., South Zone Championship, Karnataka State Championship), district/local/city/town (e.g., Bangalore First Division Football League)
Disciplines: Single discipline (e.g., All England Open Badminton Championships), single-discipline multisport (e.g., World Athletics Championships), multidiscipline multisport (e.g., Paralympic Games)
Participant type: Individual (e.g., US Open Tennis), team (e.g., ICC Cricket World Cup)
Participant status: Amateur (e.g., NCAA), professional (e.g., PGA), pro-am (e.g., certain golf events)
Participant affiliation: School (e.g., inter-school cricket league), collegiate (e.g., inter-college football tournament), corporate (e.g., BCCI Corporate Trophy), club/franchise (e.g., Indian Super League), nationality (e.g., Olympic Games), service (e.g., World Military Games)

Participant characteristics: Gender (e.g., FIFA Women's World Cup), age (e.g., Sub-junior National Swimming Championship), qualification (e.g., Karate Black-Belt Championship), Weight category (e.g., World Heavyweight Boxing), Disability class (e.g., Paralympic Games)

Event characteristics: Sanctioned (e.g., Indian Premier League), unsanctioned (e.g., Indian Cricket League), private (e.g., NBA), open (e.g., Open Nationals), invitational (e.g., Invitational Swimming Championship), exclusions (e.g., non-medallist swimming meet)

Objective: Qualification (e.g., FIFA World Cup Qualifiers), ranking (e.g., Junior National Badminton Ranking Tournament), championship (e.g., Rugby World Cup), friendly (e.g., International Friendly Football fixture), exhibition (e.g., demonstration events at Olympic Games)

Venues: Single venue (e.g., Wimbledon), single-city multivenue (e.g., Olympic Games), single-country multicity (e.g., FIFA World Cup), multicountry (e.g., ICC Cricket World Cup 2011)

Frequency: One-off (e.g., Golden Jubilee Test Match), annual (e.g., Super Bowl), biennial (e.g., FINA World Aquatics Championship), quadrennial (e.g., Commonwealth Games)

Structure: Tournament (e.g., ICC Women's T20 World Cup), series (e.g., Border-Gavaskar Trophy Test Series), season (e.g., F1 Grand Prix), closed league (no promotion or relegation, e.g., Professional Kabaddi League), open league (e.g., Premier League)

Progression methodology: Single elimination (e.g., French Open tennis), double elimination (e.g., NCAA College World Series baseball), round robin (e.g., Premier League), round robin + knockout (e.g., ICC Cricket World Cup 2023), round robin + hybrid play-offs (e.g., Indian Premier League), knockout + round robin, round robin + round robin + knockout (e.g., ICC Cricket World Cup 2007)

Black and white

Categorization and classification of competitors are at the heart of designing a sports competition. Categories are designed to allow participants to demonstrate the skills the sport requires. The event must also remain interesting for competitors and provide for personalized styles, expressions and approaches from a wide pool of participants.

Classification involves creating various baskets of certain shared characteristics and placing them in the same category. When there is a healthy balance between certainty and uncertainty, two results will flow: the outcome is not predetermined by the design of the contest, and factors other than the sport-specific skills do not influence its result in a significant way. Eligibility criteria—who gets to play and in which event—reflect classifications and influence competition design.

Certain physical characteristics of competitors can be used to determine competition categories. These include gender, age and weight, among others. Paralympic and disability sport disciplines classify competitors by the nature of their disability. In key Paralympic athletic disciplines such as running, wheelchair racing, jumps and throws, athletes who have disabilities causing approximately the same amount of inactivity are placed in the same class. To be eligible to participate in Paralympic disciplines, an athlete must have an eligible impairment type, and the impairment must be determined by an official classifier to be severe enough to have an impact on the athlete's performance.

This classification system aims to minimize the impact of eligible impairments on the outcome of the competition. It is designed to ensure that athletes do not succeed simply because they have an impairment that causes less of a disadvantage than their competitors. As each sport requires different activities, the impact of the impairment on each sport also differs, and hence disability classification is done in a sport-specific way.

While some physical characteristics are considered for the purpose of classification, many others are not. This is so even though they could have a significant influence on outcomes. Height is an example. No sport event classifies competitors by how tall they are, even though this can provide a significant advantage in jump events, basketball, swimming, fast bowling, etc.

First move

Gender is probably the most pervasive basis of sports classification. Name the competition, and it is likely to have different men's and women's events. The relevance of gender as a generic, rather than sport-specific, basis of classification usually goes unquestioned. This despite gender no longer being understood in a binary manner, with growing recognition that it can also be fluid and, sometimes, ambiguous. When gender is used as a binary classifier in sport, questions will arise on where and how to draw the line between the two. Should a person who transitions from male to female compete in female competition? Which traits differentiate male from female—is it the sex organs, chromosomes, testosterone levels? These questions have no ready answers, but sport is called upon to answer them when it designs its competition regulations.

There is a historical, physiological and social context to all of this.

Sport as a widely pursued state- and business-sponsored project began with the Industrial Revolution. It was seen as an effective means to socialize boys into the values of hard work, sacrifice, teamwork, discipline and obedience. These were considered vital for men working in factories.

Women were prohibited from competing at the first modern Olympic Games held in 1896 in Athens. They began competing in a few events at the 1900 Olympics in Paris, and have participated at every edition since. Today, with the exception of certain sailing and equestrian events, all Olympic events are classified based on gender. For a few editions of the Olympic Games, the 'men's shooting' events were treated as 'open', and allowed entry to both men and women. A woman, Zhang Shan of China, won gold in the skeet shooting event at the Barcelona 1992 Games, but overall, it was found that women participated in smaller numbers when the competition was open to both sexes. The event was split into men's and women's skeet from the next Olympic edition onwards.

Does the historical exclusion of women from sport justify continued segregation? What happens when a sport remains gender-segregated? Is there enough evidence to show that the key physiological differences are material advantages across all sports? Are social factors, like stereotypes and structural inequalities, also relevant?

Kings and queens

The opinions of influential men were what originally kept women out of sport. 'No matter how toughened a sportswoman may be, her organism is not cut out to sustain certain shocks,' said the founder of the modern Olympic Games, Baron Pierre de Coubertin. Women were perceived as being too weak for sport, particularly endurance sports such as marathons, weightlifting and cycling. The exclusion apparently came from concern for their safety, especially their reproductive health.

They were gradually 'allowed' into sport, first in the disciplines that were deemed not damaging to their health and then, progressively, into all the rest. Due to the physiological differences, for women to have a shot at success, a separate competition had to be created for them. However, this history alone cannot explain why most sports have remained gendered despite the passage of time, social progress, scientific research in physiology and a greater understanding of the human body.

At the simplest level, the argument in support of the gender binary has been physiological. Male hormones such as testosterone drive the development of male characteristics, which include larger hearts and lungs, more haemoglobin, denser and differently shaped skeletons, less body fat and increased muscle size and strength.

Much of this development occurs in the teenage years. Many of the resulting advantages that men have are insurmountable even by the most skilled women athletes. If you pooled everyone together at matched competitive levels, men would almost always win. Given this, what would the incentive and motivation be for women to participate? If women chose not to compete, this would reinforce the gender divide rather than bridge it. With the social role of sport, can we afford to have half the population lacking opportunities to succeed and role models to emulate?

On the other hand, there might be some sports in which women might be better than men. Long-distance swimming, horse riding and rifle shooting are known examples. Here, it is argued, open competition might cause different problems. Men can find it socially embarrassing to lose to women, and this could result in men's self-exclusion from events where this is a possibility. These sports then risk being characterized as 'feminine' sports. Instead of fighting stereotypes, gender desegregation can end up introducing or reinforcing them.

Another suggestion is that the gender binary must be encouraged because it enables two very different styles of sport to be played. An example often used is men's and women's tennis—both played by the same rules and on the same courts, each shaped by the participants' physiology and social conditioning, each attractive and appealing to the paying and watching spectator in different ways.

Sociological differences can also play a role. In most countries, men and women receive disparate treatment, not just in sport but also more generally within society. In such situations, distinct opportunities for women are a matter of equity.

Despite all the arguments against desegregation, is it time to seriously consider the merging of both sexes, at least in some events? The question rests on the argument that, as a result of gender segregation, women's sport risks always being seen as inferior, both in quality and in importance. Would sports like archery and shooting and chess, where physiological differences are not as relevant, benefit from being gender desegregated? When support is available in an equitable manner, do the differences in skills, capabilities and other factors affecting performance remain, or do they dissipate and, even, disappear?

Efforts to de-gender sport can begin with small steps. Deeper scientific questioning can help us understand which sports disciplines are genuinely gender-affected and which ones are not. In sports where gender affectation has been acknowledged, efforts can be made to understand the age at which physiological differences start playing a material role. Then, junior-level sports can be mixed-gender until the age when boys begin to enjoy insurmountable advantages over girls. Premature classification by gender will be avoided. When sport defaults to non-segregation by gender, then the role of science is to step in to justify when and where girls and boys, women and men, should play in separate competitions.

Coming back to the chess study, the drop in performance when women know they are playing men is attributed to what is known as 'stereotype threats'.[2] This suggests that women adopt different roles when playing against men. They can adopt a more defensive style and be less self-confident and win-oriented. They can be cautious of angering men and having to deal with their aggression. This puts women at a motivational and performance disadvantage, not because of their inherent cognitive abilities but because of their own internalization of social stereotypes.

Chess is a sport that does not, intrinsically, need to be classified by gender to ensure competitiveness. In fact, it has a universal rating system, the Elo ratings, that takes care of that. Unlike other sports that separate men's and women's events, chess categorizes tournaments as 'open' and 'women-only'. This is a purely social decision, targeted at encouraging and fostering participation among women and enabling their growth. Is this a permanent state of play or a means to ultimately integrate and unify competition?

Sport is generally seen as reflecting the society we live in. Can it also play a more active role in changing stereotypes? Equal treatment of athletes, regardless of gender, can be one of those areas in which sport can influence culture.

Check

With the gender binary firmly in place, sport has to confront difficult questions on gender and eligibility. Among these, two are particularly thorny—the appropriate treatment of female athletes with the natural condition of hyperandrogenism, and the classification of transgender athletes who have transitioned from male to female.

Ad hoc gender testing was first practised at the Berlin 1936 Olympic Games. This was to counter what was considered 'gender-cheating' by participants—for example, a man named Hermann participated in the high-jump event in Berlin as Dora.

Mass testing of female athletes was first implemented by the world athletics body, the International Amateur Athletic Federation (IAAF, which since 2019 has been known as World Athletics), in 1946. In 1948, the International Olympic Committee (IOC) followed suit and implemented its first formal policy for female gender determination. In these early iterations, female competitors in sports events were required to provide 'medical certificates of femininity' to be eligible to compete. However, the IAAF and IOC provided no standard criteria for making this determination and exercised no oversight. Allegations of gender fraud and rumours around the injection of male hormones into female athletes continued over the years.

To guard against the possibility of men entering women-only events, the IAAF adopted standardized tests to determine gender in the mid-1960s. These required female athletes to parade nude before a panel of physicians and submit to a series of gynaecological examinations in order to confirm their femininity. Polish sprinter Ewa Klobukowska, a gold and bronze medallist, was the first to formally fail a sex test at the Tokyo 1964 Olympic Games. Gender verification of female athletes became a part of the pre-competition protocol in all IAAF-certified events.

However, rising protests and criticism from female athletes against the IAAF-prescribed test standards for gender determination led the IOC to devise less invasive methods. From 1968 onwards, all female athletes were required to undergo the 'Barr body test'. This consisted of acquiring a 'buccal smear' from inside the athlete's cheek and then examining the cells for the presence of a chromatin mass (known as the Barr body)—something found only in women.

If the test was positive, the athletes were issued a 'certificate of femininity'. However, if the test results were negative, a complete chromosomal examination was conducted on a blood sample of the female athlete and was supplemented by a thorough gynaecological examination. This test continued until it was phased out and a new protocol was issued by the IOC in 1992 which consisted of the 'polymerase chain reaction' (PCR) test that searched for the sex-determining Region Y gene.

Although the PCR technique was supposed to identify unique male DNA sequences, further examination revealed that at least one of the DNA sequences used in the PCR test was not really exclusive to males, and may have contributed to a large number of false positive results, such as in the case of eight female athletes in the Atlanta 1996 Olympic Games who were wrongly identified as male.

When the IOC switched over to the PCR test, the IAAF did not follow suit. Instead, the IAAF decided to abandon mandatory sex testing and instead granted authority to a medical delegate to 'arrange for the determination of the gender of the competitor should he judge that to be desirable'. Soon, the IOC and most other SGBs abandoned all forms of routine gender testing of female athletes and switched to this 'suspicion-based' standard devised by the IAAF.

This was invoked in the case of Indian sprinter Santhi Soundarajan, who failed a gender determination test conducted by the Olympic Council of Asia at the 2006 Asian Games in Doha. Later, South African sprinter Caster Semenya was subjected to a gender determination test after the 2009 IAAF World Championships.

The approach faced strong criticism on grounds of the inherent subjectivity involved in the identification and targeting—with potentially racist undertones—of test targets. This eventually led to governing bodies such as the IAAF issuing bright-line policies on the treatment of ambiguous cases. For reasons we will examine, these turned out to be no less controversial.

Variation

Testosterone has an effect on human muscular and physiological development. Men's bodies generally produce more testosterone than women's bodies. Hyperandrogenism is a natural condition in certain individuals due to which higher levels of hormones are produced by their bodies. When hyperandrogenism is found in intersex women, it can lead to the prevalence of testosterone levels much higher than the average for females.

In 2011, the IAAF introduced testosterone-level-based eligibility regulations for female athletes with hyperandrogenism who wanted to compete with other women. These rules were endorsed by the IOC prior to the London 2012 Olympic Games. Though not attempting to determine a participant's sex or gender, the rules were issued in the name of preserving the safety, fairness and integrity of women's competition.

In 2015, the regulations were successfully challenged in the Court of Arbitration for Sport (CAS) by suspended Indian sprinter Dutee Chand.[3] The CAS ruling found that insufficient evidence had been provided to show that testosterone increased female athletic performance, and notified the IAAF that it had two years to provide the evidence. Dutee Chand's suspension was revoked and she was able to run again.

The Dutee Chand case forced the IAAF to go back to the drawing board, and it issued new regulations for female classification based on a 2017 study in the *British Journal of Sports Medicine*.[4] This study was supported by the IAAF and conducted by Stephane Bermon and Pierre-Yves Garnier, the current and former directors of the IAAF's Health and Sciences department.

The new regulations applied only to intersex female athletes with XY differences in sex development, having testosterone levels in the male range and normal androgen receptors, and who compete in middle-distance track events (all events from 400m to 1500m) at international competitions. Athletes with naturally high testosterone faced a choice: they could take oral contraceptives, go through hormone therapy or have a gonadectomy to keep racing the middle distances, or move to sprints or longer races.

Under the regulations, no athlete could be forced to undergo assessment and treatment. The way these regulations play out, the same person can be eligible to compete against women in the 100m or 200m dash and yet be ineligible to compete in the 400m or 800m women's races within the same athletics meet.

Caster Semenya challenged the new regulations before the CAS. The CAS upheld them on the grounds that they were necessary, reasonable and proportionate in order to preserve the integrity of female athletes in the restricted events and to ensure fair competition. Her attempt to have the CAS holding overturned at the Swiss Federal Tribunal did not succeed either.

Notably, after the Tokyo 2020 Olympic Games, Bermon and Garnier—the authors of the supporting 2017 study—issued a correction.[5] They acknowledged that they had overstated the impact of testosterone on performance and that, while there was a correlation between high testosterone and performance, their data did not demonstrate causation. In lay terms, they accepted that their study counted for nothing.

Meanwhile, Semenya wasn't about to give up. She took the matter to the European Court of Human Rights (ECtHR), alleging a failure on the part of the Swiss legal system to afford her an effective remedy against discrimination and the right to respect for private life. In July 2023, in *Semenya v. Switzerland*,[6] the ECtHR ruled in her favour by a majority (four votes to three). It determined that Semenya had not been afforded sufficient institutional and procedural safeguards in Switzerland to allow her to have her complaints examined effectively, especially since her complaints concerned substantiated and credible claims of discrimination as a result of her increased testosterone level. It recognized that the high stakes involved for Semenya should have led to a thorough institutional and procedural review in Switzerland, and that Semenya had not been able to obtain such a review.

This is a complex issue of significant import. The world's best athletes are all outliers in some way. Many have unique physical characteristics that provide performance advantages over others. Others work harder or smarter with what they have.

Sport's attempt to define a line between the male and female classification and to find objective markers is fraught with risk. However, the way sport is structured means that it must take up the task. It's not called a binary without reason. The trajectory of gender regulations also raises questions on the role, reliability and independence of scientific studies, and our still-incomplete understanding of how our bodies work and the factors that influence human performance.

How should sport classification deal with natural biological variations like hyperandrogenism? There are no right answers. There are only battles between two seemingly incompatible values: inclusion on the one hand, and competitive balance and notions of fairness on the other. It is impossible to please everyone.

Yet, these edge cases present an opportunity—for sport, and also for the societies we live in—to reassess deep-rooted notions about gender that are past their expiry dates.

Transition

Similar issues play out in another sphere: when athletes transition from one gender to the other. Here, the attitudes and responses to gender transition in sport can be compared with those relating to other ways in which athletes change eligibility.

Many societies have recognized an individual's autonomy to identify with gender as they choose. The Supreme Court of India has affirmatively recognized the rights of all persons to declare their self-perceived gender identities. The Indian Parliament also passed the Transgender Persons (Protection of Rights) Act, 2019. This law recognizes that assigned sex at birth and gender can be different, and respects one's ability to transition from one gender identity to another.

Within the gender binary of sport, the inclusion of trans athletes can be controversial, especially so in women's sport. It is a challenge for SGBs to balance trans athletes' right to be included in sport opportunities with their governance objective of 'fairness' and the rights of potential competitors. To understand such complexities, consider the example of a trans athlete who has transitioned from male to female and may have retained certain developmental advantages over women athletes who have been female by birth.

Should a swimmer, who has been male for the first sixteen years of their life, be permitted in female swimming events after they have transitioned to female? If so, under which conditions? The issues here are different from the cases of hyperandrogenism we discussed earlier because, here, the athlete is making an affirmative decision to go through a gender transition.

The evolving discourse led to anatomical changes not being made a precondition for transitioned athletes to participate in the new category. In 2015, the IOC Consensus Meeting on Sex Reassignment and Hyperandrogenism did two things. It agreed that those who transition from female to male are eligible to compete in the male category without restriction. In respect of those who transition from male to female, it said that they are eligible to compete in the female category subject to certain conditions. First, the athlete must have declared that their gender identity is female (a declaration that cannot be changed, for sporting purposes, for a minimum of four years). Second, they must be able to demonstrate that their total testosterone level in serum has been below 10 nmol/L for at least twelve months prior to their first competition (subject to case-by-case exceptions that might be longer). Finally, the athletes must maintain such levels throughout the period of desired eligibility to compete in the female category.

The IOC Consensus also stated that compliance with these conditions may be monitored by testing and that, in the event of non-compliance, the athlete's eligibility for female competition would be suspended for twelve months. The International Cricket Council (ICC) introduced almost identical eligibility conditions for transitioning cricketers, while also specifying that no player should be forced to undergo any medical assessment or treatment.

This approach tried to balance the individual autonomy of the transitioned player with the safety of other competitors and notions of fairness. It used testosterone levels as the marker of transition. It used testing limits, time periods for maintenance of levels and cooling-off periods for return to prior gender as guardrails.

Such measures remain subject to scientific substantiation that links testosterone levels to the continuance of historical anatomical and performance advantages. With the gender binary remaining firm, the inclusion of transitioned athletes in female competition has understandably been the subject of controversy, even hostility, from many quarters. There are the rights and interests of competitors on the other side of the debate. Why should they be forced to compete against a person who carries male developmental advantages?

In the middle of the raging debate, the IOC soon saw the inappropriateness of identifying a generic standard based on testosterone for all sports disciplines within the Olympic movement. It recognized the assumptions implicit in this approach, i.e., that transgender women have an inherent, and potentially lasting, advantage over cisgender women across all sports disciplines.

After undertaking multiple years of consultations and study, the IOC changed tack. In 2021, it issued the IOC Framework on Fairness, Inclusion and Non-Discrimination on the Basis of Gender Identity and Sex Variations. This placed the responsibility of establishing guidelines for inclusion on each individual sport and its SGBs. It urged SGBs to not make presumptions about sporting advantages that trans athletes and those with sex variations have. It suggested that they use an evidence-based approach instead. It also urged SGBs to impose restrictions only after undertaking robust and peer-reviewed research, encouraging them to be sure that any basis for ineligibility reflects a consistent, unfair and disproportionate performance advantage or unpreventable risk to the physical safety of other athletes.

The IOC advocated for inclusive and welcoming sport environments for all without discrimination, while signalling the primacy of athlete health, safety, bodily autonomy and right to privacy. Predictable responses followed.

World Athletics (formerly the IAAF) issued new guidelines prohibiting athletes who have gone through what it called 'male puberty' from participating in female world rankings competitions. World Rugby and World Aquatics (formerly Fédération Internationale de Natation or FINA) implemented changes in their policies that would entirely exclude the participation of transgender players in 'female' competitions in their respective sports. The British Triathlon Federation restricted transgender athletes from participating in the sport under the 'female' category and instead allowed them to compete in an 'open category'. Other international federations began reviewing their policies and undertaking studies. Blanket restrictions on transgender participation are likely to be put in place across more sports. Separately, several US state legislatures have passed laws that limit participation in female sports on the basis of gender identity, citing reasons of health and public safety.

In India, the Kerala High Court took an interesting approach in the case of *Anamika v. State of Kerala*,[7] holding that where organizers have not made alternative arrangements for transgender participation, transgender athletes must be allowed to participate and compete in sports in their chosen gender identity. Here, the court shifted the onus of creating inclusive events on to event organizers and SGBs.

In August 2023, World Aquatics announced that it would debut 'open category' races for transgender swimmers at the World Cup in Berlin later in the year.[8]

Fédération Internationale des Échecs (FIDE), the international chess federation, decided that it was not going to sit around and do nothing on this issue. In August 2023, it announced its new policy[9] that transgender women would be barred from competing in official women's chess competitions until further notice and a full review by FIDE, which would be completed within two years.

This move is an interesting one and is bound to reignite the gender debate in non-physical sports like chess.

Knight swap

Gender is not the only aspect in which athletes can transition their eligibility. Nationality and disability classifications are two others.

Some athletes have dual nationality while others might move residence and change their nationality and citizenship in the course of their lives. SGBs have rules on eligibility for such athletes.

The IOC provides that any competitor representing a country in the Olympic Games must be a national of that country. The Olympic Charter provides that a competitor who has represented one country in the Olympic Games, in continental or regional games or in world or regional championships, and who has changed his or her nationality or acquired a new nationality, may participate in the Olympic Games to represent his or her new country so long as at least three years have passed since the competitor last represented the former country. This cooling-off period also applies to athletes having dual nationality who wish to switch to representing another country at the Olympic Games.

Sports like cricket take a wider approach, recognizing citizenship, birthplace and residence as criteria for representing a national team in an international match. In the case of the ICC, the Player Eligibility Regulations state that, besides citizens, a person who has their primary and permanent home in the relevant country for the immediately preceding three years can represent that country's national cricket team. Legal resident status is not an essential condition; factors such as time spent, purposes of absences, whether the person works in the country or owns or rents property therein and can demonstrate permanent ties to the country are considered.

The ICC also makes provision for exceptions to the three-year residence requirement in exceptional circumstances, such as when the player studies in a different country from where his or her parents are resident. For changing nationality after having represented one nation competitively, the ICC requires a stand-out period that can vary based on the membership status of the original and new nationality, to retain more flexibility at the Associate Member level where the game is still developing. No stand-out period is required for a player who has previously represented an Associate Member but does not want to represent a Full Member. So a cricketer can move from playing for Singapore to playing for Hong Kong without serving a waiting period.

All other variations of switches between and among Associate Members and Full Members require a three-year stand-out period. A cricketer who has played for Singapore and wants to now play for Australia, or vice versa, or wants to play for England or New Zealand after having represented South Africa, must serve the waiting period. The ICC also puts a limit on the number of switches permitted, limiting this to one switch unless the second switch is back to the first nationality.

While these provisions are not inherently controversial in the same way as those relating to transgender participation are, the leeway can enable opportunism and marketization of citizenship. It also raises deeper questions of culture, ethnicity and nationhood. Yet, most criticism around nationality transitions is directed at countries seen to be 'acquiring' the allegiance of 'mercenary' and 'gun for hire' elite athletes.

Some of these athletes come from relatively poorer nations and are willing to switch to a new flag for better opportunities, support, the prospect of financial gain and an improved quality of life. Think of Saif Saaeed Shaheen, formerly Stephen Cherono, a Kenyan-born runner and world record holder in the 3000-metre steeplechase event. After having won gold at the Manchester

Commonwealth Games in 2002, he transitioned to represent Qatar and won the World Championships gold in the event in 2003 and 2005. Others move from nations with such deep talent pools that they are unable to rise to the top. Thus, numerous Indian-, Pakistani- and Caribbean-origin cricketers have gone on to play for the US and Canada, among others.

Interestingly, the FIFA World Cup 2022 in Qatar featured a record 136 players representing countries other than the ones in which they were born. Most of these played for Africa's five teams at the World Cup. In these cases, athletes might bring several inherent advantages of their birth country, but will take away opportunities from a local athlete who has had to develop their skills within the constraints of the sporting system they were born in.

Of course, nationality is not a binary and changes in nationality or residence do not bring new or additional contestants into contention within the global sports pyramid, but they certainly do impact certain segments of this pyramid.

Resentments around eligibility have played out in India, and the government eventually issued a notification that only holders of an Indian passport—and not even Overseas Citizens of India or Persons of Indian Origin—could represent national teams, regardless of the eligibility criteria of the sport.

Paralympic sport also permits change of eligibility classification, both when an athlete might first become disabled and when the athlete undergoes a change in disability level. The International Paralympic Committee sets the standards for eligible impairments.

Except for intellectual impairments—which it requires must be present before the athlete turns eighteen—the International Paralympic Committee accepts impairments that occur at any later age. For instance, it accepts both congenital limb deficiency and amputation as eligible impairments.

To compete in para-sport, every athlete must go through an evaluation process. They must be certified as having an eligible impairment and meet the minimum impairment criteria for the specific sport. Then, the athlete receives a classification that factors in the extent to which he or she can execute the specific tasks and activities fundamental to that sport.

A change in the nature or degree of an athlete's impairment may mean that a review is needed to ensure that the classification allocated remains correct. This is done through a medical review. Examples include where the effect of surgery or some other medical procedure has resulted in a change in the athlete's ability to execute the specific tasks and activities relevant to a sport—either positively or negatively—or when the athlete has a new condition or eligible impairment.

A medical review is also required if a change in the nature or degree of an athlete's impairment changes their ability to perform the specific tasks and activities required by the specific sport in a manner that is clearly distinguishable from changes attributable to levels of training, fitness and proficiency.

The classification system provides the flexibility to classify an athlete based on their ability to perform specific tasks or activities. Largely, it takes athletes as they come during the evaluation process. This means that it is possible that an athlete who has trained for many years as an able-bodied athlete and then acquires a disability—such as the loss of a limb—might be competing with an athlete who has had a limb deficiency from birth. A cooling-off, stand-out or waiting period is not required, regardless of the direction in which the classification changes.

In transitions of eligibility on matters such as nationality and disability class, the balance between fair play and autonomy can be found in a manner that is flexible, inclusive and broadly accepted in the public discourse. While society and science grapple with the issues of gender variation and transition, classification by gender remains fraught with seemingly intractable challenges. This reflects how much more entrenched—from cradle to grave—gender is as a human marker when compared to other significant ones like nationality, allegiance and disability.

Is it any surprise, then, that women deal with 'stereotype threats' during a game of chess?

Checkmate

Organized sport is a global sandbox, and perhaps the world's largest social experiment. It plays on the frontline of many thorny issues, especially on matters of gender—inclusion, access, equal pay, safety and fairness, to name a few.

For sports governance, a conflict, contestation or challenge anywhere is relevant everywhere. Forced to make common rules around the world, sport must encounter many complex issues head-on. Often, it must do this before many societies and legal systems do. It navigates these complexities and finds balances. Those balances will keep changing, as we have seen, but they do play an important role.

The decisions made in organized sport resonate across the world of sport, from school playing fields to the World Cups. They also begin to cascade through society at large. They may be 'just' sports rules, but they are much more than that. They give us the chance to reflect on social roles and labels, learn about each other and, indeed, about ourselves. Where do our social boundaries lie? Where should they? When sport plays its moves carefully, it has the power to catalyse social change.

On a chess board, there are only two pieces that are obviously female—the queens. They are the most versatile and powerful of all the pieces. Off the board, many women still believe that men play better than them, simply because they are men.

Check.

Your move, sport!

Chapter 7

On Integrity

What happens when both teams try to lose a match?

The women's doubles badminton event at the London 2012 Olympic Games produced a rare spectacle. A couple of matches during the group stage involved four of the best pairs in the world, two from South Korea and one each from China and Indonesia. By this time, all four teams had already won enough matches to qualify for the knockout stage.

All of them battled hard to lose their last group match. Why? They felt that the losing teams would get the benefit of a more favourable draw in the next round of competition, by avoiding difficult opponents. It was an unabashed race to the bottom. The teams were booed by the crowd for making basic errors, unexpected from Olympic contenders.

In one of the matches, between the top seeds Yu Yang and Wang Xiaoli from China and their South Korean rivals, Jung Kyung-eun and Kim Ha-na, the players repeatedly hit shots wide or served into the net, with the longest rally of the match being four shots. The booing got progressively louder, and the referee warned the players over their conduct. The farce continued and the Korean pair went on to win, which meant the 'losing' Chinese pair could avoid their second-seeded Chinese compatriots until the final (if both teams made it that far).

The Badminton World Federation (BWF) disqualified all four pairs for having tried to 'tank' their matches. Their actions were seen as a breach of the spirit as well as the principles of the integrity of sport. Each player was found guilty of 'not using best efforts' and of 'conducting oneself in a manner that is clearly abusive or detrimental to the sport'.[1] They could not take any further part in the Games. The two South Korean teams were banned for life by their national federations, though their bans were later reduced to six-month suspensions on appeal.[2]

This episode put the spotlight on some interesting questions. Do athletes—particularly those in representative sport at the highest levels—have an obligation to try their best to win every match they play? Do their motives matter? What standards should we hold them to?

Fair play

Authenticity and unpredictability are at the heart of organized sport. Players keep audiences engaged by the display of their skills and the degree of their mastery over them. Everyone wants to see who the best in the field is, what he or she does better than the rest, and why. Unlike music, dance, theatre or movies, neither the participants nor the audience know how things are going to play out. Sport is like a laboratory experiment, one in which you know there will be a result but don't know what it is going to be—and that principle is central to its purpose.

As we have seen earlier, the 'spirit of sport' involves a commitment to compete by the rules, while respecting the values and purpose of sport. Authentic, unpredictable and entertaining competition is supported by a level playing field, with common rules applied uniformly. For a lab result to be meaningful, the environment must be clean, the variables controlled, the inputs unadulterated and the protocols followed scrupulously.

Throughout the history of sport, many inappropriate shortcuts and underhanded methods have been used to gain unfair advantage. The professionalization and commercialization of organized sport, and the vast gaps between the fortunes of successful and contender athletes, have contributed to a hyper-competitive and outcome-obsessed ecosystem. Results have immediate, life-changing economic and social consequences. Corrupt commercial interests can also influence participants and the competition itself. In such an environment, challenges to the sanctity of competition are inevitable.

These challenges can come from unlikely places and in unusual ways. Who is playing? Are they eligible? How are they playing? What methods are fair? Are they doing all they can to win?

The pyramid of sport, the sports industry and the ecosystem of organized sport are built on the foundational pillars of fair play and integrity. If organized sport is to serve its public purpose, many different aspects of its architecture must be protected from manipulation and contamination.

Baseline

The gateways to organized sport are protected by consistently applying and enforcing the classification, qualification and eligibility rules of sporting events. These are point-of-entry requirements that ensure that the participants are playing in the right competition and that they deserve to be there. The pool of competitors can then be constituted properly. Only permitted ingredients must be allowed in the lab, and they should be what they claim they are.

Unprotected gateways can skew competition outcomes and affect deserving and eligible participants. Contamination of lab results follows. Checks on age, nationality and gender, among other grounds of eligibility, protect fair competition. With developments in science, technology, record-keeping and research, the rules, evidentiary standards and protocols for testing and verifying these continue to evolve.

With gender and nationality having been discussed in the previous chapter, the issue of age verification deserves attention here. Age fraud involves the fabrication of age-proof documentation, or the use of other means of misrepresentation of a competitor's age, to enable their participation in an age-restricted competition.

During the early stages of an athlete's development, age differences can play a significant role in determining outcomes. Older athletes have gained more physical, mental and strategic maturity and experience. An advantage of a year or two, in areas such as height, strength and analytical capabilities, can give them a material advantage that can negate any superior skills that younger athletes may have. An eighteen-year-old cricketer or footballer playing at the under-sixteen level can overwhelm younger players' skills and technique by dint of brute strength and power. Sadly, age fraud is rampant across Indian junior sport.

Age fraud disturbs system competitiveness and can also, perversely, slow the progress of overaged athletes when they eventually transition to senior sport. When the same eighteen-year-old is playing in a category below their real age, their use of strength and power reduces their focus on improving their skills—the competition does not demand it. Players like this get found out at the senior level once their strength and power advantages dissipate. In some team sports, age fraud may even result in over-extending athletes' careers beyond their best years, especially where selectors are reluctant to drop iconic athletes.

Age fraud is more common in countries like India, where birth records are not systematized and many children do not enter formal institutions such as schools and colleges. This leaves the door open for the fabrication of birth records through falsification of affidavits and other documents. This systemic weakness is exploited not only by sport; it extends to various spheres—among them the defence services, the bureaucracy and the judiciary—where careers can be extended, earning capacity enhanced and promotions earned beyond what is legitimately due under the system's guidelines.

Age fraud in sport not only breaches the rules and regulations of events but also takes away the opportunities of deserving athletes within the relevant age bracket. Every ineligible athlete who participates through deceit might beat players younger than them, limiting the latter's progression. They also take the spot of an eligible candidate in the particular competition, possibly eliminating them from the progression pathway towards elite sport. Once age fraud becomes pervasive, it changes the normative structure of sport and can result in lower moral friction. As more of it happens, the practice is normalized and further entrenched.

Age verification protocols rely on the science of the day. The widely used Tanner-Whitehouse bone age test involves radiography of the left hand and wrist to assess the relative maturity of the subject. The test has its limitations, and errors can occur. Its tolerance levels impact the degree of predictability and the age until which it can be used.

In the cases of *Board of Control for Cricket in India v. Yash Sehrawat*[3] and *Lokniti Foundation v. Union of India*,[4] the courts have held such testing to be reasonable and representative of the best available and most accurate scientific methods. SGBs have also tried to supplement testing with policies to limit and disincentivize age fraud. One of the measures involves recognizing only birth certificates issued within a year of the person's birth. Another, employed by the Board of Control for Cricket in India (BCCI), was to limit the number of times a player can participate in a particular age-limited event, such as representing India at the ICC Under-19 World Cup. Some SGBs, like the BCCI and the Badminton Association of India, have announced moratorium periods for rectification of age records through self-declaration. They state that no penal action will be taken against players who voluntarily correct their birth records during these periods, but have threatened severe consequences thereafter for those who don't.

Recognizing the seriousness of the issue, the Sports Ministry issued a National Code Against Age Fraud in Sports in 2010. This was incorporated by reference into the Sports Code, and all NSFs were required to adopt methods to prevent, detect and penalize instances of age fraud and manipulation of documentation. SGBs have the power to impose disciplinary action on a player found guilty of age fraud, including suspending or banning the player and purging all of their records.

These measures can get more complicated in the case of events that have been completed and in team sports. For example, Delhi-based Manjot Kalra represented the winning Indian team at the ICC Under-19 Cricket World Cup 2018, scoring a match-winning century in the final. Some months later, he was suspended by his state association from age-restricted cricket for two years and other forms of cricket for a year on the basis of a complaint alleging that he had misrepresented his age.[5] The suspension from senior cricket was eventually overturned. The results of the ICC event, and Kalra's records, stood unaffected.

Kalra's case is not an isolated one, and cricket is not the only sport affected: given the endemic nature of the problem, there is barely any Indian sport that isn't affected by age fraud. When a person is found to be overage only after an event is complete, they may lose their medals and their results, but the players they beat and denied progression opportunities to have no remedy. In this environment, pre-emptive testing and exclusion become vital.

Despite the scale of the issue in countries like India, age fraud receives less global attention than other forms of sports corruption do. This could be because it is less likely to occur in countries with better record-keeping systems. Any attempt at prioritizing integrity in Indian sport has to begin with building a cogent, robust approach to the maintenance of clean and accurate age records.

An ecosystem encouraging and rewarding youngsters who cheat is built on a poor ethical foundation. It also involves conspiring coaches, parents and officials, or those who deliberately look the other way when they know what is happening or, worse still, actively participate in the fraud. No child can cheat at this scale without adult support. When adults give children the message that winning is all that matters, their further moral decay is not only possible—it is likely.

In youth sport, age isn't just a number. It can be the difference between a future champion found and one lost to sport forever.

Double hit

One of the prime objectives of competitive sport is for participants to reach a defined goal more effectively than their opponents or co-participants. To do this, they must use the advantages of ability, physicality, skill, focus and more. Sport will want to ensure that any such advantage is gained fairly. In turn, this requires a definition of what constitutes 'unfair advantage'.

Fairness is coded into rules governing sporting competition, the violation of which will result in adverse consequences for the participant. In the lab that is organized sport, the methods employed are central to the enterprise.

The use of prohibited substances and methods to enhance performance are rule violations. Doping is a catch-all term for such practices, which date back to ancient Greece. Athletes were known to consume animals' hearts and testicles to increase testosterone, snack on mushrooms and hallucinogens and drink 'magic potions'. Those who were found out were banned for life from competitions and publicly shamed.

In the modern sporting era, the IAAF was the first international federation to ban doping in 1928. Testing was introduced many decades later but became more common only in the 1970s. Regular testing showed how rampant doping had become. Instances of state-sponsored doping in Eastern Europe and elsewhere also came to light.

In February 1999, the International Olympic Committee (IOC) convened the First World Conference on Doping in Sport in Lausanne. The conference resulted in the Lausanne Declaration on Doping in Sport, a document that provided for the creation of an independent international anti-doping agency to be operational for the Sydney 2000 Olympic and Paralympic Games. As a result, the World Anti-Doping Agency (WADA) was established in 1999 as a private foundation based first in Lausanne and later relocated to Montreal. Today, it governs the anti-doping framework through the World Anti-Doping Code (Code). The Code first came into effect on 1 January 2004 and has undergone a few revisions over the years.

The Code defines various anti-doping rule violations, including the presence of a prohibited substance in an athlete's sample; possession, use or attempted use, or the trafficking or administration of such substances or methods; the evasion, refusal or failure to submit to sample collection; tampering with any part of the doping control process, and failure to notify whereabouts for out-of-competition testing.

Compliance with the Code is mandated under the Olympic Charter as a condition for participation in the Olympic Movement and the International Paralympic framework. All international federations and National Olympic Committees are expressly required to adopt and implement the Code. Nation states are not signatories to the Code, but are bound by the Code as a result of being signatories to UNESCO's International Convention Against Doping in Sport.

In India, the Sports Ministry established the National Anti-Doping Agency (NADA) as an autonomous and independent anti-doping organization in November 2005. In 2022, the National Anti-Doping Act was passed to constitute NADA as a statutory body and to give legal recognition to the National Dope Testing Laboratory.

Anti-doping is a cat-and-mouse game. Doping attempts can be diversified, sophisticated and ingenious. Even as official bodies discover new doping techniques and find ways to test for them, ambitious transgressors move ahead and find new ways to work around those testing methods. Testing institutions and their methods must respond proactively. While athletes employ novel methods such as blood transfusions to increase oxygen levels in their blood, testing agencies devise methodologies like developing an athlete's biological passport—a tool that monitors selected biological variables over time to reveal the effects of doping—rather than attempting to detect the doping substance or method itself.

Dope testing can be undertaken during competition and out of competition, with certain athletes in registered testing pools being required to inform anti-doping authorities regularly of their whereabouts to enable surprise tests to be carried out. To keep it current with the science, WADA updates the 'Prohibited List of Substances' from time to time, and monitors anti-doping programmes during major international sports events. An athlete failing a doping test can be banned from sport for a period of up to four years.

The anti-doping regime works on the principle of strict liability and the individual athlete is responsible for all substances ingested into their body. An athlete who is the subject of an adverse analytical finding bears the onus of establishing a viable defence to avoid a ban or receive a reduced ban.

In the interest of the health of athletes, the WADA framework provides for 'Therapeutic Use Exemption' to enable athletes to pre-apply to use medication required for the treatment of a health condition that would otherwise constitute a doping violation. With prior clearance, for instance, an asthmatic athlete may be permitted to use certain medication to respond to their disease even if it contains steroids that are on the Prohibited List of Substances.

The global anti-doping system has shown how poorly it is resourced to respond to proven cases of state-driven and state-sponsored doping that destabilize and destroy the sanctity of major global sports competitions. Russia's state-sponsored doping programme is a case in point.[6]

The enforcement of sports equipment regulations also forms an important part of integrity efforts. Regulations set standards and technical specifications of permissible equipment. Along with the general rules of the sport, they can also specify the manner in which the equipment can and cannot be used in the course of competition. Such regulations try to leave room for innovation in equipment development. This can improve sporting performance and bring other benefits such as safety and fan engagement. For instance, the javelin throw specifications had to be redrawn to reduce the distance the javelin travelled after throwers began achieving distances that would endanger runners who might be on the 400-metre track at the same time as the javelin competition. The iterative development of cricket helmet design since the 1970s and 1980s is another example.

Equipment regulation also tries to maintain a balance between the relative roles of the equipment and of human skills in determining the sporting outcome. Differences in equipment capabilities can play a significant role in sporting outcomes. To retain the primacy of human skills in outcomes, it is important to limit the role such variations can play.

Mechanical or technological doping involves the use of equipment and other clandestine measures and methods that breach the competition's equipment guidelines and other rules. The intentional breach of the regulations is seen as a form of fraud, and sports governors are responsible for not just issuing regulations but also monitoring and enforcing them.

The doping framework protects the inputs that go into competition, whether in preparation or in play. For instance, the fraudulent use of motors in competitive cycling has forced the international cycling federation, the Union Cycliste Internationale (UCI), to respond with more thorough checks. Swimsuit design from companies like Speedo and shoe technologies from the likes of Nike have advanced at a pace that challenges the fine balance between equipment that is supportive and that which provides a distinct and unfair advantage.

In 2009, FINA wiped out all world records created using the NASA-designed hi-tech Speedo LZR Racer swimsuits, after twenty-three of the twenty-five records broken at the Beijing 2008 Olympic Games were by athletes wearing these suits. The use of Alphafly running shoes from Nike, which had three carbon plates and a highly cushioned midsole, was limited within official races. Nike proceeded to adapt the shoe and released the Vaporfly, which was used by thirty-one of the thirty-six podium-finishing athletes at major marathons in 2019.

Such performance-enhancing equipment puts sports governors and the technical guidelines they issue in the spotlight. There is already technology that sends low electrical currents to regions of the brain, claiming to enhance athletes' ability to maintain stronger neural signals throughout a competition. This is known as transcranial direct current stimulation. How much will we allow scientific advances like these into the human pursuit of sport?

Maintaining the integrity of sport asks difficult questions of sport itself. What is the skill being promoted, recognized and rewarded? Which external influences, like good nutrition and meditation, are acceptable inputs, and which ones like doping and souped-up equipment are not? To what extent do we want the achievers to use their own agency to earn and deserve the accolades we give them?

Integrity maintains a balance between the past, the present and the future of any sport. Advances in human skill and performance are at the core of the sporting endeavour. Advances in equipment technology, materials, design and the like are inevitable. Someday, sport might end up becoming a battle of scientific and technological capabilities. But today isn't that day, and the skill of the athlete must remain front and centre.

String along

The right competitors are in the fray. The appropriate equipment is being used. No prohibited substances, equipment or methods are being employed. A sports competition is now primed to deliver outcomes and results that are based on the relative skills of the participants. What could possibly go wrong?

Oddly enough, it is something we should have been able to take for granted—that everyone is playing with the intent to succeed and the desire to win. Is the lab working at full capacity or is there anyone trying to sabotage and manipulate the experiments? Every day, extraneous factors and influences work to corrupt professional sport. These can often come from organized crime rings that use sports corruption to further their objectives. Athletes and officials are key targets and end up becoming core participants.

Match manipulation or 'fixing' involves the pre-determination, influencing or alteration of any aspect of competition through improper acts or omissions. It includes match-fixing (the deliberate loss or compromise of the result of a contest), session-fixing (the contrivance of a particular phase of the contest), spot-fixing (the pre-determination of a specific incident at a pre-determined phase of the match), sharing of privileged/inside information with outsiders, deliberate misapplication of rules by match officials, and similar conduct involving one or more participants in the match.

While motivations can vary, most often, they are driven by either financial benefit or sporting advantage. Match manipulation is often linked to betting, both legal and illegal. Participants conspire with bookies to predetermine aspects of their performance that the bookies then use in the betting markets as an illegally gained advantage. The participant-manipulators and the bookies share in the illicit gains of the information asymmetry, with the participants usually receiving a fixed and predetermined payment in exchange for complicity.

Manipulation for 'sporting advantage' involves a team or a participant underperforming in a match to gain a competitive advantage later in the event, for a better draw or progression pathway, for impacting the relegation of another person or team, etc. Such match manipulation may not be linked to betting markets, but it can also have financial implications. It can determine which other teams qualify, alter the allocation of prize money and impact in-stadium spectatorship, television viewership and brand value.

There can also be personal or political motivations for 'tanking', i.e., deliberately throwing a game. It could be motivated by trying to oust or eliminate a disliked opponent or team, or to avoid an opponent from a political rival nation, but these incidents tend to be rarer.

SGBs and event organizers monitor patterns of play for unusual activity and suspicious behaviour using data analysis and artificial intelligence. They also issue codes of conduct and anti-corruption regulations. In some countries, these rules and regulations are supplemented at the national level by laws providing civil and criminal sanctions that view match manipulation through the lens of existing fraud, corruption and cheating provisions.

In a few cases, national governments have deemed existing laws inadequate, and enacted specific legislation criminalizing match manipulation. In 2014, the Council of Europe introduced the Macolin Convention, an international treaty specifically addressing match manipulation. It has over thirty nation states as signatories, with nine nation states having ratified it since it came into force in 2019. Its objective is to enhance the exchange of information and national and international cooperation between public authorities, sports organizations and sports betting operators to prevent manipulation of sports competitions. It calls on sports organizations and competition organizers to adopt and implement stricter anti-corruption rules, and on governments to adopt necessary measures to deal with match manipulation, including legislation.

Service over

India's response to repeated and systematic manipulation of its favourite sport, cricket, tells its own story. The sport has seen a few major scandals, from the match-fixing cases of 2000 involving Indian and South African international cricketers to the IPL 2013 spot-fixing controversy.[7] How these incidents were investigated and prosecuted is illustrative of the difficulties faced in safeguarding sports integrity within the current legal framework.

In 2000, allegations of deliberate underperformance and match manipulation were made against multiple members of the senior national men's cricket team, including players and support staff. Despite finding evidence of players accepting money from bookmakers in exchange for favours on the field, the Central Bureau of Investigation (CBI) was unable to establish a violation of any penal legislation and could not proceed with prosecution. While the act was morally repugnant, there was no specific law of the land that it was seen to contravene.[8]

The Disciplinary Committee of the BCCI banned the support staff member and the players,[9] including former Indian captain Mohammad Azharuddin. Azharuddin's life ban was later lifted by the judiciary on the grounds that the BCCI's disciplinary proceedings did not follow due process and contravened the organization's own rules.*

In the IPL 2013 spot-fixing case, multiple players (including Indian national team player S. Sreesanth) were alleged to have executed predetermined no-balls and wides in return for financial incentives from bookies or to have committed other related acts or omissions. The BCCI imposed bans on them, a couple of them for life.[10] The players were also charged with participating in 'organized crime' under the Maharashtra Control of Organised

* This case is examined in more detail in Chapter 18.

Crime Act, 1999 (MCOCA) and cheating under the Indian Penal Code, 1860 (IPC).[11]

Again, the prosecution could not provide sufficient evidence to prove the players' participation in a crime syndicate for penalization under MCOCA. The Delhi District Court also found that an offence of cheating was not made out as the conduct of players did not cause any wrongful loss to spectators, nor did it involve any transfer of property from the deceived party. Even though quantifiable loss might have been caused to bettors, betting is illegal in India and they would not be able to make a legitimate claim. A few years later, the BCCI Ombudsman set aside the life ban on Sreesanth and passed an order reducing it to a period of seven years.

Unlike some other countries, India does not have a legislation or regulation that specifically actions match manipulation. There have been calls to change this. The Justice Mudgal Committee, the Justice Lodha Committee and the Law Commission of India[12] have all separately recommended that match-fixing should be criminalized, and also that sports betting should be legalized and regulated in order to better detect match-fixing.

Over the years, especially in the immediate aftermath of major match-fixing scandals, legislators have drafted and proposed multiple bills for tackling match manipulation and corrupt practices in sport, such as the Prevention of Dishonesty in Sports Bill, 2001, the Dishonest Practice in Sporting Event (Prevention) Bill, 2013, the Prevention of Sporting Fraud Bill, 2013, the National Sports Ethics Commission Bill, 2016 and The Sports (Online Gaming and Prevention of Fraud) Bill, 2018. However, none of them has been passed into law.

Into the net

The criminalization of sports fraud is not seen as urgently necessary. Unlike those in governance positions, athletes in the sports pyramid are not seen as performing 'public functions' in the eyes of the law. They are encouraged and incentivized to act in their own private interests and to do everything within their control to succeed.

Treating athletes as public functionaries for the purpose of anti-corruption law could result in risk-averse behaviour, meaning less freedom and spontaneity in play. However, would we give scientists in a publicly funded laboratory the same leeway? What if they were deliberately contaminating the lab or fabricating results?

Like sports governors, athletes are also insiders, accessing scarce opportunities within the pyramid of sport, itself an intentionally exclusionary monopoly structure. This explains why the Badminton World Federation decided to disqualify players losing strategically to gain an advantage in the next round. The issue is not a simple one, although it was neither new nor unpredictable.

Three decades earlier, football had encountered the same issue in the 'Disgrace of Gijon'. This was a group match between West Germany and Austria in the FIFA 1982 World Cup in Spain, played at the El Molinon Stadium in Gijon. If West Germany won by one or two goals, both they and their opponent Austria would qualify for the next round, based on goal difference. If the Germans won by four goals or more, Algeria—which had beaten them earlier in the tournament—would qualify and Austria wouldn't. If the Germans won by a margin of three goals, progression would come down to the goal difference.

The Germans scored in the first ten minutes and after that, neither team made any effort to score during the rest of the match, which deteriorated into a farce. FIFA ruled that neither team had broken any rule, and both teams progressed. Here, FIFA took responsibility for the design of its event and chose to not punish teams for responding to the incentives they had been presented with.

This incident, however, prompted FIFA to change the structure of future editions of the World Cup. Ever since, all the final matches from the same qualifying group have been held simultaneously.

The badminton players could argue, similarly, that they had broken no rule and that the flaw was not in their conduct but in the tournament's architecture, which rewarded such conduct. Badminton's governors took a different approach from FIFA, holding that the players were responsible for upholding fair play, whatever the circumstances. The BWF's contention was that the players must not only play by the rules but must also not do anything that would cause detriment to the sport. The BWF did change the format for the next Olympics, however, inserting a random draw to determine match-ups after the qualifying stage, and thus 'subtly' admitting its error.

Being a representative athlete is a privilege that comes with a set of responsibilities towards others: fellow citizens, competitors, aspirants and also those who are watching and following. If a top-flight match is reduced to one that both teams are trying to lose, two crucial pillars of sport—authenticity and fair play—are threatened.

Audiences have paid good money for tickets, and young people all over the world are watching, waiting to emulate what they observe. Broadcasters and sponsors also have an interest in ensuring that matches are played fairly; authenticity is a critical aspect of keeping fans interested and protecting the commercial value of the sports property. Organized sport, especially at the very top of the pyramid, cannot afford such a spectacle. There is a line beyond which the ends—here, a path ahead that is perceived to be easier—do not justify the means.

The badminton players probably would not have been sanctioned if their sporting underperformance had been only for a phase of the match, for tactical reasons within the match itself (e.g., to tire out a more skilled but less fit opponent and elongate the match to a third set) rather than for reasons extraneous to the match itself, even if they were related to the tournament (e.g., an easier opponent in the next round). The lines may not be easy to draw, but they do exist.

Four decades apart, the relative handling of the FIFA and BWF cases shows the increasing role that public expectation plays in setting standards of fair play for all sport participants—a subject we will dive into later in this book.*

Break point

Despite calls for sports frauds to be made criminal offences, Indian criminal law has shied away from dealing with sports integrity matters head-on. It has tried, often unsuccessfully, to force fit these into existing offences against property, such as 'cheating'. However, such offences require clear identification of a victim, deceit and proof of actual loss. As the cricket-related cases have shown, such elements of a crime are not easy to establish in a court of law, especially in a country where sports betting is illegal.

The search for specific victims of match manipulation mischaracterizes the nature of the offence and the impact it has on other contenders and on those who are shut out, not even getting the chance to compete. These violations must be seen as offences against common property, with principles similar to 'trespass' applied to cases of age fraud and other eligibility offences, and those similar to 'mischief causing damage to public property' and 'breach of public trust' made applicable to offences such as doping and match manipulation.

In the absence of specific laws, most efforts at maintaining the integrity of sport are controlled by SGBs within their

---

* See Chapter 14.

own rules and procedures, through disciplinary proceedings, bans, etc. These are generally rooted in the 'bad apple' theory of identifying and eliminating the 'cheats' rather than being self-reflective and uncovering systemic inadequacies and misaligned incentives that give birth to and promote the fraud.

To believe that governments, governors, policy and system design are mute spectators to sports fraud is a simplistic view that masks—rather than reveals—the reality. While there are bound to be athletes who make their own decisions to cheat, they do so within the milieu of hyper-competitive environments where there can be little support for the process and preparation a sportsperson puts in to succeed, and large bounties and disproportionate rewards set aside for the winners. To a contender, it may appear that there is little to lose and everything to gain from indulging in sports fraud. Worst case, they get caught and stay in their current situation; best case, they don't and have a greater shot at success and its rewards.

Poorly paid athletes, especially those competing against and playing among better-paid compatriots, also become soft targets for bookies. There are parents, coaches, administrators and even governments looking to build their names and fortunes on an athlete's talent. Their incentives might not always be aligned with the best interest of the athlete, and their joint involvement in schemes of doping and age fraud can, perversely, make the athlete even more dependent on them and subject to lifelong exploitation. The lack of clarity in progression pathways and the disproportionate media and selectorial attention given to specific events, such as performances in an ICC Under-19 Cricket World Cup, can also exacerbate issues such as age fraud.

Cheating is as old as organized sport. Sports fraud of any type dilutes the unpredictability and the public expectation of fair play that together underpin sport. It undermines sport's cultural, social and economic foundation and its ability to deliver on its societal promise. As the stakes grow higher, the cheating can get more sophisticated. Especially when systems are weak and incentives are misaligned, markets fill gaps without reference to morality. Then, new norms can develop rapidly in a race to the bottom.

Any government or sports organization that takes a hard look at itself will see opportunities to strengthen not only its integrity programmes but also its governance, developmental programmes, competition structure, progression pathways, culture, incentive structures and commerce. Cheating and fraud will not be eradicated from sport, but they must be fought every single day and in every possible way.

Sports fraud is a window into human personality. What price are we willing to pay for economic and social rewards? There is an incongruity in an athlete living a lie while being admired and celebrated for pursuing a truth.

Sport's distinguishing asset—and also its Achilles' heel—is authenticity. The same could also be said for each one of us.

Chapter 8

On Skill

Why is sports betting illegal in India?

In India, betting on horse racing is legal. So is playing fantasy sports for stakes. On the other hand, it is illegal to bet on a game of dice or roulette. It is also illegal to bet on sports like cricket and football. Sports betting looks a lot like horse racing and fantasy sports, so why is it treated like dice and roulette?

The outcome of any sport or game is determined by a combination of the participants' skills and the elements of chance implicit in the game itself. The nature of the activity, the context and circumstances in which it is undertaken, and the degree of control players exercise on what happens in the game can all impact the relative extent to which skill and chance influence the results.

When you look at all games on a spectrum, at one end are games of 'pure chance' such as dice or roulette, and at the other end are games of 'pure skill'—perhaps chess is one of the few that might fit this bill. All other games fall on the spectrum as 'mixed skill and chance'. Skills are the aspects of games the participant can influence or control, and can use to respond to the uncertainty within the game. Everything else that happens is the subject and product of chance.

The skill or chance question in Indian law has its origins in a colonial-era anti-gambling law, the Public Gambling Act, 1867 (Gambling Act). Representing Victorian morality, the Gambling Act criminalized the offering of and participation in gambling activities, but games of 'mere skill' were granted a specific exemption from the application of this law. After India's independence, the Gambling Act's structure was adopted in most states' laws on regulation of betting and gambling. Thus, across most of India, it came to be that it was illegal to bet on games of chance but legal to place stakes on games of skill.

How does the law differentiate between skill and chance? Why does it make such a distinction? The legal treatment of sports betting in India tells a story.

In the money

The distinction between chance and skill is key to the law's application to games. Offering or playing games of chance can get you jail time, while games of skill are entirely exempted from application of the gambling laws. However, the Gambling Act and the state laws do not explain or provide guidance on which games qualify as games of skill or which tests must be used to define and differentiate them from games of chance. This has put the ball squarely in the judiciary's court.

Recognizing that few, if any, games fall into the pure- or mere-skill category, the Supreme Court established a standard using the concept of 'predominance'. It held that the 'games of skill' exception would apply in all cases where skill, rather than chance, played a dominant role in determining the winning outcome of the game in question.[1]

To qualify as a 'game of skill' under this test, the chance element need not be absent; it just needs to play a smaller role than skill in influencing the outcome. At the other end of the spectrum, courts have also recognized that 'games of chance' are those where the results are 'wholly uncertain and doubtful', and where a human being would be incapable of applying their mind to estimate the result.

The test is whether it is the basket of skills or the bouquet of chance that is predominant in determining the outcome of the game. For instance, the final resting place of the ball is the sole determinant of who wins and who loses at roulette—but a player cannot apply their mind to determine where the ball will end up when it comes to a stop on the wheel. Again, in a game of dice, one can only make guesses and hope for the best. Nothing the player does can influence the outcome. It may be possible for players to bet strategically or hedge their bets smartly, but this still does not affect the game's outcome.

Ultimately, skills must operate within the game's architecture and rules. Game architectures may have physical elements of chance designed into it, and rules to infuse chance (such as a coin toss on who gets to begin play), or could simply leave the game's outcome subject to some of the vagaries of the world, either natural or manufactured.

The use of dice and cards, for example, brings chance into the gameplay. That is not to say that there is no skill in determining probabilities in a dice-based or card-based game and thereby increasing the odds of winning. It is just that the participant cannot influence the result of the dice throw or the fall of cards, and this increases uncertainty. Of course, this can be likened to sports and games that use a coin toss to begin proceedings, handing the toss-winning team a significant advantage, e.g., a cricket team putting the opponents in to bat in bowler-friendly conditions.

This is where the concept of 'predominance' plays a role. Though the coin toss is a matter of luck, the outcome of the game is still going to be driven by the skills of the players who may or may not use the initial advantage to deliver a favourable result against their opponents, who also bring their own skills to the table. For instance, it is one thing to win the toss and ask the opposition to bat first in bowler-friendly conditions, but the opposition batters might, with the use of good skills, surmount that disadvantage and post a big score.

To determine whether skill or chance is predominant, one needs to determine which of them contributes more than 50 per cent towards the winning outcome. This is a question of fact and not of law. In many cases, the Indian courts have been asked to step in and make this determination.

In 1967, in *State of Andhra Pradesh v. K. Satyanarayana*,[2] the Supreme Court opined that rummy was a 'game of skill'. The court held that despite players having no way to influence which cards they were dealt, they had to memorize the fall of cards, and the building up of rummy requires considerable skill in holding and discarding cards.

While courts in other jurisdictions have relied on expert witnesses, data and academic studies in arriving at their decisions, Indian courts have seemingly made their determinations by simply looking at the rules and structure of these games and building a 'sniff test' of sorts. Does it look and smell more like a sport or a lottery?

Front runner

Skill can include strategic elements such as understanding the rules of the game, the risks, probabilities and dynamics involved, researching opponents and their styles, practice and preparation, and figuring out how to increase one's likelihood of winning.

General skills include physical and mental fitness and training—strength, agility, adroitness, increased attention and better reflexes. Skills are often used in combination. Knowing the rules and understanding what it takes to win can help with preparation and training. Fitness and practice can lead to dynamic use of judgement. Discernment and analysis can help filter options in real time and improve in-game decision-making. Skills are a package deal.

In the 1996 case of *Dr K.R. Lakshmanan v. State of Tamil Nadu*,[3] the Supreme Court decided that betting on horse racing involves greater skill than chance. Of course, horse racing is widely acknowledged as a game of skill involving coordination between horse and jockey. The Supreme Court went a step further. First, it recognized that participants successfully staking money on the outcomes of these races have considerable knowledge of the pedigree of the horse involved and their past performance, and also noted that there are many publications with information about horses and horse racing that assist participants with their predictions. Next, it held that all these factors materially contribute to the outcome of the game. Again, there was no indication that it used any statistics or data science in arriving at this conclusion. Based on its findings, it concluded that betting on horse racing was a game of skill and did not per se fall foul of anti-gambling statutes.

Courts have had a tougher time classifying different formats of poker. In some cases, they have recognized poker as a 'game of skill' while in others, they have deemed it to be a 'game of chance'. Like many other games, poker is designed to allow information to only flow imperfectly or incompletely between participants. The asymmetry of information requires players to make considered decisions on whether to continue playing and staking or to fold, without knowing which cards their opponents hold.

Here, the chance elements include a combination of the information architecture of the game as well as the playing cards used. Contrast this to a game of perfect information like chess, where each player knows the opponent's present position before having to make their next move. The players enjoy equal and transparent information on the state of the game at all times. In comparison, a poker player must contend with large information gaps throughout the gameplay. Understandably, when employing the sniff test at different times, judges can get whiffs of different scents; poker has faced this reality.

Multiple courts have also classified a format of fantasy sports as a 'game of skill'. Fantasy sports is a game in which participants assemble virtual teams comprising players who are actually competing in a real-world sports match, gain points based on how the players do in the real-world match and try and outwit others' virtual teams. The logic used by the courts was not too different from what was employed in the case sanctifying betting on horse racing.

In *Varun Gumber v. Union Territory of Chandigarh*,[4] the Punjab and Haryana High Court noted that fantasy sports required successful users to exercise superior knowledge, judgement, attention and adroitness in understanding the rules, acquainting themselves with the past performance and the physical state and form of athletes available for selection across multiple categories, assessing the relative worth of an athlete and the anticipated statistics arising out of the athlete's performance in the underlying real-world event, and devising an overall strategy in selecting and playing the fantasy sports game.

It also held that greater experience and training provided a user with greater insight into strategies for success and a better understanding of the game's dynamics and operational constraints, and in itself heightened and attuned the element and exhibition of skill on the user's part, thereby having a material influence on generating a successful winning outcome in favour of the user. On these grounds, it concluded that the element of skill has a much greater and predominant influence on the outcome of the game than any incidental chance.

Odds and ends

Sports betting has not received as enthusiastic a reception. It is regularly prosecuted as a gambling offence and is seen as a 'game of chance'. Currently, only the state of Sikkim permits sports betting under strict licensing conditions through a local intranet for participants located in the state.

If there is adequate skill involved in evaluating and placing bets on horses on the basis of their breed, age and previous performances, or in assembling virtual teams based on the abilities and current form of players, surely the same logic should hold for betting on sports like cricket and football? All of these require an understanding of the underlying sport and its rules, evaluation of the athletes or teams involved, and factoring of their past performances, the conditions and context into the decision to draft and back certain players or teams. As fantasy sports has shown, these sports are the subjects of far more coverage and freely available statistical information and expert analysis than horse racing is. What, then, explains the different treatment two similar activities receive under Indian law?

By the time the Supreme Court was called upon to decide on the legality of betting on horse racing in 1996 in the *Lakshmanan* case, the activity had a legacy of over a hundred years in the country. Attending the races and being seen at the racecourse was a favourite pastime of the British in colonial times, and was soon adopted by Indian high society after Independence.

Multiple racecourses had been constructed and were being operated by racing clubs that admitted the relevant city's elites as members. They also employed hundreds of staff, from administrative and event managers to trainers, professional jockeys, cleaners and many more, from different strata of society.

Betting was undertaken on the day of the race, in regulated surroundings in a separate enclosure at the race club tote or through licensed bookmakers. The competition, the odds and the payment structures were overseen by managing committees of the racing clubs, elected from among the elite members. The turf clubs themselves operated under a licence from the relevant state government under state racecourse licensing laws. Holding betting on horse racing to be illegal would have brought this party to an end.

There is a very different hue that sports betting—particularly betting on cricket in India—has taken on over the decades. Cricket has always been a betting-friendly sport since it was first played in its vestigial form. One of the legendary greats, the Englishman W.G. Grace, was even accused of betting on the matches he played in.

With the passage of time, however, such activities were deemed as not quite 'playing the game'. And over time, as betting on cricket began to be increasingly frowned upon, it went underground. In India, sports betting came to be associated with organized crime, the underworld, match manipulation, addiction and resulting social ills. It has flourished as an underground, shadow activity, with widely espoused negative effects on people and society. Betting's connection with multiple match-fixing scandals in Indian cricket is undeniable. Regardless of the activity's inherent characteristics or its similarity to betting on horse races (as argued in the 2017 case of *Geeta Rani v. Union of India*,[5] which remains pending before the Supreme Court), the moral milieu in which sports betting existed made it far easier for judges and law enforcement agencies to give it a different label—to characterize it as undesirable, non-productive and deservedly illegal.

In 2018, the Law Commission of India published its 276th report on Gambling and Sports Betting Including in Cricket in India. It trod carefully, recognizing the state of the public tide and accompanying undercurrents, including the possibilities of addiction, debt and social unrest. It cautiously expressed its preference that sports betting be strictly regulated over being left uncontrolled in the shadows. The Union Parliament has not taken the bait.

Horse racing and sports betting may seem very similar in fact, but to a judge, they can look—and smell—very different. One can be seen as elite, organized, already regulated, socially accepted and offered in a carefully managed and supervised architecture, and the other as shady, damaging, socially dangerous and so widely distributed that it is impossible to monitor and control. Also, horse racing had been legal for decades and the inertia was in its favour.

The trope that cricket betting is shady has become self-perpetuating. The sports betting industry has not helped its own cause, employing underhand techniques and ambiguous business models. The latest of these is the manner in which online sports betting has been offered by offshore providers operating out of tax havens and dodgy jurisdictions. It would take a brave judge to author change on a topic like this.

Judges, too, are products of the societies they live in and their societies shape their opinions and world views. When they handle cases, they are not immune to the prevailing social context, reality and pressures. Unlike the judges in the BCCI case we visited in an earlier chapter, the judges in these cases have played safe, preferring the conservative route.

In the running

So, how did fantasy sports get the legal nod when sports betting hasn't? It all comes down to how the law has characterized the position and role of the participant in the activity.

Sports betting and fantasy sports are both reliant on the occurrence of real-world sporting events, where the underlying discipline is also a game of skill, like cricket or football. Participants must understand probability and assess the likelihood of performances in the real-world event.

Yet, a few things distinguish their classical versions. While there are other formats of sports betting, the stake is typically placed on a single, binary matter such as a prediction of who will win a match or score the first goal. In contrast, fantasy sports contests require players to make multiple decisions while drafting a virtual team. They usually derive their statistics from an entire match, multiple matches or even an entire season.

In the case of a binary bet on a single event, the outcome is deemed to be outside the hands of the participant. The participant is seen as a mere bystander staking on the performance and work of someone else. How is fantasy sports further down the chance-skill spectrum? How is drafting eleven out of twenty-two players into a virtual team not just a multipronged sports bet?

The law looks at the fantasy sports player differently, assessing the number of drafting choices to be made from a range of options, defined by the pool of all potential combinations within the rules of the game. When participants select a virtual team consisting of the same number of players as prescribed for the real-world team (e.g., eleven cricketers) and the contest operates for the entire duration of the underlying real-world sports event (i.e., a full cricket match), the courts have recognized this as a distinct, derivative game, a label they haven't given sports betting.

Here, fantasy sports participants are seen to be staking not on the match but rather on their own skills in the fantasy sports contest—those of drafting and assembling the team—after having conducted research and following the game rules and squad composition guidelines. Just as in sports betting, there is uncertainty involved here too, but the law recognizes the agency of the fantasy sports participant in a way it doesn't with someone betting on sport.

The issue boils down to strategic drafting versus mere prediction. Looking at curtailed versions of fantasy sports might explain why.

What if you had to pick only five players out of twenty-two, or the fantasy contest was around events from just five overs or thirty minutes of a real-world match? How will courts look at these formats?

Reducing the number of selections (say five instead of the original eleven) or the applicable match duration of the underlying match (a block of overs or time period instead of the whole match) introduces new and interrelated dynamics into a virtual contest.

As the drafting choices to be made in a fantasy sports contest decrease, the influence of chance increases. Each event in the underlying match takes on a larger significance. Fewer decisions to be made mean reduced opportunities for the statistical normalization of stray chance elements across the drafted pool.

A few unpredictable wickets here or an expensive over there can have an outsized influence on the outcome of the fantasy contest. They cannot be set off by other events that might occur if there were more players involved. The game starts to look more like a prediction game and less like a drafting or strategy game. Again, as the relevant period of underlying play is reduced, the number of players realistically in a position to earn fantasy points—those in the zone of drafting consideration—can also reduce significantly.

In a sport like cricket, with its role definition and specialization, there are only two or three players prominently involved in a play at any given point in time (the batters and the bowler). If the fantasy contest were to be reduced to a single-innings game, the first six batters of one team and the five likely bowlers of the other team would be the main players in the zone of contention to generate fantasy points. In a five-over period of play, all batters who have been dismissed and all bowlers who have finished their quota of overs are also removed from the roster of likely points generators.

In such a situation, the two batters at the crease and the two or three bowlers who will bowl those overs are the players most likely to generate fantasy points. This then reduces the meaningful decisions a fantasy player needs to make. For more players to come into the zone of consideration to generate points, a specific incident such as a wicket falling, a bowling change, or a catch or a run-out involving one of the other players, must occur. In themselves, these are unpredictable events. Whether and when they occur is outside the control of the fantasy sports participant. Again, with reduced underlying gameplay, statistical normalization gets a shorter window and single events can have a disproportionate impact on end outcomes.

This is the 'predominance' theory at work. In a fantasy game involving an entire cricket match, the skill of the player in reading match conditions, the form of the players available for selection and related factors predominate. Against that, if the game is reduced to events across a single over, or a short period of play, choice becomes more about luck and chance than skill.

While this seems clear enough, the lines between skill and chance can be difficult to satisfactorily establish. The answer lies in data. We have more data available, and more statistical and analytical capabilities at our disposal than ever before. We must move beyond the sniff tests and make these determinations in a rigorous, statistically supported and scientific manner.

Thoroughbred

Now on to a couple of fundamental questions: Why do we prioritize and reward skill? Why do we disparage pursuits involving chance?

We can all work on improving our skills. As we progress, we can be more productive and lead better lives. Others can benefit from our skills, learn from them, emulate them. The skills we have acquired can be retained for future use. They equip us for the challenges that lie ahead in different spheres.

We can't, however, set out to improve our luck. Another person's luck, as much it may fascinate us, cannot benefit us. Being lucky once is no guarantee of future performance. In these truths lie some answers to the questions of why sport and society are partial to promoting skill-based activities.

It is natural for the official sports pyramid to organize competitions primarily around the skill of participants. The legitimacy of competition rests on identifying and rewarding those who are more skilled than others. Though luck and chance are implicit in sport, as they are in life, if organized sports used chance as a key metric, it would not be able to morally justify its exclusive and exclusionary nature; not to those who are eliminated from competition, and not to those outside the pyramid, such as taxpayers and governments. If sports results were based on luck or chance, sport would lose its political and social legitimacy.

Sport doubles down on its commitment to promoting skill. As we have seen in previous chapters, it goes to great lengths to create and protect level playing fields for competition. Through classification and eligibility criteria, it determines who can participate and compete. The integrity of the structure prevents cheating. These structures and protocols are put in place to ensure that competitors' skills and performances can shine through and determine results.

While unpredictability is a desirable feature of sport, the sports system also requires reassurance that it is the most talented and skilled who prevail. The random influence of chance and external factors must be acknowledged, but not foregrounded. Then, efforts are made to reduce and curtail luck's impact. This encourages participants to enter the pyramid. It demonstrates that putting in effort is worthwhile and will be rewarded.

As much as we may want to be lucky ourselves, and are curious about others' good fortune, we do not genuinely respect the luckiest person on earth. There is no world championship of luck. Chance remains a concept we do not fully comprehend whereas skill we do understand and appreciate, at least to a large extent. Sport is our collective quest to explore, to test and to—eventually—know where our human boundaries lie.

Beyond the finish line

Fatalism is woven into Indian culture and risk-taking is a part of everyday life. Yet, there is a broader societal aversion to profiting from luck: the deceit and unfairness of chance, the addictiveness, the teasing of winners who are made to believe that luck is repeatable, the impact on impressionable minds, and the economic impact on the families and the vulnerable. Society—right from the age of mythology—has thus highlighted cautionary tales of people and families ruined by chance, beginning with the Pandavas.

In the *Lakshmanan* case on horse racing, the Supreme Court quoted the Vedas and the Mahabharata, saying, 'We find it difficult to accept the contention that those activities which encourage a spirit of reckless propensity for making easy gain by lot or chance, which lead to the loss of the hard-earned money of the undiscerning and improvident common man and thereby lower his standard of living and drive him into a chronic state of indebtedness and eventually disrupt the peace and happiness of his humble home could possibly have been intended by our Constitution makers to be raised to the status of trade, commerce or intercourse and to be made the subject matter of a fundamental right guaranteed by Article 19(1)(g).'[6]

Sport has its reasons to prioritize skill over chance. The reasons for society's broader approach on gambling, betting and luck are not that different.

The principles of fairness and just deserts underly the moral position on luck. Labour begets rewards. Gains should never be unearned. The law thus weaves a social fabric that promotes improvement and also rewards value-positive initiatives. This is done to keep society vibrant and dynamic.

The sports and games we play are a microcosm of our larger world. Through rules and formats, we construct common realities within which we can all participate. We identify goals, lay out rules and frame the challenges. Our skills then become our expression. Society agrees to celebrate and reward this expression. This promotes a targeted striving, both personal and societal.

Many sports and games, and the skills they purvey, may seem mundane, even inane or pointless. Yet, in a chaotic world in which the trajectory of our lives can seem random and inexplicable, they provide us opportunities to demonstrate causality between our efforts and the rewards we receive.

This common striving comforts us. It breeds connection, empathy and respect. It helps us acknowledge that we are all on a journey together. It gives us reason to believe that we aren't just dice in someone else's grand game. Isn't that how we all like to roll?

Chapter 9

On Innovation

Should Dhoni own the 'helicopter shot'?

Dick Fosbury goes over the bar backwards and his eponymous 'Flop' revolutionizes the high jump; K.S. Ranjitsinhji plays the leg glance and opens up a new part of the field to the half-volley on or outside the leg stump; Antonin Panenka comes up with his light touch penalty kick to befuddle the goalkeeper; Elena Produnova produces her high-degree-of-difficulty vault to rack up artistic gymnastics points; M.S. Dhoni uses his cricket bat like a helicopter's rotor blade to transport the full ball from off and middle stump to over the square leg boundary.

Introducing radical new 'ways of doing' to sport requires creativity, practice and innovation. It adds to the known set of possibilities within the sport and expands the universe of our understanding and imagination.

What motivates on-field innovators? What does this teach us about incentives and rewards? Welcome to the world of intellectual property and sports moves.

Driving ambition

Creativity and innovation are strange bedfellows with the law, brought together by the intellectual property rights regime.

Under this system, governments grant legal monopolies to creators and inventors, giving them exclusivity and control over their intellectual creations for specified periods.

Patents protect innovations and inventions; copyrights protect literary, dramatic, artistic, musical and other creative works; designs protect original designs applied to objects; and trademarks protect names and marks used in trade and commerce—each of these protections prohibiting unlicensed use by others. Once the term of protection expires, these intellectual properties enter the public domain, available for anyone to use without the permission of the creator, inventor or other owner.

The law strikes a bargain when it grants intellectual property rights. The exclusive rights are offered as an economic incentive for people to go beyond known and established ways of doing things by innovating, creating and then publicly disclosing.

Intellectual property law recognizes that many of the things it protects need time, effort and investment to create but, once known to the public, can be copied at close to no cost. The printing press originally made copying and distribution at scale possible. Digital technologies have made things even easier and cheaper, with the digital copy having practically no marginal cost of production or distribution. In a second, an almost-perfect copy can be made of a painting that took days to paint, a song that took weeks to compose and produce, a book that took months to write or a medicine that took years to formulate.

Would paintings, books, songs or pharmaceutical products be created by their authors if anyone could copy them and make money off them? The intellectual property system believes not. On this basis, it protects the intellectual goods from free copying. It creates a legal moat around the work, which gives its owner the right to control its use. It is left to the owner to decide whether—and on what terms—a photograph or a book can be republished, a song performed or a medicine reverse-engineered. Anything of the sort done without the owner's licence would amount to infringement, with compensation and other remedies following.

Thus, ideas and creative expression that might not have seen the light of day are brought into the public domain. Art, literature and science can progress, with more being created and made public. The short-term social cost of patent monopolies and copyright control is seen as legitimate social expenditure towards achieving net overall societal utility. After all, innovation and creativity replenish the public domain and change—even improve—the way we live. It is difficult to imagine a world without the classics, the epic movies, life-saving drugs, motor vehicles, airplanes and everything else that receives intellectual property protection today. If not for this protection, might we have missed out on many of these?

Society's attitude towards 'unjust enrichment' also supports intellectual property protection. Shouldn't creators of value be protected from 'poachers', 'pirates' or 'free riders' who are looking to appropriate and extract value without effort? Why should anyone get 'something for nothing'? The focus of such an argument isn't whether the creator 'deserves' the right to their creation; it is why a stranger should have the benefits of its use. As we have seen in the previous chapter, society prioritizes reward for skills and effort. It doesn't like gain without pain.

Similarly, the labour theory of property furthers the principle that an individual has a property right in their own person and deserves to enjoy the fruits of the labour of their body. The argument is that the effort expended by the individual in participating in the activity is owned by the individual and, therefore, the results of the effort should be, too.

A more esoteric version of this argument is one rooted in personal autonomy. It says that in order to be truly free, each person must exercise control and dominion over their own creations, not because of the effort spent on creating them but because it is an inseparable extension of the creator's autonomy.

Whatever the theory, society promotes its own growth and development using the intellectual property system as one of its drivers. It seeks a balance between private and public rights, short-term and long-term availability, and the control of ideas and their free expression. How does this apply to sport? What rights should we give Dhoni and company over their creations?

Playing it my way

Intellectual property exclusivity—and resulting private control—is used by owners to create markets and generate economic value through licensing and merchandising. This shores up the sports business model. Different types of intellectual property rights support media rights sales, sponsorship deals, licensing and merchandising transactions and athlete endorsements.

Audio-visual match content can be the subject of copyright and broadcast rights. As we will explore in later chapters, the media rights sold exclusively to television and media companies underwrite the sports event; this brings funding to sports development more generally, and intellectual property ownership protects this model.

Intellectual property rights also protect innovative sports equipment—like a new golf driver, training and recovery tools like massage guns and other devices like wearables and motion tracking vests—from unlicensed copying and use. Innovation in sports equipment can also support athlete performance, make sport safer and refereeing more accurate. Think of the latest gym equipment, protective gear like pads and helmets and video-assisted refereeing systems. These innovations tend to be supported by the patent system.

Brands are created around the names and logos of teams. This helps build fan following, goodwill and commercial opportunities. What follows are sponsorship and licensing agreements, sports merchandise and other collectibles that create additional revenue streams. In certain cases, clothing, sports equipment and sports-allied tools can receive design protection.

Intellectual property rights protection plays a vital role in supporting sport in these different ways. When it comes to happenings on the field of play, however, the relationship between sport and intellectual property rights is complicated.

An athlete's journey is best described as the quest for continuous improvement. Every so often, this results in them finding new ways to play their sport. Do athletes need the promise of intellectual property rights to create, innovate and improve? Should they be given the ability to own and control their creations, and the right to stop others from 'copying' them? What can we learn from the answers to these questions?

Cutting edge

By definition, outliers push boundaries and create 'new normals', redefining what we can do and how we can do it. Innovative moves can revolutionize a sport, result in new world records and add to the vocabulary of human capabilities.

The bicycle kick was used for the first time in football over a hundred years ago in South America. The move became popular among Chilean footballers in the early twentieth century. This was used as much for show as for effect. Chilean forward David Arellano famously died of an injury sustained while performing one of his aerial moves during a tour of Spain in 1927.

Pelé brought the bicycle kick back into the limelight, and Diego Maradona was another famous exponent of it. Could the Chileans have stopped Pelé and Maradona from performing the move on intellectual property grounds? Does anyone own the rights to the move? Should they?

In the mid-1990s, US lawyer Robert Kunstadt was among the first to ask the question of whether a 'sports move' could and should receive intellectual property protection.[1] A fair bit of academic writing followed, evaluating whether various sports moves were the appropriate subject matter of copyright and patent protection, i.e., whether they met the thresholds of originality, inventiveness, utility and the like.

Hard work, thought process, strategy and innovation often go into doing something that has never been done before. Dhoni would have practised his helicopter shot, Warne his *zooter* and Muralitharan his *doosra* many times over in the nets before they used these in a cricket match. Other innovations might emerge interactively within competition when an athlete is pushed to the limit, resulting in a moment of magic.

Many commentators have argued that the thresholds of both copyright and patent are capable of being achieved on the sports field as much as anywhere else. Despite Dick Fosbury never seeking to protect his high jump innovation, the Fosbury Flop is held out as an example of an invention that had all the required elements of patentability—novelty, an inventive step, utility and non-obviousness. The standard counterpoint to this is that nobody should ever enjoy exclusive rights over ways in which to use the human body, even if limited to a specific context.

If treated like choreography, artistic or dramatic works, then sports moves could theoretically be eligible for copyright protection. A few individual non-interactive sports, such as figure skating and gymnastics, have elements of scripting. These might have a stronger case for such protection.

In the 1997 case of *NBA v. Motorola, Inc.*,[2] the United States Court of Appeals for the Second Circuit held that no copyright lies in a game itself, even if a broadcast of the same event could gain legal protection. In India, in the case of *Institute for Inner Studies v. Charlotte Anderson*,[3] the Delhi High Court held that yoga *asanas* cannot be copyrighted, opining that sports fell short of the copyright requirements of fixation and predictability.

Another strand of thinking is that sports moves could be eligible for 'method' or 'process' patents, which have been granted for various ways in which the human body interacts with equipment. The argument to support this says that when the standards for the grant of patent rights are met, sports moves should be extended protection since their technical utility and commercial value are self-evident.

If creators and inventors can be protected in other contexts, why not in sport? It is a good question.

Beating the field

The formats and complexity of different sports can vary. Some involve interactivity and others do not. For instance, while badminton and boxing involve multiple moves to be used in interactive sequence, one-shot sports like shooting and the high jump need just one move to be employed at a time (of course, these moves may need to be repeated over different rounds). Whatever the format, organized sport is designed to get the best out of athletes within competitive environments. This makes all sports performances context-specific, even when they are scripted in advance.

Dhoni must pick the right ball for the helicopter shot after assessing the risks and rewards of playing it in the match scenario. An athlete's performance is impacted by how others—including fellow competitors, referees and audiences—behave or perform. If, for instance, the bowlers focus on short-pitched deliveries at Dhoni, he will have to pick another stroke instead.

Performance can also be influenced by the weather conditions and the playing environment. The size of the leg-side boundary and whether the ball is swinging will influence Dhoni's shot selection. Many track and field athletes have been denied world records because their performances were held to be 'wind-assisted'.

Despite the amount of practice and preparation that elite sport requires, original and creative in-match performances can often be instinctive, reactive and raw. This is an inherent feature of sport. Situational innovation is a response to the opportunity and the circumstances of competition. The application of moves and techniques cannot always be planned. Match situations, pressure from opponents and support from teammates can provoke athletes to do things even they had not thought of before. So it is unsurprising that athletes have been excluded from the Indian copyright law's definition of 'performers' who are entitled to *sui generis* performers' rights, even though the list does include conjurers and snake charmers![4]

As in other cases, it may also be unclear whether the invention or work in question is entirely the result of the athlete's own labour and creativity. The competitive context adds value. The coaching received by the athlete draws upon pre-existing and passed-on knowledge. There are also resources, institutions and technologies supporting athlete training and performance.

Should the athlete who completes the chain—places the last pieces to complete the jigsaw puzzle—be given wide-ranging and exclusive rights? The 'romantic authorship' concept uses the rhetoric of a solitary creator, being based in individual entitlement. In reality, it may not always be possible to separate and reward the individual contribution to the final product. Glorifying the athlete-author can result in a system that trivializes or ignores others' contributions to their performance.

Calling the shots

Imagine a world in which certain moves and techniques, once displayed or published, could be locked up and controlled for extended periods by individual athletes who were the first to think of or express them. What if Dhoni could decide whether, who and when another cricketer could play the helicopter shot? Any use would require a licence from Dhoni. Besides being a logistical nightmare, it would alter the competitive balance of many sports by taking parts of the vocabulary out of use or raising their price. Participants may also end up handcuffed, unable to operate instinctively, driven by their muscle memory.

A batter who doesn't have Dhoni's permission to play the helicopter shot could play other shots to the same ball. However, the control of the owner over a unique move could be determinative in other sports that are premised on a single effort rather than extended and multiple segments of play. For instance, the high jump competition would be heavily skewed if Fosbury was the only one allowed to use his move for two decades. Competition results would be more predictable and, as a result, less engaging for participants and spectators.

Despite these complexities, some believe that it is appropriate and fitting to incentivize sports creators or inventors. They argue that there are remedies available to reward the athlete for their ingenuity while keeping the move in use by everyone. If Dhoni owned the helicopter shot, the BCCI could license the move from him in a deal that allowed anyone to use it in the IPL.

Of course, this would come with costs that the system must bear and will, eventually, pass on to its participants. There are also transaction costs involved, with licences to be negotiated. Battles in conference rooms will precede those on the playing field. Infringements would have to be policed across amateur and professional sport—hardly an attractive proposition for anyone other than player agents and lawyers!

If certain moves are taken out of play or made exclusive, learning is hampered. So is improvement and further innovation of such techniques and methods. Sport is learnt at every level of the talent pyramid through observation and emulation. School kids learn movement from physical education teachers. These teachers may have played sport at some level or might teach their wards using a vocabulary of movement passed on to them from a previous generation. Aspiring youngsters learn sports technique in camps from coaches who have often been athletes themselves. Elite athletes learn from certified coaches trained by the system, and from peers and competitors.

The Kenyan athlete Julius Yego was unable to find a coach who could teach him to throw the javelin, so instead, he learnt how to do this by watching YouTube videos. He went on to become African, Commonwealth and World Champion and won silver at the Rio 2016 Olympic Games. Google him and you'll find his nickname—Mr YouTube.

Creativity at any rung of the pyramid quickly reverberates through the system. It is learnt, aped, modified and improved upon.

In many ways, Dhoni's helicopter shot has its origin in a long line of prior ways of doing so—Azharuddin and VVS Laxman's on drives, Ravi Shastri's *chapati* shot, Kapil Dev's *Natraj* shot and Ranjitsinhji's leg glance, each building on the prior art. The freedom to copy without concern or cost is at the heart of the pedagogy of sport. This is especially so in resource-limited countries where coaching talent is limited and much of the learning is done by watching elite players on television and then attempting to emulate them. If certain moves were granted protection and locked away, young athletes on the learning path would first be exposed to the move but then told they may not use it. This is a type of 'pre-alienation' that puts options and ideas into the mind but takes them away even before they can be experimented with.

A truly exceptional innovation that impacts performance permits one to rise through the ranks quickly. In 1968, Dick Fosbury won the gold medal at his first Olympic Games while still in college. Equally, the athlete who first uses a move may not be best at exploiting it. Another athlete could perform the move with better technique, more strength or another element, each of which could result in a performance better than the move's original author is capable of.

Although Fosbury won the Olympic gold, it was another American jumper, Dwight Stones, who first used the Flop technique to break the high jump world record in 1973. Fosbury's career-best jump was 2.24 metres. The high jump world record stands in the name of Cuban jumper Javier Sotomayor, who

Flopped over the bar set at 2.45 metres in 1993, almost 10 per cent higher than Fosbury ever managed. The world record was set twenty-five years after Fosbury first used his technique at the Olympics and has stood for over three decades.

Others who came after Fosbury refined his Flop and expanded what was possible with it. And none of this may have been possible, limits may not have been pushed and new records may not have been set, if the use of the Flop were restricted to Dick Fosbury alone.

When the intellectual property system seeks to find balance, it looks at the rights of the inventor or creator on one side and at collective social interests on the other. In the bargain, individual rights can be overlooked and neglected. Sport cannot afford this.

Privatization and control of the building blocks of sport—the ways of playing—would have significant social costs on those trying to learn sport, improve and progress during the period in which intended exclusivity, protection and control are enjoyed by their owners.

The 'aggregative approach' to social good that favours intellectual property protection is unable to understand or show sensitivity to the predicament of the individual athlete. The public domain may be replenished in the long run by giving athlete-inventors control of their unique moves, but a whole generation of athletes would be denied the use of a technique already known to the sports community. This flips the 'tragedy of the commons' on its head, the suboptimality resulting from the—albeit temporary—private ownership of the public domain.

Every athlete borrows freely from the past and expects to lend to the future. Leaving a legacy is among an athlete's greatest compensations. The social rewards of creating something unique in sport are ubiquitous and real. The spontaneous linking of the athlete's name to the exceptional and unique move—think of the Fosbury Flop, the Produnova, the Panenka and similar—also gives them a lifetime, and beyond, of acknowledgement. History and folklore remember and honour the inventor, providing compensation and reward that cannot be measured in monetary terms, indeed transcending such terms.

At the close of play

The quest to be the best that one can be, to be better than everyone else, is at the heart of competitive sport. This plays out within the preset universe of the rules of sport that lay out a challenge, create a framework for conduct and provide a platform for possibilities to play out. They call competitors to test their mettle against each other. By keeping track of performance records, participants may also be compared to those who have played by similar rules in the past.

The rules bind and frame behaviour on the field. Every option permitted under the rules must always remain available to all participants if sport is to achieve its objective of pushing, and eventually determining, the boundaries of human capability. When a 'way of playing' is removed from currency, it reduces the range of choices and dilutes the overarching role of the rules in crafting the universe of permissible and encouraged behaviours. This impacts outcomes and results. The spontaneity of sport leaves no time and options for evaluating whether the cost of licensing a move is worth the benefits of using it in a situation that might last no more than a fraction of a second.

The sports system is set up for participants to find new ways of playing within the rules and to improve on their—and others'—performances, methods and skills. It is also set up to reward them along the way.

Athletes inspire, connect with and entertain the rest of us. We are all curious about what we are capable of as a species. What is the collective capacity of the human body, mind and spirit? Where are our boundaries? Sport provides us with answers that we can understand, that we believe in and that move us.

The fundamental question the intellectual property system must ask is whether the behaviour it seeks to incentivize would occur anyway even if the protection were not given. On the field of play, the answer is a resounding 'yes'.

Organized sport has internal reward systems. If the application of a new sports move has value in the context of the rules, there will be points scored or an advantage gained within the game. Dhoni's shot will soar for six, Produnova's degree of difficulty will win her more points than the competition and Fosbury will literally 'up the bar'. All these contribute to in-game success and enable winning outcomes. These outcomes have rewards—financial, reputational, social and personal. Prize money, brand value, endorsement fees and national rewards lie in store. Besides, athletes enjoy intrinsic personal rewards from achievement and excellence.

Granting sports moves intellectual property protection is unlikely to bring more people to sport or to change their motivations or behaviours. Keeping intellectual property rights off the sports field is not going to hinder innovation or result in stagnation in sports methods and processes. Such protection delivers little social value in an internally coherent, rule-bound environment that adequately rewards improvement and innovation. On the field of play, net overall societal utility is best served by free and open gameplay.

Sport and intellectual property law have similar goals and serve similar purposes—to get the best out of humans in the service of humanity. Sport, with its clarity, coherence and objectivity, presents a valuable sandbox for intellectual property policy. The question is not simply whether an activity has value or 'deserves' protection. If the incentives are unnecessary to nudge a certain type of human behaviour in an upstream supplier market, exclusivity should not be granted to defend value in the downstream consumer markets. Protection becomes an unnecessary and non-utilitarian social cost.

In recent times, there have been many questions asked of intellectual property laws and institutions. Why do we have them? What do they do for us? Are there any alternatives? Globalization has upped the pressure to strengthen protection, and economic interests push for more subject matter to be covered by intellectual property laws and for longer periods. Controversy rages over the patenting of human genetic materials, life forms, lifesaving vaccines and computer programs, with inventor companies pushing for stronger intellectual property protection and others pushing back. Intellectual property overreach is a challenge faced around the world and across a variety of industries.

How and why athletes improve their skills on the sports field can be an effective case study in using a 'back-to-basics' approach that dispassionately evaluates public and private costs against the public benefits of intellectual property protection.

Any serious reassessment of our laws can learn from sport. When we all get behind a common pursuit, people can be motivated by much more than exclusive rights and commerce.

Dick Fosbury, K.S. Ranjitsinhji, Antonin Panenka, Elena Produnova and M.S. Dhoni have left an indelible mark on their sports. They—and the moves they authored—are talked about years after they have retired. Whether or not they earn a royalty, they continue to be treated like sports royalty. They gave us their new moves. They also give us food for thought on the motivations and incentives that drive human creativity, innovation and progress.

Chapter 10

On Value

How did the IPL thrive while other Indian leagues didn't?

The Indian Premier League (IPL) was launched in 2008 with eight teams, each owned and operated by a private franchisee. The Board of Control for Cricket in India (BCCI) was its official sanctioning body, franchisor and event owner, all rolled into one. The league brought in private investors as active—and significant—stakeholders. It gave them decision-making powers of a nature that had no precedent in Indian sport. It divested to them the right to own their brands, select their teams and run their businesses. The IPL has now grown into a prominent ten-team league and sits among global sport's most significant commercial properties.

Observing the success of the IPL, multiple other Indian sport governing bodies (SGBs) have tried to launch copycat leagues in their sports disciplines. Badminton, tennis, cue sports, wrestling, hockey, football, basketball, volleyball, arm wrestling, kho kho—name the sport, and a franchise-based league has either been attempted or announced. With the Pro Kabaddi League and the Indian Super League for football being prominent exceptions, most other leagues have not survived beyond a season or two, with some like hockey having had multiple iterations and reincarnations, all with limited success.

How did the IPL succeed while most other leagues faltered? How does the sports business work and what lessons does it have for all of us?

Markets and economies have grown around the identification, development and marketing of athletes, the hosting of events, the communication of sports content to spectators and viewers, and the engagement of fans. The industry is built on the premise of connecting athletes to audiences. It addresses the symbiotic human desires to explore one's capabilities and achieve results on the one hand, and to be entertained, engaged and inspired on the other. Various intermediaries are involved in these markets. They service athletes, audiences or both.

Sports industry participants can be categorized into three broad categories: talent businesses on the athlete-supply side, event businesses that create connecting platforms, and media and fan engagement businesses on the audience-demand side. As we shall see, these work in interconnected and interdependent ways.

Show me the money!

How do athletes make a living?

As amateurism gave way to professionalism in global sport, the ability to find talent, nurture it and make it competitive increased along with the commercial value involved. Athletes are key assets. Significant resources and attention go towards supporting their development, sustaining their livelihoods and rewarding them for their achievements.

The demands of high-performance training, equipment, coaching and travel can make professional sport an expensive pursuit. While athletes may play for pride and satisfaction, they also aspire to recover—and gain from—the financial investments they have made. This can happen only when their income exceeds their outflow.

Successful athletes can be among the wealthiest professionals in the world. *Forbes* reported that, in 2022, the top fifty best-paid athletes in the world made a total of almost $3 billion in income, with the top ten earning almost $1 billion of that total. The list includes footballers like Lionel Messi, Cristiano Ronaldo and Neymar, basketballers LeBron James, Stephen Curry and Kevin Durant, and tennis player Roger Federer.

Their on-field and off-field incomes are all closely tied to popular sporting events. Events like professional football leagues, the NBA, tennis Grand Slams and the golf Majors are successful professional events that compensate participants and winners well. Other premium events like the Olympic Games are lucrative for organizers but do not directly compensate participating athletes. Their international salience drives national governments and markets to sustain athlete development and livelihoods, and their 'solidarity' model is oriented to distribute revenues across sports and countries, including those without sustainable economies surrounding them.

Many athletes make their living off their sporting income alone. In sports that have not been commercialized, this may be inadequate, and athletes must find supplementary incomes from other jobs or sources. Chess Grandmaster Hikaru Nakamura makes more income from streaming his chess analysis and commentary online than he does from competition. Not all contenders will succeed at sport, and the sports industry will support their pursuit to varying degrees. Over a career, athletes rely on a patchwork of funding sources, and each athlete's commercial journey is likely to be unique.

Professional athletes in team sports are contracted to play for a club or a regional or national team. Their total playing fee might be fixed, or can be contingent on match participation and personal or team performance bonuses. In the Premier League, the average of first-team footballers' annual earnings is almost £3 million. In the case of cricket, the BCCI issues central contracts to a select group of players across different grades and categories, and the payments under these contracts act as guaranteed retainer amounts. In addition, they receive per match fees that vary by format (Test match, One Day International and T20 International) and also share in a specified percentage of the BCCI's revenues from broadcasting and sponsorships. These amounts are supplemented by the incomes that they might receive from their franchises for playing in the IPL.

In some team sports, iconic players can have playing contracts that entitle them to royalties from sales of the team jersey bearing their name. When David Beckham moved to the LA Galaxy in 2007, a large part of his income was related to the sale of team jerseys, and the team went on to sell an average of 3,00,000 Beckham jerseys per year in his five-and-a-half-year tenure.

Beckham was also given an option to own an MLS club as part of his deal, an option he exercised in 2020 when he became co-owner of Inter Miami. In 2023, Inter Miami signed the 2022 FIFA World Cup-winning captain of Argentina, Lionel Messi, in a deal not dissimilar in structure to what Beckham had.

Where there is a transfer market, players can receive a share in transfer fees that are paid by their new club to the club releasing them. Player compensation can be determined through draft systems, auctions or through open market negotiations. In some cases, they could be unilaterally determined—say, by an SGB—and, in others, may be negotiated by a players' union. Athletes can use agents to negotiate fees where these are open to mutual agreement. Agents make commissions on the deals they close and are thus incentivized to get the best value for the player.

In individual sports, premier athletes attract audiences and raise the profile of an event. They can command compensation just for turning up, and are often paid appearance fees by events. Such fees are common on the professional golf and tennis tours. Outside the Majors and the Grand Slams, players like Tiger Woods, Roger Federer and Rafael Nadal can be paid significant amounts by tournament organizers regardless of how they perform.

This can be taken a step further in sports such as professional boxing, where heavyweight championship contenders can receive shares in the bout's pay-per-view revenues. In their 2017 Money Fight bout, Floyd Mayweather and Conor McGregor made $275 million and $85 million, respectively, a majority of which came from their share in pay-per-view profits.

Some contracts also include a share in ticketing revenue from the matches played. For instance, NBA players receive around 50 per cent of league revenues as part of their compensation. The structure and size of these payments vary significantly based on the profile of the sport, its format, the economy surrounding it, the profile of the athlete and their ability to negotiate.

Participants, whether individuals or teams, can also be rewarded with prize money that depends on their (or their team's) performance in the event. While some events such as the tennis Grand Slams might pay prize money to all participants, including qualifiers and first-round losers, others might reserve prize money only for the winner or the finalists.

Over the years, prize money at major professional events has grown rapidly, especially for those who win them. For instance, at the Wimbledon Championships in tennis, the men's singles winner received £2000 in 1968, £1,00,000 in 1984, £5,00,000 in 2001 and £2.35 million in 2023 as prize money. The women's singles winner received £750 in 1968, £90,000 in 1984, £4,62,500 in 2001 and £2.35 million in 2023, with equal prize money for men and women in place since 2007.

Athletes can have sponsors who support them. In exchange, they wear the sponsor's logo on clothing and equipment or agree to use and promote their products. They often receive a share of team sponsorships, either as part of their playing fees or shared separately. Athletes also tend to be popular endorsers, paid to tell others to buy products and services.

For many of the top athletes, endorsement income can far outstrip playing income. In 2020, Virat Kohli stood sixty-sixth on the *Forbes* list of the World's Highest Paid Athletes, with salary income of $2 million and endorsement income of $24 million for the year.

Athletes can also receive fees to make appearances at product or store launches, inaugurations and events, both in person and digitally or virtually. These events want to capitalize on the attention that the endorser's involvement brings or the media following that they enjoy on traditional or social media. Most athletes use marketing agents and agencies to negotiate these deals, paying them a commission or success fee in return.

Besides athlete earnings from these sources, they can also receive support towards their training and competition expenses. Thus, in some countries, Olympic hopefuls are supported by their SGB, which might receive funding from their international federation, through Olympic Solidarity funding or from the government. Governments might also fund athlete training directly through special programmes and schemes.

In India, the Target Olympic Podium Scheme supports the top Olympic and Paralympic aspirants through financial support to cover training expenses and also provides them with monthly stipends. There is also a grassroots scheme called the Khelo India Talent Development Scheme, which works at the talent identification and nurturing level and provides scholarships and stipends to a larger pool of young athletes. The government also funds the Annual Calendar of Training and Competition of various NSFs, and these funds are meant to support athletes in their training and competition.

Some athletes may receive scholarships and financial support from private sources such as foundations, non-profits and individuals who are interested in supporting sporting journeys and enabling athletes' achievements as part of their programmes. These scholarships might cover training and competition expenses and could also include a stipend.

Athletes can also take on freelance work or other regular jobs that give them some flexibility to train. In India, athlete employment has been made possible through the mandate given to various public sector undertakings such as the Railways, Services, Customs, oil marketing companies like Indian Oil and Bharat Petroleum, and banks like the Reserve Bank of India, State Bank of India and others, to recruit and engage promising athletes as employees.

They have the flexibility to train alongside their job commitments, being tasked with a few non-sport responsibilities. Public sector jobs provide a steady source of income during the athlete's sporting career and an assured post-career professional opportunity. For many decades post-Independence, Indian sportspersons were sustained through these public sector jobs.

National and state governments often set up reward structures for athletes who succeed at prestigious international events. Under the Sports Ministry's 'scheme of special cash awards to medal winners in international sports events and their coaches' issued in 2020, the Indian government committed cash rewards of Rs 75 lakh for the winner of an Olympic or Paralympic gold medal, Rs 50 lakh for a silver and Rs 30 lakh for a bronze. This is supplemented by rewards from the state governments, some of which can be even more generous. In 2021, the Punjab state government announced that it would reward such achievements with Rs 2.25 crore for a gold, Rs 1.5 crore for a silver and Rs 1 crore for a bronze medal. Comparatively, US Olympic medallists are rewarded $37,500 for gold, $22,500 for silver and $15,000 for bronze by the United States Olympic & Paralympic Committee.

Government honours may also have a cash component. Each year, the Indian government presents athletes and coaches the National Sports Awards. These include the Khel Ratna and Arjuna Awards that, as of 2020, carried Rs 25 lakh and Rs 15 lakh each as the cash award components. Additional award components include free train travel for life on the Indian Railways.

In sum, in most cases, athletes must rely on diversified sources of income, many off the field of play. This can result in inequality between athletes and among teammates.

Sport is the sole source of livelihood for many athletes and their families. It can be lucrative for some at the top and, equally, a source of concern, insecurity and worry for most others who enter the sport pyramid.

Where talent meets opportunity

Time and resources are required to find young talent, develop it and prime it to compete and excel. This is typically done in academies, coaching centres or clubs. These organizations can come in different shapes and sizes. They can involve a single coach or an entire set-up, including multiple talent scouts, administrators and trainers. The facility could be owned or rented and could be associated with an educational institution or sports club.

A thriving sports system requires that its talent nurseries be healthy, since these talent development organizations work with youth who would not yet have reached their playing, earning and paying potential. This can make running a talent development business commercially challenging.

Venue-related costs can include the cost of land, rentals, building of infrastructure and maintenance. Operating outflows include equipment, administrative costs, technology costs, insurance costs, travel costs and marketing costs. Human resource costs include the hiring of coaches and other staff. Academies will try and spread these costs across their trainees and generate other sources of revenue as well.

Coaching and subscription fees charged to trainees and their parents or guardians are their basic source of revenue. An academy might hold events and tournaments, raising registration revenue and sponsorships. It might attract brand sponsorships and enter into strategic partnerships with schools, colleges and clubs. These partnerships can bring brand value, recognition and a broader market reach as well as stable revenue.

Avenues may also be open for academies to receive financial support—either as general donations or project- or programme-based grants—from philanthropists, foundations, companies, members of the local community and even the government. Keeping in mind the financial challenges that academies and training centres face in a country like India, the government puts in place various schemes, such as the Khelo India Scheme and the National Sports Development Fund. Through these, academies may be entitled to government support to cover athlete support and development, construction and renovation or improvement of facilities.

Recognizing the need to ensure a strong pipeline for the sport, certain global governing bodies like Fédération Internationale de Football Association (FIFA) have developed innovative deferred compensation structures such as training compensation fees and solidarity payments that benefit coaching and developmental organizations at the grassroots.

Under FIFA's regulations, when a football player first registers as a professional in a country different from the one in which they were trained, the club undertaking their registration must pay training compensation fees to each club that contributed to the player's training between the ages of twelve and twenty-one. This fee is also payable to the immediately prior club on any transfer involving the player until they turn twenty-three years old, except under certain exceptional circumstances, such as if the player is transferred to the lowest category of clubs specified in FIFA's regulations.

This compensation can be accessed by any club and academy that has participated in the player's progress and has registered them in FIFA's player registration system. The training compensation is calculated on a sliding scale, depending on the geographic region and the status of the club signing the players, and is adjusted from time to time by FIFA.

Similarly, whenever a professional footballer is transferred—temporarily or permanently—from a club in one FIFA member federation to a club in another member federation while under contract, up to 5 per cent of the transfer fee is to be withheld and paid by the transferee club to the clubs involved in the player's training during the years between their twelfth and twenty-third birthdays. Unlike training compensation fees, these solidarity payments are due for the entire duration of a player's professional career. The payment is to be divided proportionally among the clubs involved in the player's training and education.

Payment structures like these can be a useful source of revenue not only for standalone academies but also for those associated with professional clubs. They incentivize investments in grassroots coaching, coach development, talent scouting, player development and facilities, and also rebalance the commercial reward between the places and systems where talent is developed and where it is commercialized.

FIFA has a well-established player and club registration system that enables the tracking of each player's journey. This is an important aspect of market-making and talent pipeline management that football does better than most other sports. Although the FIFA system has some critics who claim that the fees act as a tax on player mobility and value, the system enables a wide pool of players to receive high-quality training at below-market cost when they are young. It also helps sustain economies for talent across geographies.

Best v. Best

At the top of the sports events pyramid are global events organized by bodies such as FIFA, the International Olympic Committee (IOC) and the International Cricket Council (ICC). These involve participants—individuals or teams—who have been successful at national and continental events and have met various qualification criteria. The commercial model of sport plays out on these platforms, and the revenues sustain the sports pyramid through a trickle-down of grants and disbursements to regional, national and subordinate bodies.

With this funding, these bodies are expected to hold events, develop infrastructure and invest in athlete development programmes and other projects. The IOC's development and assistance budget for 2021–24 for Olympic Solidarity is $590 million.

It can be expensive to produce and organize a sports event. Athletes and officials must be brought to the same place, stadiums and venues might have to be built, tickets have to be sold and the spectators seated. Also, facilities must be made available to broadcasters and media personnel to take the event to audiences outside the stadium. The typical Olympic and Paralympic Games or FIFA World Cup requires many billions of dollars in investment. Despite the costs, some events can achieve commercial success through a calibrated revenue structure.

The event organizer and owner is often the SGB itself. In cases of major sporting events, the SGB may partner with a host city or nation. It will transfer several event responsibilities to the host. In addition, the event owner also has to cover a number of costs and has its own sources of revenue. Many of the costs, such as international travel, might be borne by participating athletes and teams and their national federations and governments, though some might receive federation support or subsidies from the event organizer to cover this. The expenses outsourced to others are as good as revenues earned. Besides minimizing costs, the event owner also looks to raise revenues from various sources.

Participating individuals or teams can be charged entry fees to take part in the event. In other cases, such as franchise-based leagues, these can be franchise fees. The event organizer can also sell tickets to spectators in attendance at the stadium. Many stadia will have premium seating and corporate boxes that are sold in blocks, along with hospitality services and travel packages. Food and drink may be sold during games and the concessionaires will pay for the right to sell in the venue.

Besides ticketing and hospitality, the main sources of revenue for the event owner are media rights, sponsorships, and licensing and merchandising. These can add hundreds of millions of dollars for each event. A broadcaster might be willing to pay for the exclusive media rights to transmit—usually live—the footage from the event to audiences outside the stadium. Media rights can be sold at sizeable values that underwrite the event costs and more. The media rights owner, in turn, sells on-air advertising and sponsorship to try and make a profitable return on the investment it has made. We will look at this sports broadcast model in more depth in a subsequent chapter.

Prominent events will sign up sponsors who pay for visibility within the venue, to interact with attendees and otherwise claim association with an event, its goodwill and brand. The value of these sponsorships can go up if the event is being broadcast as there will be a wider audience available for brands to reach.

Fans within the venue and others outside it might purchase merchandise, such as clothing and apparel, that bears event logos or the names of participating teams or players. The right to use event branding and other intellectual property may also be licensed to those selling other products and services that are unrelated to sport, like automobiles, beverages, hotels, airlines and the like. We will examine how sports sponsorships work in a later chapter.

Cheerleaders

The media industry and sports broadcasters play a key role in taking sport to global audiences. The universal, live, competitive and unpredictable nature of sport is uniquely attractive for broadcasters. It gives them access to a mass audience that is interested in the same thing at the same time. Few other global events command this type of simultaneous attention. FIFA reported that 3.572 billion people—more than half the world—watched the 2018 FIFA World Cup.[1] Sports events attract viewership and advertising, and subscription revenue flows from eyeballs and the attention economy.

Traditionally, the live aspects of sports broadcasts command the most value, though the right to transmit replays, highlights and clips can also generate fees. The rights are given exclusively to a broadcaster, and this enables it to concentrate viewership and monetize the rights.

Sports broadcasters regularly engage in bidding wars for the media rights to prime sports events. These deals are usually concluded through private negotiations, tender systems or auctions. The successful broadcaster signs a media rights agreement with the event owner. The agreement grants licences to the broadcaster to transmit and distribute content from the event, both live and deferred, in exchange for a fixed rights fee.

Having paid for the right to broadcast, the media rights holder will try and generate revenues that exceed the fee it has paid. Revenue comes from selling on-air advertising, branding and channel subscriptions. The broadcaster will sell the visibility of the broadcast to advertisers who would like to be noticed by these audiences.

In the US, advertising around the Super Bowl has attained significant status, not just in commercial terms but as a launch for many major advertising campaigns. In 2022, a single 30-second Super Bowl ad spot cost more than $7 million. Selling the advertising inventory can be an art and a science—it involves knowing what value to sell at, how much of it to pre-sell and how much to retain for sale closer to the event.

The manner and timing of advertising might be the subject of limits and protocols that are prescribed by the event owner and contained in the agreement granting the broadcaster the rights. This can include guidelines on when ads can and can't be played (ideally, in breaks only and not during the live action) and the amount of real estate they can occupy on screen (whether it is a logo, an ad insertion, etc.). These impact the viewership experience and perception of the brand, which are important elements of keeping the event watchable, entertaining and widely followed.

Securing sports media rights can drive up channel subscriptions among viewers. Broadcasters may use large sports events to attract subscribers to their platforms with the hope of retaining them as subscribers beyond the completion of the event. Sports rights can, therefore, be over-valued, as they might not always render profit to the broadcaster on a stand-alone basis.

Having outlined how the two-sided sports business structure works, let's see how things played out in the IPL.

Each ball is an event

Over its first decade and a half, the IPL has demonstrated the commercial potential of sports business in India when the fundamentals are strong and the strategy is well-conceived. The value of the IPL has grown off the enthusiasm of the world's best players to participate, the production quality of the event, the excitement of its followers within stadia and at home, the value of broadcast and sponsorship rights and advertising slots, and the willingness of investors. Despite their very different circumstances, other Indian sports have tried to adopt the IPL's franchise-based business model. Things have not quite worked out as well for them. Let's see why.

Franchising is a popular business model across a variety of industries. By inviting and involving the capital and efforts of others, businesses grow and scale in new territories and markets. Franchisees are attracted to established business formats and intellectual properties. There is already a proof of business potential, and the franchisee does not need to invest anew in research, product and brand development. Advertising and marketing can also be centralized, and this brings the benefits of economies of scale to franchise participants.

Given that the franchisor will support and guide the business, the franchisee also does not require prior experience, and there is a stability in structure and business potential that eases access to credit and capital. The model is popular with 'businesses in a box', where repeatable products and processes can bring about a relatively standardized consumer experience across franchise locations. International fast food giant McDonald's, the hotel group Marriott International, the Indian retailer Fabindia and the playschool EuroKids are examples of franchised businesses.

While commercial models differ, the franchisee will often pay the franchisor a one-time fee, an annual fee and a share of revenue. In return, the franchisor will license the use of the brand, logos and protocols, and might commit to undertake a certain amount of centralized branding and marketing activity.

It could also provide raw materials and inputs to the franchisee and other business support. Many successful businesses have been built and expanded using the franchise model.

The IPL franchise contract requires each team, for its first ten years of existence, to pay a predetermined annual franchise fee (prorated based on its original bid) to the BCCI. In addition, the franchises also commit to paying their players from the designated player purse, with the BCCI setting minimum and maximum total spends on players from time to time.

Besides the payments it gets from franchisees, the BCCI has retained the right to sell the broadcast and media rights and central sponsorships, including the league's title sponsorship and naming rights. A percentage of these central revenues is shared in equal proportion with all participating teams, with the percentage reducing over the years as the teams stabilized their respective businesses and the IPL brand and valuations grew. From the get-go, the IPL model ensured financial stability for the league and a path to profitability for the franchises. If things went well, the upside would be shared by everyone.

In the early stages, although the franchises relied significantly on the central distributions for their sustainability, they were also allowed to raise their own team sponsorships for display on playing jerseys and within their 'home' stadia. Franchises were also entitled to retain ticketing revenue from their 'home' games in addition to other revenues from team merchandising and local partnerships.

From each team's eleventh season onwards, the model changes for the franchises. The annual franchise fee is replaced by an obligation to share a fixed percentage of annual franchise revenue with the BCCI. This comes with the franchise's share in the central revenues from media rights and central sponsorships reducing when compared to the first decade.

With two additional teams introduced in the 2022 season at many times the value of the original franchises, it is hard to believe that the BCCI had difficulty finding willing buyers of the original franchises in 2008—but it is a fact. At the time, there were no guarantees that the business model would succeed or that broadcast valuations, sponsorship and ad rates would rise to where they stand today. The IPL hit a sweet spot in terms of the market for talent and audiences, and its timing, in an aspirational and upwardly-mobile India.

The world over, most successful professional leagues are organized in a hierarchical structure. At the top is the premier, first or major league, with other feeder leagues sitting below as minor or lower division leagues. These lower divisions not only act as stabilizers and feeders of talent to the upper divisions but also enable the promotion and relegation of teams: top performers move up a division in the following season, and those at the bottom of the standings move down.

While the IPL is a 'closed' league with no promotion and relegation, it has had the Indian domestic cricket structure and ready access to the world's best cricketers as a source of talent supply. The BCCI negotiated a calendar slot for the IPL during which not only would the Indian men's national team not play, but there would also be limited bilateral cricket between other teams. This ensured the availability of Indian and international talent, as the players would not have other competing commitments during the IPL.

The Indian board also negotiated terms of release with other international boards such as Cricket Australia and Cricket South Africa, which would receive a payment to issue no-objection certificates and release players from their national teams and systems to play in the IPL. The BCCI also chose to not release active Indian-registered players to play in any other T20 league in the world. This prevented the creation, elsewhere, of a league directly competing with the IPL.

With IPL player salaries rising to substantial levels over the years, the league became the aspirational platform for professional cricketers from across the world. It was the place to show their wares and commercialize their talents. Many other cricket boards, including Australia, South Africa, England, Pakistan and the UAE, have similar leagues, but none compares in scale, brand value or commercial stature with the IPL.

On the demand side, cricket was already a compelling, widely followed and watched product. In fact, the IPL wasn't even the first mover—the unofficial Indian Cricket League (ICL) had been operating for a while, much to the chagrin of the BCCI. The BCCI protected its turf by banning any cricketers who participated in the ICL and blocking access to its stadia and official channels for ICL organizers.

When it launched the IPL, the BCCI did not have to invest in educating and building an audience. It merely served the existing audience for cricket a repackaged product—one that was entertaining and engaging. This allowed broadcasters to forecast potential revenues and make an investment with a degree of confidence. It also leaned on the healthy sponsorship and advertising market that was already in place for international cricket in India.

The IPL used franchise capital effectively, as expansion capital, and the franchise system for growth. It also enabled a diverse set of first-time stakeholders to invest their respective businesses in a common project, while the central brand IPL and the team brands grew in salience in an interdependent manner. The ownership group included prominent business leaders and Bollywood personalities.

The franchise system not only helped widen the reach of cricket but also localized and democratized the administration of the game through competitive private participation while also aligning commercial and governance incentives. Not only were the sources of economic reward diversified, so was the risk. Given that the BCCI was the sole sanctioning authority, franchisor and event organizer, this permitted singular control and coordination as well as aligned incentives.

In this model, the BCCI did not have to bear the costs of expanding the game. After putting in the work to set up the IPL, it could sit back and enjoy the significant upsides of its success. All it had to do to unlock massive value for itself and its members was to play an enabling and regulatory role. The size of the overall pie grew and the commercial strength became a source of governance influence. This altered the BCCI's international standing in the ICC structure. As the BCCI gained in stature, it could use its regulatory clout to strengthen and protect the IPL proposition further. This created a virtuous cycle—for the BCCI, at least.

As a platform business, the IPL was able to tap the potential of the two-sided sports economy—the markets for talent and audiences—without having to invest heavily to create either. As this happened, it retained self-perpetuating control of both markets.

If the IPL franchise system was an established model, why did it not work out for other sports leagues in India?

In a league of its own

The contrast between the environment in which the IPL was created and the situation in other sports in India is telling.

The pool of talent and domestic tournament structure in non-cricket sports in India is not comparable with Indian cricket's riches. Many federations struggle to hold their annual national championships on a regular basis. Broadcast rights for non-cricket sports are rarely considered prized commodities and are not bid for competitively. In certain cases, rather than buying media rights, the broadcaster must be paid to carry the product, moving media coverage from the credit to the debit side of the balance sheet.

Sponsorship markets are also intrinsically tied to broadcast value and remain tepid while viewership is limited. Without healthy media rights and sponsorship valuations, the franchise business model comes under severe stress, and it is difficult to provide franchises with a pathway to break even, let alone attain profitability. The hard numbers are where all the action is, especially once the novelty and vanity of team 'ownership' wears off.

Most other sports in India did not have the luxury of a prototype, a mature talent market or a readymade audience base they could build on. They had to invest in finding and upgrading the talent needed for a league, and spend on marketing to educate viewers on their sport and build audiences. These are both expensive pursuits and difficult to pull off at the same time. It meant that unlike the IPL, which could use franchise capital to expand cricket, most of the other Indian sports leagues had to use it as start-up financing.

The governance-risk alignment was also missing. Most of these other leagues were launched with private promoters purchasing the rights to operate the league from the relevant NSF. These promoters had to navigate the business risk of a nascent product and also the regulatory risk in dealing with the sanctioning authority. If the league failed, it was their baby. If it succeeded, the promoter risked it being unilaterally appropriated by the sanctioning authority.

Most of these leagues were able to pull off one or two seasons while the experience was still novel for the team owners. Once balance sheets began talking, the willingness of the franchises to continue to invest waned quickly. Other than the Pro Kabaddi League, which did have some of the elements of a grassroots structure and mass following, most others that had been launched with fanfare wound themselves down with barely a whimper. Even a globally popular sport like football has struggled commercially, with Indian Super League franchises continuing to bleed a decade into their existence.

It is a common impulse to mimic a product simply because it is successful. In the bargain, it is easy to forget that each product has its own features, levers and peculiarities. Just as architects like to build with local materials and chefs prefer using seasonal ingredients from the vicinity, every sport must also understand its own context before choosing its business architecture. Aping a model from another sport just because it has worked there suggests a lack of imagination.

India is not a single-sport nation—and the corollary is that the broad spectrum of sport is ripe with opportunity. A careful consideration of culture, systems, contexts and people can help unlock its business potential.

Sport can bring fame and fortune in no small measure. It can also provide valuable management lessons for any business. Not every ball can be hit out of the park. Not even in the IPL.

Chapter 11

On Agreement

Do you get a full ticket refund if a match is washed out?

In November 2005, the M.A. Chidambaram Stadium (also known as Chepauk) in Chennai was slated to host the third match in a five-match series of One Day International matches between the Indian men's cricket team and the visiting South Africans.

The Tamil Nadu Cricket Association (TNCA), a member of the Board of Control for Cricket in India (BCCI), was the designated hosting association. The series was nicely set up, with the teams having won one match each. November is typically the wettest month of the year in Chennai, and the glorious uncertainties of cricket were overshadowed by the relative certainties of the weather. The not-so-cold November rain put paid to any hopes of a contest, and the match was washed out without a single ball being bowled.

An abandoned match is a dampener in more ways than one. The players don't get to play and there is no live action to broadcast or to watch. Lots of money and time have gone into preparations for the match: getting the venue ready, the travel and stay of players and officials, and event management costs. All of this comes to naught in an abandoned match like this one.

Tens of thousands of tickets have also been sold to the public. What happens to this money? Do the organizers get to keep it or are ticket-holders due refunds? Would things be different if the match had commenced and the rain had intervened later? How can the rights of the event organizer and those of ticket-holders be balanced? All of this comes down to what we believe ticket-holders are buying and the risks they should bear.

The TNCA had sold the match tickets with standard terms and conditions printed on the back. These terms included a clause stating that there would be no refunds under any circumstances. The TNCA stood its ground and did not process refunds. Feeling like they had been left out to dry, a few ticket-holders came together and filed a writ petition in the Madras High Court seeking a refund of the ticket costs from the BCCI and TNCA.

The TNCA, supported by the BCCI, argued that the tickets were a binding contract and that they owed no refund obligation. The petitioners acknowledged the no-refund clause but argued that such a condition was against public policy, void under Section 23 of the Indian Contract Act, 1872 (Contract Act) and thus could not be binding. The Madras High Court was left to consider these two opposing positions. Would the court intervene and override clauses in the ticket terms?

Before we get to that, let's understand what contracts are and the roles they play.

The ties that bind

It is difficult to imagine our lives without contracts. We enter into them practically every day, and they are embedded in most of our interactions. For most of the history of industrialized society, goods and services have been created and distributed through markets facilitated by contracts. Contracts ensure order, certainty and the ability to plan and transact. They help bridge information gaps, reduce transaction costs, overcome trust deficits and bring to life relationships that might otherwise not have existed.

The basic legal requirements of a valid contract include two or more parties, their mutual promises, their legal capacity to contract and the consideration that must be involved. These legal requirements sharpen the focus of contracts, moderating their role and impact.

Sports contracts that individuals enter into can vary from being entirely operational (such as coaching, training, playing and management contracts) to those facilitating commercial relationships such as scholarships, grants, sponsorships and endorsements. Hosting sports events involves multicontract frameworks including hosting agreements, stadium and venue agreements, media and broadcast rights agreements, event sponsorship agreements, licensing and merchandising agreements, ticket terms and conditions and media accreditation terms, among others.

The ability to choose one's interactions and the autonomy to order one's own world are at the core of human freedom. Contracts enable private citizens to foresee, regulate and maintain their relationships and transactions. The law strikes a balance by recognizing the mutually supporting principles of 'freedom of contract' and 'sanctity of contract'. Through these, the state defers to the will of the parties while supporting the bargain and holding the parties to their promises.

The freedom and sanctity of contracts provide parties with the space to regulate themselves and create specialized, smaller pockets of privately crafted rules to govern their interactions and transactions. For instance, they may give up certain rights and abstain from doing certain things in exchange for promises from the other party, or some other consideration. As an example, two neighbours might agree to refrain from parking their cars on the street in front of each other's houses, even though no law stops them from doing so.

Contracts also allocate risks and agree on mechanisms to work through foreseeable uncertainties, respond to unforeseeable changes to circumstances and resolve disputes. The parties will keep in mind that there will be known knowns, known unknowns and unknown unknowns, and try to create mechanisms to address them.

Think of an agreement between a fruit wholesaler to purchase a certain quantity and quality of oranges from a farmer at a specified price, with this bargain being struck three months before the harvest. At the time this contract is made, both parties know that there will be oranges that form part of the harvest, although it is unknown whether it will be a good harvest, whether the oranges will be sweet and juicy or not, etc. There might also be unpredictable incidents preventing the harvest from being sold, such as a blockade or a change in the law. The contract will have to factor in the uncertain aspects of the deal and the parties will have to agree on how to handle it. Once a contract is validly executed, the parties must perform their respective duties under the contract unless they are legally excused from performance.

State recognition of these contract principles is granted through legislation. In India, the Contract Act is the framework law. Special legislations and regulations govern particular types of contracts such as the sale of goods, property, insurance, consumer credit, the carriage of goods and building and construction. Typically, these specialized statutes focus on context-specific terms while leaving the Contract Act to govern the formation of contracts and the remedies for breach.

The judiciary is tasked with ensuring that valid contracts entered into in accordance with the law are enforceable, while unlawful contracts are not. The availability of such remedies gives comfort to parties negotiating and entering into agreements that private promises will mean something, with the state bearing witness and agreeing to assist with enforcement.

However, the autonomy granted to contracting parties is neither unfettered nor unlimited. The state places certain limitations on this autonomy in situations where one party is liable to be taken advantage of or misled, or where the transaction might result in material and negative externalities on other people, markets or institutions. In these cases, the state allows an affected party to invalidate certain contract terms and refuses to use its institutional power to enforce these, even if they were entered into voluntarily.

The world of organized sport presents opportunities for us to understand this interplay between private freedom and public guardrails. When not a single ball of a match has been bowled, should a court enforce the no-refund clause in the ticket terms? Before we get there, let's take a look at other cases where the state does step in.

Little master

A fundamental principle of contract law is that, for a contract to be valid, the parties must have the legal capacity to contract. This protects persons who might not be capable of making decisions from being exploited or harming their own interests in a situation of obviously unequal bargaining power. In such cases, the contract law limits the enforceability of such a contract, and the party lacking the capacity to contract will not be compelled to perform their obligations.

One of the key aspects of the capacity to contract is the age of the party. Minors, i.e., individuals aged under eighteen, are considered incompetent to contract under Indian law and in most other jurisdictions. If an individual is a minor while entering into a contract, the contract is deemed void, i.e., it would have no legal effect. The minor is generally seen as not having the maturity to make binding promises and the judgement and experience necessary to negotiate and take on binding obligations.

The capacity to bind minors to contracts assumes significance in the sporting realm for obvious reasons. It is not uncommon for athletes to turn professional while they are minors, especially in sports such as football and tennis. With the limited windows that sports careers present, this gives them a head start, especially if they are ready to take on the competition. Developing an athlete to reach their full potential involves a significant investment of time, money and energy, often during the years of their youth. Many of these investments will fail, but without them, the star athlete is unlikely to emerge. How does one incentivize these investments for academies, clubs, teams and sponsors if the minor athlete, while being the subject of investment, cannot be bound to any commitments in return?

Early in the career journey, contracts with minors could involve funding, development and scholarship agreements that cover the athlete's coaching, training and travel expenses. As they progress, mature and excel, there could be playing contracts with clubs or teams and marketing and representation contracts that seek to commercialize the athlete's name, image, publicity rights and goodwill through endorsements and partnerships. While these contracts play an important role in developing talent and building the talent pipeline, there is an inherent legal risk in entering into such contracts directly with a minor.

The minor's agreement is void ab initio under Indian law (i.e., not valid from the point it was entered into), and it is not enforceable against the minor. Such a contract cannot even be validated by ratification once the athlete reaches the age of majority.

In India and certain other legal systems, such as the UK, the practice has generally been to enter into contracts with the legal guardian of the minor on the minor's behalf. This is possible as a legal guardian is expressly permitted to contract on behalf of a minor. However, only agreements that are within the competence and power of the guardian and that operate for the benefit of the minor will be valid—and they can be enforced only to the extent that they provide some benefit to the minor and do not impose any obligation on the minor.

The contract counter-party deals directly with the guardian in respect of the minor's affairs until the minor reaches the age of majority. Such an arrangement does not eliminate the risks of contracting in relation to a minor.

Once the minor hits the age of majority, the legal guardian loses the power to contract on their behalf. Contracts previously entered into on the minor's behalf by the guardian will no longer remain in effect. While the legacy contract will often explicitly provide that the guardian shall cause (or use best efforts to cause) the minor to enter into a fresh contract upon attaining majority, this clause cannot be enforced against either the guardian or the athlete. A fresh contract with new consideration is needed, meaning the athlete who reaches majority has the full right to walk away, even to engage with a competitor.

Also, if a guardian breaches a contract entered into on behalf of the minor, the only remedy available to the counter-party is to initiate legal proceedings against the guardian for breach of contract and seek compensation for any damage suffered.

The minor remains shielded from any action and cannot be made personally liable or compelled to perform the contract entered into by the guardian.

Entering into a contract with the guardian is not the only avenue used by sports enterprises contracting with minors. Certain contracts with minors can be structured as contracts for 'necessaries'. Under Indian law, 'necessaries' are defined as goods reasonably necessary to support a minor's extant position in life and are relative, to be determined with reference to the circumstances of the minor and the purpose of the contract.

For example, certain terms of academy and training contracts that provide allowances for food, transportation and accommodation could qualify as agreements to provide the minor with 'necessaries'. In such cases, the other party to the contract would enjoy limited rights to receive compensation for delivery of necessaries. While this kind of agreement provides for limited remedies, it too does not compel the minor to perform or continue to be bound by obligations on attaining majority.

The law may seem to operate in an onerous manner with respect to those contracting with minors, giving them little effective protection. It does this to prioritize the best interests of minors. In reality, sports service providers continue to offer services to minors and contract with respect to minors' participation in sport. The legal position incentivizes them to treat the minor with respect and care in commercial relationships, as the delivery of quality services helps build lasting relationships. This can often fructify into long-term, mutually beneficial commercial relationships once the minor gains contracting capacity. Most athletes do not forget their early sponsors, and many of them continue these relationships throughout their careers, sometimes even at a discount on their prevailing market price. M.S. Dhoni used a variety of bats bearing the logos of his various early sponsors at his swansong international event, the ICC Cricket World Cup 2019, without seeking any compensation from them. There is, after all, a market for loyalty.

Sport governing bodies (SGBs) have no trouble binding minor athletes to their rules, such as anti-doping and other regulatory matters. These are presented to all participants as conditions to participation rather than as contracts.

Concurrently, these bodies bring an element of balance to the treatment of minors through their regulatory functions. As we saw in the previous chapter, FIFA's solidarity payments and training compensation structure provide deferred bonus compensation for those who invest in the talent at the early stages. Concurrently, FIFA's restrictions on the transfer of minors protect against trafficking by eliminating the incentives to commodify talented minor footballers. Such measures provide additional layers of incentives and constraints that keep the sports system balanced and healthy.

While contracts play a critical role in enabling transactions and commercial interactions, they are not the only mechanism to build trust and healthy relationships. A focus on protection, benefits and the best interest of minors can incentivize healthier treatment of vulnerable adults-in-waiting. Sport shows us that this is possible.

'Broad' contract terms meet Yuvraj Singh

By virtue of the exchange of promises in a contract, each party hopes to exert control over the others—to be able to influence how they act and how they don't. In this bargain, how much control is too much? When does the state no longer agree to enforce terms? This is a vexing question, particularly in the context of restraining behaviour after the contract has come to an end: either having expired or been terminated. For instance, a team might try and restrict the behaviour or transactions of an athlete after a playing contract has expired, such as preventing them from playing for a competitor. If a player has agreed to such a condition in the contract, will this be enforced against the player?

Clauses that try to restrict, limit, prohibit or prevent certain actions are known as 'restrictive covenants'. These can include 'exclusivity' and 'non-compete' clauses that limit the ability to deal with others, 'right of first refusal' and 'right to match' clauses that bias the continuity of contractual relations. Other examples are 'gardening leave' requirements that force an employee to not work at all for some months after completing a job, and 'unilateral extension' clauses where one party gets the right to increase the term without the other's consent.

Such clauses are purportedly used to protect the integrity of the contract relationship from disruption or dilution by competing interests. They try to protect and maximize the value of the parties' investment. When certain clauses operate during the term of the contract, these are generally seen as part of a fair exchange. The issue isn't as straightforward when the same clauses are intended to apply after the contract term expires or terminates. What is the difference and why does it matter? Understanding how sports contracts work might give us some clues. First, let's start with some background.

In the Indian context, to be enforceable, restrictive covenants must satisfy the requirements of the Contract Act. The Act invalidates contracts that it deems to be against public policy and voids those that restrain another from carrying out a legitimate trade or profession. When it comes to matters impacting a trade or profession, Indian courts have consistently held that restraints imposed during the term of the contract are acceptable so long as they are reasonable.

To assess the reasonableness of such restraints, courts may look at the territorial scope of a non-compete, its length, the power equation between the parties, etc. If, on balance, these are seen as reasonable, they will be enforced. However, if they are too broad, too long, too widely conceived or have the potential to severely limit the employability and livelihood of the party, courts will refuse to enforce them. Also, if the restraint acts beyond the term of the contract, i.e., after it has expired or been terminated, courts have deemed it to be void, and no evaluation of reasonableness is required to invalidate it. The timing of when a restrictive covenant operates then becomes a key consideration for legality.

Indian sport has produced a few interesting case studies over the years. An early one involved cricketer Zaheer Khan, who had signed a promotional agreement with management agency Percept D'Mark. The contract included a clause that prohibited Khan from accepting any offer from a third party to provide services relating to managing his commercial affairs, not only during the contract term but also for a period of 180 days thereafter, without first providing Percept the details and a right to match such other offer.

In *Percept D'Mark (India) Pvt. Ltd v. Zaheer Khan*,[1] the Supreme Court held that the clause was void and unenforceable to the extent it applied to the 180-day period after the term. It was deemed a clear restriction on the player's freedom of contract and, therefore, against public policy. The Supreme Court held that, with post-term restraints like this, no evaluation of reasonableness was necessary. It said that a relationship between an athlete and a sports management agency is a relationship built on mutual faith, confidence and continued trust. It held that any order compelling Khan to enter into an agreement would be against his will and therefore against the spirit of contract law.

Another similar case involved the same agency. Here, it was Percept's attempt to enforce a similar 'right of first refusal' clause in its promotional agreement with cricketer Yuvraj Singh that extended beyond the contract term. In *Percept Talent Management Pvt. Ltd. v. Yuvraj Singh and Globosport India Pvt. Ltd.*,[2] the Bombay High Court held the clause to be void and unenforceable as a 'post-termination negative covenant in a personal services contract'.

The court reasserted the legal position that all such post-contractual negative restraints are void and that neither the test of reasonableness nor the principle of restraint being partial would apply to the case. Taking a leaf from the Supreme Court's observations in the Zaheer Khan case, the Bombay High Court noted that an agreement such as one between an athlete and a player management agency is founded on the pillars of trust, confidence and the basic principles that underlie a fiduciary relationship. It observed that a relationship cannot survive if these don't exist between the parties.

There have also been sports-related cases using similar principles around the termination of contracts. Typically, termination clauses in contracts enable the premature severing of contractual ties before the original full contract term expires. Termination can be for cause (where the other party has breached the contract or failed to perform its obligations) or without cause (simply because a party would like to move on, with no explanation or trigger required).

When the rights of termination are not mutual in nature, i.e., one party enjoys a certain right of termination while the other does not, courts have chosen to intervene. For instance, in the case of *Infinity Optimal Solutions Pvt. Ltd. v. Vijender Singh*,[3] the Delhi High Court stepped in to ensure that boxer Vijender Singh was not boxed into his contract with the management agency IOS.

While IOS enjoyed certain rights to terminate the ten-year 'exclusive' management and representation contract, there was no provision in the document for the pugilist to exercise such a right. Four years in, Vijender wanted to exit the agreement and sign a deal with Percept, the agency involved in the Zaheer Khan and Yuvraj Singh cases described earlier.

The court held that Vijender, too, could exit the contract unilaterally, despite there being no such clause in the contract. It opined that where a contract is entered into for mutual profits and gains, the right of unilateral termination of the contract cannot be restricted only to one of the parties. In deciding thus, it stated that although specific performance or injunctive relief could not be claimed, if it is ultimately found that the termination was in contravention of any term or condition of the agreement, IOS could be granted compensation in the form of monetary damages. This holding furthers the principle of mutuality seen in the previous cases.

A similar approach has been taken in the case of contracts that provide one party with a unilateral right to extend the contract. This has been likened to a post-term negative covenant where one party has little choice but to accept the other party's will. In 2013, a dispute arose between Nike and its brand ambassador Virat Kohli. The endorsement contract contained a clause that provided Nike with the option to extend the contract for one additional year after the expiration of the contract period, upon the same terms and conditions applying in the final contract year of the initial contract period.

When Kohli rejected the one-year extension, Nike filed a suit, seeking to prevent him from entering into an endorsement contract with its competitors and requesting the court to ensure that he honoured the contract extension. In *Nike India Pvt. Ltd. v. Virat Kohli*,[4] the Karnataka High Court initially granted an order requiring the parties to maintain the status quo for a period of four weeks.

Later, when it found that Kohli had already signed with a competitor, it proceeded to vacate the stay and denied Nike's request to have Kohli specifically perform the contract during the extension period. The court held that giving such relief would be contrary to 'public policy and amounts to bonded labour'. As in the Vijender Singh case, the court did not discount the possibility of Nike being granted compensation in the form of monetary damages, but made it clear that it would not mandate Kohli to perform the contract with Nike or limit his ability to deal with other companies.

As these cases show, the law is ready to override the parties' agreement in certain circumstances. It does this when it feels there are negative public externalities that would result from enforcing such contracts.

The legal system recognizes the importance of each person enjoying the freedom to choose their own profession or vocation and being paid a fair wage for it, the freedom of the worker to productively use their skills without encumbrance, and the critical function of keeping a healthy and competitive labour market replenished with available talent.

Contract law and public policy balance freedom of contract with the freedom of trade and profession. Together they prioritize the public interest over private freedoms, where deemed important. Similar principles play out in contracts between sports organizations and the teams and the athletes they contract with—a subject that will be discussed in the next chapter.

Form is temporary

Standard form contracts are predetermined terms and conditions drafted by one party in a 'take it or leave it' form for the other party. The only options before the other party are to either accept the terms and enter into the contract, or reject them and not transact. You can't negotiate or bargain on terms.

Standard form contracts are common where a party has to contract with several individuals or entities on a similar basis. Airline terms and conditions, the privacy policy of various websites one visits, the terms on which one downloads an app—these are standard form contracts. In the sports context, match tickets, membership terms of a sports club, subscription terms to an academy and IPL player contracts between a franchise and players are all examples of such types of contract.

In accepting the legality of standard form contracts, the law recognizes that they provide an efficient way of transacting with many consumers at a time. Standard terms avoid the transaction costs that would come if terms had to be individually negotiated and finalized with each consumer.

Given the lack of negotiating opportunities, the law recognizes that standardized forms of contracts are likely to be one-sided in nature and may include terms and conditions that are overly favourable to the party drafting them. This can be further exacerbated when the party drafting the terms enjoys monopoly-type powers, which is often the case in sport. The absence of alternatives and competition can embolden the party drafting the terms and enhance the inequality in power dynamics between the parties.

To counterbalance this, the law provides protections and safeguards for the party that is susceptible to structural exploitation and disadvantage. In doing so, it adds contextual nuance to the principles of freedom and sanctity of contract.

In standard form contracts, the law steps in regularly on the interpretation of so-called exemption clauses. Many such clauses are aimed at excluding liability and, in sport, they can be found in documents like liability release forms and match ticket terms.

Organizers try to restrict their potential liability for any harm or loss caused to participants or spectators. For instance, spectators could be injured during a match because of being hit by a cricket ball, a projectile thrown by another spectator or a stampede in the stadium. The organizer will usually disavow any liability for such incidents and their consequences. They will usually have included a blanket release from liability in the terms of entry on the ticket.

However, on grounds of public policy, the law restricts any limitation on liability where the harm is caused by a reckless or intentional act of the organizer. Overly small boundaries in a cricket stadium, failure to provide security at the gate and in the venue and poor crowd control could factor into a holding of recklessness or a breach of the duty of care. In cases of reasonably foreseeable risks that have not been adequately mitigated, the law will not support a victim's release of claims or an organizer's exculpation from liability. It would see such a clause as being against public policy. After all, there is no public interest in giving a safe harbour to gross negligence or intentional misconduct.

The law also steps in when there is ambiguity in a standard form contract. The doctrine of '*contra-proferentem*' states that when a contract provision can be interpreted in more than one way, the court will prefer the interpretation that is more favourable to the party who has not drafted the contract. This encourages the drafter of the contract to be as clear, precise and explicit and to consider as many foreseeable situations as possible. It also reflects an inherent rejection of onerous or unfair clauses in standard-form contracts, and allows room for the interpretation and enforcement of the standard-form contract as a balanced document.

Taking a rain cheque

So what does this discussion tell us about the rights of ticket-holders to receive a refund of ticket fees in case of a rained-out cricket match? Will courts enforce the terms of a 'standard form' contract such as the one appearing on the back of a match ticket?

The Madras High Court took up the petition described earlier in this chapter and, in the case of *N. Chandrasekar v. The Tamil Nadu Cricket Association*,[5] recognized the validity of the ticket as a contract. It also opined that the TNCA cannot 'enrich itself' based on the ticket terms.

It suggested to the TNCA that a refund would be appropriate in the circumstances, while recognizing that the TNCA spent money towards organizing the match. It directed that the TNCA must make a refund of one-third of the ticket price to bona fide purchasers of the match tickets. In so doing, the court attempted to find a balance between the interests of the organizers of the match and the interests of the general public.

This case points to the treatment that cricket fans received in a previous era. With the massive demand for cricket in India—and, so, for match tickets—the interests of fans could be taken for granted without consequences. One would be hard-pressed to find reports of fans taking their concerns or grievances to consumer court, suggesting that even they probably didn't consider themselves to be 'consumers' in the legal sense.

It wasn't until the IPL was launched that fan comfort and fan engagement were acknowledged as vital to the health of the product. The Lodha Committee Report, too, brought up the need to enhance the treatment of fans at match venues and in general. Its suggestion to establish the position of BCCI Ombudsman to hear complaints from fans was actualized by the Supreme Court.

Since the office was created, there are no reported fan-promoted cases that the ombudsman has taken up. Yet, there have been changes since that wet day at Chepauk and, today, the ticket terms and conditions issued by the BCCI for IPL matches state that a refund of ticket fees is available if the match is cancelled or abandoned without a single ball having been bowled.[6] However, once a ball has been bowled, the match is deemed to have taken place and there is no refund available under any circumstances. This is also the prevailing practice when any BCCI member association hosts a Test match, One Day International or T20 International match.

This prompts another question: what exactly is a ticket purchaser buying as part of the bargain? This is sport, and uncertainty is an essential part of the purchase, but uncertainty of what sort and to what extent? In a team event, people are perhaps purchasing nothing more than an entitlement to enter the stadium and occupy a designated seat to watch the contest between the competing teams or players in person. They are not purchasing the right to witness a particular outcome or even a guarantee (in team sports) that a particular player will be selected, take the field for the match or perform to expectations.

As much as an Indian fan would like to see Virat Kohli play and score a century in a winning cause for India, there is no question of a refund of ticket fees if Kohli is rested, doesn't get to bat, scores a duck or if India loses. Yet, the ticket-holder is purchasing something substantial, and a single delivery being bowled does not quite fully capture the bargain struck.

A few other international cricket boards have determined that there is more to this, and have adopted dynamic ticket refund policies for incomplete matches. In case of rain-affected or disrupted matches, the England and Wales Cricket Board's policy provides for refunds to be calculated on a sliding scale, depending on the number of overs completed in the match or on the day (if a Test match), and also factors in cases where no result was obtained. The policy also considers the circumstances leading to the non-completion of a match. Refund amounts range from 50 per cent to 100 per cent of the ticket price paid.[7]

Cricket Australia[8] has a similar policy. Typically, if there are less than ten to fifteen overs played in a day when a result is not achieved, it provides for a full ticket refund, and also provides for a 50 per cent refund if less than twenty to thirty overs are played without a match result. These ranges change marginally for T20 matches.

The Cricket West Indies refund policy is similar to Cricket Australia's. It also earmarks and separates the hospitality and cricket viewing components of tickets, making the refund policy applicable only to the latter.[9]

These refund and compensation structures suggest that there is indeed a baseline higher than a single ball of cricket that underlies the match ticket purchase. They attribute value to a reasonable spell of play occurring, and recognize that spectators are invested in witnessing a definitive result. Fans are given some ammunition on the thorny issue of an 'act of God'.

The law of contract encourages parties to establish healthy, flexible and dynamic relationships. It does this by respecting their autonomy and freedom.

It also keeps its nose to the ground to determine how such autonomy and freedom are used. Where it smells a risk to fairness, balance, public interest or systemic health, it jumps in to reset the bargain.

As we discuss a rainy day in Chennai, an adage on the limits of human freedom comes to mind: 'You have the right to twirl your umbrella in the air, but it cannot hit me. Your freedom ends where my nose begins.' That smells about right.

Chapter 12

On Competition

Which defence kept Dhanraj Pillay at bay?

Dhanraj Pillay is regarded as one of India's best hockey players ever. He made quite a splash on the world stage as he dribbled his way past the most formidable defences. However, there was one citadel he couldn't quite breach. It was that of the Indian national hockey federation.

Between 2011 and 2013, Pillay was among a group of players who took on Hockey India, the body recognized as the Indian national sports federation (NSF) for hockey by the sport's world governing body, Fédération Internationale de Hockey (FIH). The players wanted to participate in World Series Hockey (WSH), a new city-based franchise league organized by Nimbus Sport (a private broadcaster) and the Indian Hockey Federation (a body previously recognized as the national federation by FIH).

Soon after WSH was launched, Hockey India and FIH issued regulations stating that players participating in 'unsanctioned tournaments' would face disciplinary action, including a possible playing ban. Hockey India also announced its own league. Pillay and the others initiated a complaint alleging that Hockey India was violating Indian competition law by misusing its position as the NSF to promote its own league at the expense of WSH.[1]

The episode raises existential questions: Can players be banned or penalized simply because they play in a tournament not recognized by the official NSF? What is competition law and what is its role in sport? How does it apply to the conduct of NSFs and other sport governing bodies (SGBs)?

Open play

Competition or anti-trust laws aim to ensure that competitors in a market have an equal opportunity to compete fairly, to thrive and to deliver the best quality goods and services at optimum prices to customers and consumers.

Why do we need these laws? Why can't we just trust open market forces to deliver these results? After all, markets are thought to be self-correcting, able to adjust prices, quality of goods and services, product availability, etc., in response to demand and supply.

In reality, the self-correcting mechanisms of markets can sometimes fail. A monopoly (a single seller in the market), a monopsony (a single buyer in the market), collusion (competitors coming together to decide the price and supply) and similar configurations and arrangements can constrain the 'invisible correcting hand' of the market and give rise to abuse of dominance, unfair collaborations or other, similar restraints, to the detriment of consumers.

Competition law understands these phenomena as market failures. As long as market correction takes place automatically, competition law takes a back seat. However, when the market fails or there is a possibility of failure, it steps in and intervenes to protect consumers' interests.

To understand market failures and how competition law tries to remedy them, consider the example of a telecommunication services provider that enters the market with deep pockets.

It undercuts other operators and provides telecommunication services at extremely low prices. This attracts consumers in large numbers and enables it to corner a large market share. Its competitors suffer massive losses and either go bankrupt or are purchased by this new operator.

Now, there is just one operator left and it enjoys a monopoly position. It increases its prices. Consumers end up paying much more than what they were paying before. Service quality degrades, but there are no options to switch to. The absence of competition also means that the monopolist has little incentive to provide better prices or service. The market has failed. Competition law is crafted to prevent and remedy such situations by controlling certain business practices that lead to such market failures.

Competition law has several tools in its shed. The Competition Act, 2002 (Competition Act) is the law in force on the subject in India. Its provisions fall broadly into three buckets: prohibition of anti-competitive agreements, prohibition of abuse of dominance and regulation of combinations. This framework disallows agreements that restrict the freedom of other businesses or consumers, such as requiring a car buyer to purchase motor insurance alongside the car (tying/bundling) or an agreement by competitors in the cement market to engage in pre-agreed 'price fixing' (collusion). It also guards against monopolistic conduct that operates independently of the competitive market forces to determine prices or to limit or control production or supply of goods and services, as in the example of the telecommunications service provider described earlier.

Combinations are also regulated to pre-empt and prevent the creation of monopolies, monopsonies or other market situations where an entity's operation can cause anti-competitive effects. In the example of the telecommunication services provider, competition law would prevent the new operator from buying the last remaining legacy operators, as this creates a monopoly with unbridled power and will leave the consumers with no alternatives.

The Competition Act created the institution of the Competition Commission of India (CCI), which is responsible for administering the law. The CCI regulates market activities, restricts agreements or arrangements with an anti-competitive impact and limits abuses of any entity's dominant position in the market. For CCI to investigate a matter, the entity must be engaging in economic activity in a particular market, and it must be engaging in behaviour prohibited or regulated by the Competition Act in that market.

How is this relevant in the sporting context? Can sport be equated to other industries and markets?

Protective gear

As discussed at several points in this book, modern sport is powered by commerce and, in turn, also powers many businesses. Within the ambit of sport, there are markets for media rights, sponsorships and endorsements, event management, franchise rights, talent, playing opportunities, equipment supplies and more. All of these constitute economic activities, and that opens the door for competition law to step in.

While these various markets develop downstream, SGBs like Hockey India are also performing regulatory functions like issuing rules and regulations for tournaments, organizing selection trials, scheduling events, prescribing codes of conduct, supporting state-level bodies and coordinating with the international federation. These activities have commercial consequences, either direct or downstream.

Does this mean we can treat SGBs as commercial 'enterprises' and apply the general principles of competition law to all their activities? Here's where things get interesting and we meet a unique principle of sports regulation—the 'specificity of sport'.

The 'specificity of sport' or the 'sporting exception' first emerged as a 'special' sporting exemption under European Union (EU) law through the rulings of the European Court of Justice and the decisions of the European Commission. It was recognized in the Lisbon Treaty, the amended Treaty of the European Union, in 2009.

Specificity refers to the recognition of, and exception created for, certain unique and inherent characteristics of the sporting ecosystem. This includes many of the concepts covered earlier in this book—separate competition on the basis of gender, organization of competition along the lines of nationality, relative regulatory autonomy in governance, the pyramid structure from grassroots to elite level, the principle of one federation per sport, and regulation of and restrictions on participation at various levels.

These features are all recognized as intrinsic and necessary for the maintenance of the sporting system, its integrity and efficiency and to ensure meaningful competition. The specificity principle recognizes that without this treatment, if sport was treated like any other commercial activity, it would be constrained in achieving its purpose.

The concept of 'competitive balance' in team sports serves as a good example of the sporting exception. Sport thrives on uncertainty. The uncertainty of results builds excitement, ensures quality games and compels the audience to engage with, and emotionally invest in, sport. Investors in any sport are encouraged by the audience numbers, and the audience expects both quality and uncertainty. Uncertainty thus becomes important from the sporting perspective as well as the commercial perspective.

SGBs aim to promote competitiveness and maintain balance among competitors by reducing the likelihood of concentration of talent in one or a few teams. Reducing various disparities ensures that teams are of similar capabilities and skills. This increases the likelihood of competitive and engaging matches. Rules and policies that prevent the concentration of power and resources are put in place. Leagues might have a salary cap for talent that limits how much the players in a squad can be paid individually and in aggregate. They might also bundle the sale of broadcast rights at the league level and distribute proceeds equitably to participating teams rather than allowing them to sell rights to their home matches individually, keeping in mind that some teams might have larger followings that lead to higher valuations. They could also bring in financial fair play regulations that curb and equalize spending, debt and investments in talent across competing teams.

Such regulations try to level the commercial and sporting playing field so that pre-existing disparities between owners off the field do not predetermine outcomes on the field of play. Under general principles of competition law, however, each of these measures would have a high chance of being declared as a legal violation. Salary caps would ordinarily be an artificial restriction on the market mechanism of price discovery akin to price fixing; bundling of broadcast rights might constitute collusion by competitor teams to the potential detriment of the broadcasters; and financial fair play regulations could be classified as an unlawful restraint on trade that distorts markets. However, the specificity of sport creates the sporting exception and permits these restrictions in the interest of the competitive balance.

Indian dribble

The specificity of sport has been recognized under Indian competition law in many cases. The CCI has agreed that SGBs are entitled to self-regulate without the intervention of competition law in matters of a purely 'sporting' nature, such as match and event rules, team selection decisions and the grant of event organization rights.

Having recognized the sporting exception, the CCI then uses an 'inherence-proportionality' test to moderate the principle's application and limit it to deserving matters. It assesses whether the practice that is under the scanner is inherent to the objectives of the sporting entity (this is the first prong), and whether the effect of the practice on economic competition is proportionate to the legitimate sporting interest it is claiming to protect (this is the second prong). If either response is in the negative, then it may look to apply competition law principles to the matter.

What does this mean in the world of sport? The 'one-sport-one-federation' principle means that each sport is governed and regulated by a particular—and singular—body at the national level as well as at all other levels of the pyramid.

Consider the All India Football Federation (AIFF), which governs football in India. The AIFF selects various national teams (based on gender and age group), appoints national coaches, decides training schedules and the tournaments that they will participate in, and so on. The playing programme and team selections are entirely in its hands. Fans who want to follow, watch and support the Indian national football teams have no option but to follow the teams selected by the AIFF. It is the only buyer of talent and the seller of rights and viewing opportunities in this market for national team football matches, events and related spheres. This makes it both a monopsony and a monopoly.

As we have discussed above, the presence of a monopoly enterprise generally invites scrutiny under competition law. Realistically, anyone who is unhappy with the AIFF's conduct or practices has no alternative purchaser or supplier to approach. If challenged, the AIFF will attempt to show that the decisions it makes on ticket pricing or distribution of broadcast revenues are inherent to its objectives of being the sole national governing body of football as part of the pyramid structure, and that the decisions are proportionate to the legitimate sporting objective of funding, training, selecting and fielding the national football teams. In such cases, specificity kicks in to prevent external intervention in the SGB's regulatory functions.

Can Hockey India legitimately stop Dhanraj Pillay and the other players from participating in a competing, unsanctioned league by threatening them with bans from official hockey? Will the principle of specificity of sport come to its aid? Before we find out, let's understand a bit more about how SGBs' roles have changed over time.

Switching flanks

Historically, the main role of SGBs was to regulate, develop and govern their sport. The revenues they earned were minimal, incidental to their regulatory roles, and reinvested in the development and growth of the game. Almost all national and international SGBs were established as non-profit entities, charities, trusts or societies, and they continue with these structures. While commerce has always been an element of sports governance, in simpler times, the administration of sport was focused only on keeping the structure funded and healthy.

The commercial landscape has changed dramatically over the decades. SGBs are now actively involved in the running of lucrative leagues, hosting major sporting events, granting franchise rights, selling multibillion-dollar media rights and hundreds of millions of dollars in sponsorship rights. These are intentional, planned and focused commercial activities.

SGBs were uniquely positioned and empowered to respond to the altered scale and focus of commercial activities. Using their exclusive control over the game, they could impact different markets, including the market for talent. SGBs operate registration systems, require athletes to sign player contracts and often issue regulations that restrict the athlete's participation to official events approved by the SGB. Athletes are threatened with bans if they violate such regulations, and can lose eligibility to play in the official or sanctioned league or system.

Although no one can be prevented from organizing an unsanctioned or competing event, any talent that participates in such an event risks being banned from the official structure. Try as they might to justify them as necessary, not all non-compete and restrictive clauses are enforceable against the athlete.

The landmark English law decision on 'restraint of trade' in the sports realm is the 1978 case of *Tony Greig v. Insole*,[2] in which it was held that the relevant cricket board's decision to ban the English cricketer Tony Greig and other cricketers from official Test cricket as punishment for participating in the unsanctioned World Series of Cricket was unlawful and unreasonable. The court held that a retrospective ban constituted an unjust and unreasonable restraint of trade as it deprived a professional athlete of an opportunity to earn their livelihood.

Similar restrictions extend to the mobility of players across borders. When workers have mobility across national borders, talent can access more opportunities and also put pressure on domestic employers and markets to raise standard pay scales to retain talent. Closed markets have little incentive to create and sustain competitive job markets. In many sports, a no-objection or permission certificate must be obtained from the home federation of an athlete wishing to participate in the league or competition hosted by another national federation.

Thus, today, any cricketer registered with the Board of Control for Cricket in India (BCCI) who wants to participate in a domestic cricket competition in any other country needs permission from the BCCI to do so. This is a form of reciprocity that respects the exclusive regulatory jurisdiction of a national federation over its athlete within the sports pyramid. The existing policy of the BCCI involves a blanket restriction on registered male players playing in another country's T20 league. They can only do so after they retire from all forms of Indian cricket and accept that they will not have the chance to return. Not allowing a replica to be created elsewhere with talent produced in India is seen as an important aspect of maintaining the primacy of the Indian Premier League (IPL) in terms of talent, viewership and value.

SGBs justify their control of players on multiple grounds. They would argue that the pyramid system has invested in developing talent and those who invest must have the opportunity to benefit from it. Unauthorized events will also be positioned as not having regulatory frameworks that adequately protect athletes and their safety, and that the resulting integrity—and other—breaches would devalue the public confidence in the sport and the stature of the athletes.

Similarly, SGBs would claim that they are best placed, with their expertise and perspective, to manage the athlete workload and welfare. These arguments are all premised on the sports pyramid being seen as a natural monopoly—that economic and structural chaos would result if anyone and everyone could organize an event and poach athletes bred in the official system.

The specificity of sport recognizes the role played by the sports pyramid in keeping sport organized. By virtue of their nature and role, SGBs exercise dominance within various markets in their sport, not least of them the market for talent. Few other professionals have to work in an environment so stacked against them, and the moderating role of competition law is critical in sport. We would never accept a medical regulatory body forcing doctors to provide services only in the hospitals operated by it, or the bar council choosing which cases a lawyer can and cannot argue. Yet, we allow this for sport.

In the quest for a balance between SGBs' legitimate controls and the importance of free market values, the 'inherence-proportionality' test and the boundaries between the regulatory and commercial functions of SGBs come into play. As detailed below, the CCI has not shied away from assessing an SGB's activities under competition law, including the Hockey India case and other cases relating to the NSFs governing cricket, volleyball, chess and athletics in the country.

Pushback

On receiving the Dhanraj Pillay complaint against Hockey India and the FIH, the CCI agreed that there were competition law issues to consider. In *Dhanraj Pillay v. Hockey India*,[3] the CCI decided that SGBs do not have immunity from the application of competition law, and proceeded to assess whether Hockey India was an enterprise in a dominant position and if it was abusing that dominance.

Given Hockey India's regulatory powers, which it can use to sanction and approve leagues, and its ability to control players, the CCI found it to be in a dominant position in the market for organizing private professional hockey leagues in India and also in the market for services of hockey players. The CCI held that the sporting exception would apply to SGBs' regulatory actions, considering the primacy of national representative competition, the need to deter free riding by others on player investments made by SGBs and the importance of maintaining the calendar of activities and preserving the integrity of the sport.

Its decision that Hockey India had not abused its dominant position hinged on its finding that there was insufficient evidence that Hockey India had acted against the players who participated in WSH. It also reasoned that the bar on unsanctioned events was proportionate to the 'dimensions of efficiency' and could not be faulted unless applied disproportionately, for which there was no evidence in this case. Despite his best efforts, the specificity of sport was the one defence that Dhanraj Pillay—of all people—was unable to get the better of.

Given the social and commercial stature of cricket in India, the BCCI has also faced similar scrutiny. In 2010, a complaint was brought by Surinder Singh Barmi, a member of the public, alleging that the BCCI was abusing its position in the market for the 'organization of professional domestic cricket leagues and events in India' by promoting the IPL and contractually restricting itself from organizing or sanctioning any similar domestic T20 cricket tournament. In 2013, the CCI imposed a penalty of Rs 52.24 crore on the BCCI on the grounds that it had abused its dominant position in the market by restricting competition while conducting IPL tournaments and granting exclusive media rights for the broadcasting of IPL matches to one TV channel for a ten-year period.

The BCCI appealed this order on the grounds of, among other things, violation of the principles of natural justice, and the erstwhile Competition Appellate Tribunal (COMPAT) remitted the case for a fresh investigation by its director general and a post-investigation inquiry. By way of an order in May 2015, the CCI ordered its director general to conduct further investigation into the matter in accordance with COMPAT's directions. The director general filed the supplementary investigation report in March 2016.

In its November 2017 order in *Surinder Singh Barmi v. The Board of Control for Cricket in India*,[4] the CCI noted that the pyramid structure of cricket allowed the BCCI to exercise the sole authority to approve or sanction official cricket tournaments in India. It found that the BCCI enjoys a dominant position in the relevant market and noted that the IPL media rights agreement mentioned that BCCI would not organize, sanction, recognize or support a professional domestic Indian T20 competition that is competitive to the IPL during the duration of the rights agreement.

The CCI also found that the BCCI's internal rules provided that only BCCI member associations would be given permission to organize tournaments and that no member, player or match official could participate in an unapproved tournament. It concluded that such restrictions could not be said to be inherent to the objectives of the BCCI. It also held that closing the market in such a manner to protect the commercial interests of the parties was not in the interest of the development of the game and was a disproportionate measure. Here, the CCI found that the 'inherence-proportionality' standard was not satisfied on the first prong. On this basis it affirmed the Rs 52.24 crore penalty imposed on the BCCI.

Contrasting the CCI's handling of the Hockey India and BCCI cases highlights the evolution of the principle of specificity of sport in India. While Hockey India escaped penalty for restricting others, the BCCI was penalized for tying its own hands. In the BCCI matter, the CCI took a stricter view of such restrictions, looking at the intent of the regulations rather than requiring evidence of actual harm.

This approach was also visible in *Pan India Infraprojects Private Limited v. Board of Control for Cricket in India*.[5] The complainant, formerly transacting as Essel Sports, was the promoter of the Indian Cricket League (ICL), which had not been sanctioned by the BCCI. The complainant alleged that the BCCI had abused its dominant position by specifically targeting and excluding it from participating in tenders for media rights for the IPL because it had promoted the rival league. In this case, too, the CCI found a prima facie case of abuse of dominance and ordered its director general to undertake further probe and inquiry.

Similarly, a prima facie case of abuse of dominance was also found in *Shravan Yadav and Other Informants. v. Volleyball Federation of India (VFI)*,[6] a case concerning a complaint against the volleyball federation for having restricted anyone from organizing domestic volleyball leagues for a period of ten years by granting exclusive hosting rights and access to players to one specific business entity.

A case against the All India Chess Federation (AICF) threw new light on the second prong of the 'inherence-proportionality' test. Here, the complainant alleged that the federation had used its dominance to restrict players from participating in tournaments not authorized by it. This was done through terms in the player registration form that had to be completed before the AICF would nominate the player to represent the country in tournaments. Players participating in unauthorized tournaments also faced financial penalties and the removal of player ratings.

There was no provision to seek permission from the AICF or offer any explanation.

In its order in *Hemant Sharma and others v. All India Chess Federation (AICF)*,[7] the CCI agreed that such absolute restrictions were an abuse of dominance as they were neither inherent nor proportionate to preserving the integrity of the sport. The AICF had argued that the restrictions it imposed on the chess players through its player registration process were regulatory in nature. The stated objective was to 'instil discipline amongst the players'.

The CCI acknowledged the regulatory powers of AICF. However, it held that a fine balance was needed between the need for regulation and the implication of competition in economic activities incidental to the sport. It considered the nature of chess as not physically taxing, and also the limited professional life and opportunities for chess players in India, to conclude that the restrictions were disproportionate to any legitimate objectives the AICF might have, and that they were unfair and unjustified.

In *Department of Sports v. Athletics Federation of India (AFI)*,[8] concerns were raised against the AFI's 'draft' decision to act against its members, officials or athletes who encourage or become part of marathons not authorized by AFI. The CCI noted that the AFI was dominant in the 'market for provision of services for organization of athletics/athletic activities in India'.

However, the CCI did not find abuse of dominance in this case as the draft decision was later modified by the AFI. The draft decision was updated as an advisory about educating athletes in relation to events that might adversely affect them physically and financially. The CCI also did not find evidence to show that AFI had ever prevented anyone from organizing a marathon or acted against anyone for being associated with unauthorized marathons.

This case is important to understand the limits to which SGBs' powers extend, especially in respect of community, recreational and youth sport. Limiting the scope of SGBs' sanctioning and disciplinary power to the organized sports pyramid only—a position the AFI was forced to concede—moderates their powers. It also focuses them on areas and activities that are relevant to their regulatory functions.

Free hit

Competition law recognizes the power disparities between SGBs and athletes. It tries to navigate a fine balance between their use and abuse of regulatory power. It asks important questions, examining SGBs' intent and actions for good faith, objectives and reasonableness. This acts as a counterbalance to SGBs and their wide powers.

With the greater professionalization, commercialization and globalization that characterize modern sport, these debates have occupied an increasingly prominent space. There are livelihoods and business interests involved, and the specificity of sport will not insulate SGBs when they misuse their regulatory powers to protect their own extra- and non-sporting interests.

New leagues and competitions are being mooted and launched with regular frequency across sports. They promise players significant sums of money, and fans an improved experience. Examples include a domestic volleyball league in India, a football league in Europe and international golf, skating and swimming leagues. These competitions are not sanctioned by the relevant SGBs and are often presented as 'unofficial' alternatives.

SGBs' kneejerk response in most cases is to threaten, and then implement bans on, players and officials associating with such leagues. These bans are usually couched in the language of preservation of the sport, its culture, its integrity, the athletes and their safety. Unsanctioned events are presented as muddying the waters on the pathways of participation, and as being destructive to the solidarity model that funds balanced development across the sports pyramid. The attempt to launch the European Super League for football was scuttled primarily on this basis. Worldwide, competition law authorities have been on guard, growing warier of SGBs' regulatory overreach.

It is true that if the best athletes in the world are forced to choose between various disjointed leagues and competition structures, elite talent will end up being scattered and disaggregated. A takeover of competitions by entities outside the sports pyramid can also end up creating new, pervasive sites of abuse of market dominance.

At the same time, in many underdeveloped sporting markets and systems, SGBs have been unable to provide athletes with viable professional avenues to earn a livelihood. How does a wrestler, boxer or hockey player make a living in a cash-poor SGB-controlled ecosystem?

Here, alternate competitions become welcome additions to the roster of their options. In the name of specificity, competition law must be careful to not shield SGBs that are not delivering on their fundamental obligations and yet doing all they can to protect their turf. They should be prevented from using their regulatory powers as a sword to keep others from doing what they are not doing. All this shows what is at stake and the important role that nuance and context must play in the 'inherence-proportionality' analysis.

Sport has much to offer society. It needs to be regulated with care. Sometimes it requires special treatment, at other times it needs reining in.

By simultaneously protecting the values of sport and the interests of its participants, competition law plays an important role in keeping sport competitive and sustainable.

Who said all the action is on the field of play? It certainly wasn't in the case of Dhanraj Pillay.

Chapter 13

On Community

Why do we have a right to watch cricket for free?

In 2004, the Indian men's cricket team toured Pakistan for a series of five One Day Internationals and three Test matches. The 1999 Kargil conflict had caused strained relations between the two countries, and this was the first bilateral series since.

The series was going to be closely followed in both countries, and the Pakistan Cricket Board had sold the global media rights to the private broadcaster Ten Sports. In Pakistan, Ten Sports had licensed the rights to telecast the matches to the public service television provider, PTV. In India, the matches were slated to be broadcast by Ten Sports to its paying subscribers via satellite and cable.

Ahead of the tour, a consumer group filed a writ petition in the Madras High Court arguing that it was against the public interest to restrict the availability of matches played by the national team to a private channel's subscribers alone. It requested the High Court to intervene and require the matches to be broadcast on Doordarshan, the Indian public service broadcaster's free-to-air channel.

On what basis could a court accede to such a demand? Does every Indian have the right to watch cricket for free? Does this extend to other sports?

Making waves

In 1982, India hosted the Asian Games. The public broadcaster, Prasar Bharati, built the technical capability for a live colour broadcast on its Doordarshan channel—the first such instance in the country. The government permitted the import of colour televisions under stringent customs laws. Sport provided the impetus for India to communicate itself to the world in technicolour. It also paved the way for Indians to watch a turning point in Indian sport—India's 1983 Men's Cricket World Cup triumph—in all its hues.

Until the early 1990s, Doordarshan continued to enjoy a virtual monopoly over audio-visual sports broadcasting. For decades, it was the only Indian broadcaster. Later, it was the only one that had the necessary resources, infrastructure and capability to broadcast live sports. In fact, instead of paying for rights as is common practice today, Doordarshan reportedly charged the Board of Control for Cricket in India (BCCI) a production fee of Rs 5 lakh for each live telecast of its events. This is difficult to believe in today's world of multibillion-dollar cricket rights deals, but that was the reality of the time.

After the liberalization of the Indian economy in 1991, several private broadcasters entered the Indian market. Sachin Tendulkar, one of the game's greats, emerged and built up an enormous fan following. The BCCI sensed an opportunity to break free of Doordarshan's shackles and felt emboldened to deal with private entities, hoping to sell broadcast rights to the highest bidder. This proved controversial, with Doordarshan initiating legal proceedings that culminated in the Supreme Court case of *The Secretary, Ministry of Information and Broadcasting v. Cricket Association of Bengal*[1] (the CAB case).

In the CAB case, the Supreme Court ruled that the airwaves and frequencies were 'public property' and that Doordarshan did not have a monopoly over the creation and transmission of signals for sporting events. It held that for a democracy to work, no private or state entity could claim absolute ownership of or monopoly over airwaves or frequencies; that the larger public interest required the plurality of opinions, views and ideas to be protected.

The court also held that the use of this public property ought to be controlled and regulated by a public authority in the interests of the public. In 1997, an act of Parliament created the Telecom Regulatory Authority of India (TRAI) as a statutory body to take on this role.

In this changed regulatory environment, the green shoots of the Indian sports business emerged—but a potentially competitive market for cricket rights was also going to bring new challenges.

Auction reaction

Sport provides live, competitive and unpredictable action and a mass audience that is watching the same thing at the same time. Broadcast imagery can transport viewers to the venue and give them an immersive, near-live experience of the match. The economics and dynamics of sports events change when broadcasting comes into the picture. The sale of broadcasting and media rights has become the single biggest source of revenue for sport. In India, this accounts for between 55 per cent and 70 per cent of total sports revenues. Additionally, other income streams such as sponsorship also rely on sport being broadcast and followed.

The money that sport governing bodies (SGBs) make is meant to be invested back into the development of that sport. There is, therefore, a public interest in maximizing revenues. Media rights can be hot property and lead to bidding wars. The processes employed in selling such rights can influence their price.

For many decades, Indian sports media deals were based on private negotiations between the SGBs and broadcasters. A rights contract with a sports broadcaster was executed after the seller had, presumably, tested the market. There was ambiguity involved in this process, and this led to allegations of rent-seeking by rights sellers. Of course, any money that was privately extracted from the winning broadcaster or otherwise left on the table was lost to the sport.

Recognizing the potential for leakage and the need for transparency, the Lodha Committee recommended, and the Supreme Court endorsed, the use of a tender process by the BCCI. By this time, a closed bidding process was already being used in some cases for price discovery. This involved an 'Invitation To Tender' document being issued, which set out eligibility criteria and required written technical and financial bids to be submitted by eligible bidders. The bids were then opened in front of all bidders, with the highest bid from among qualified bidders securing the rights.

This tender process brought a degree of openness and transparency and removed the avenue for corruption implicit in private negotiations. This approach was largely in line with the European rules around the sale of rights for globally popular football leagues: with respect to these leagues, the law requires such rights to be sold through open and transparent tender processes for a limited duration (usually not exceeding three years), and broken down into different packages to allow several competitors to acquire rights (referred to as the 'no single buyer rule').

Though it was better than the previous version, the closed bidding process was not immune to complaints of bid rigging, collusion, potential violations of confidentiality and other forms of manipulation of the process.

The tender methodology also raised concerns that the bidders would employ 'game theory' while making one single and final financial bid. This could, in some cases, result in suboptimal pricing and lower revenues for sport. For instance, consider a situation where there are three bidders for IPL broadcast rights in a closed bid. They all know that each bidder gets only one shot. Each of them knows that a successful bid only needs to be higher than the other two bids, and they know the others are thinking the same way. While, in some cases, this tender format may encourage one bidder to place an outsized bid to obliterate the competition, usually the bidders are in a 'game', only trying to outbid each other. Though the intrinsic value of the rights will be an anchor, the general market sentiment and the expected conduct of the other bidders can determine the bid values. A lower than expected price can result. This is why SGBs often insert a 'reserve price' below which they will not accept a bid. There have even been stray instances where SGBs have annulled a tender process and re-tendered the rights because they were 'not satisfied' with the highest bid.

Prodded by a petition filed in the Supreme Court by member of Parliament Dr Subramanian Swamy,[2] the BCCI conducted an 'e-auction' for the first time in April 2018 in respect of its international and domestic rights. Bidders were given a login and password for an online portal and allowed to submit and revise their bids multiple times in real time. Eligible bidders simultaneously filed incremental bids within defined timelines until only the highest bidder was left, and the rights were awarded to that bidder. This brought unparalleled transparency and dynamism to the process in a competitive market.

Regardless of the price discovery mechanism used, the successful broadcaster signs a media rights agreement and obtains exclusive rights and agrees to obligations to telecast the event footage. It gains the rights to exclude any other person from rebroadcasting, or reproducing, the broadcast content.

Under the contract, only the host broadcaster may be permitted to bring broadcast-ready cameras and production equipment into the playing arena. The terms and tenure of the contract will have been disclosed at the time of bidding. These can have a material impact on incumbency, entrenchment, barriers to entry and competition in the market for media rights.

How rights are sold can impact transparency, public faith in the process and also the price. It can also increase or decrease the likelihood of operationally and financially stable and technically competent enterprises winning bids to become official broadcasters. After all, there is a public interest not only in the rights being fairly valued but also in having them exercised and marketed professionally and without disruption.

Fee or free

Having paid a high price for the rights, the sports broadcaster must then expend more money to purchase spectrum, create infrastructure, produce the broadcast and market the content.

The broadcaster must also invest in preventing the revenue leakage that piracy brings. With new technologies democratizing broadcast innovation, leakage can be both challenging and expensive to identify and eliminate.

The broadcaster, thus, is under pressure to recoup their sizeable investment and make a profit.

Broadcasters typically monetize rights in one or two ways—by selling on-air screening slots to advertisers and/or subscriptions to viewers. Advertisers, who pay big money for slots, would like their brands to be seen, repeatedly, by the audience. And since no single advertiser can pay the kind of money that helps the broadcaster recoup expenses, sports events typically attract multiple advertisers, all of whom are keen that their ads get maximum mileage.

The other revenue model is where the broadcaster uses a major sports event as a hook to acquire subscribers. Here, the idea is that the subscriber who has signed on in order to watch a sports event will remain a subscriber even after the event concludes, thus allowing the broadcaster to commercialize the customer beyond the duration of the event itself.

The two models, however, often find themselves in conflict. The advertiser expects the message to be seen repeatedly; on the other hand, a paying subscriber tends to dislike too much commercial intrusion—especially repetitious ads—into their viewing experience. Satisfying the advertisers' demands thus leads to dissatisfied subscribers. This, in turn, impacts the long-term business model of the broadcaster.

Though advertisement-only free-to-air models and subscription-only ad-free premium services do exist, the most common models are hybrid, with paid-for advertisements being broadcast to paying subscribers.

This two-pronged approach acts as a diversification strategy for broadcasters who do not want to become too reliant on a single source of revenue. Because part of the income comes from the advertiser, the broadcaster can keep subscription rates low. Low rates lead to mass adoption—which, in turn, is a prerequisite for healthy advertising slot rates.

In a hybrid scenario, the broadcaster needs to carefully manage pricing, availability and piracy challenges in their markets. The ability of the rights holder to make a return on its investment also factors into the valuation of rights in the future.

TRAI again

In determining monetization strategy, the rights holder must also contend with the broadcast regulatory environment. In India, TRAI undertakes tariff controls, setting maximum limits on the pricing of a la carte channels offered as part of a bouquet, and barring the mixing of free-to-air channels with paid channels in subscription bouquets.

For instance, the 2017 tariff order provided that the broadcaster must declare the monthly maximum retail price of each channel. It said that no pay channel that is part of a pay channel bouquet can be priced above Rs 19. Also, it put a floor on the price of a pay channel bouquet, providing that it may not be less than 85 per cent of the aggregate cost of all its constituent pay channels if bought separately.

In practice, this means that a channel like Star Sports, if it is being sold as part of a larger package, must price itself at no more than Rs 19. Let's say there are five sports channels in the Star Sports Channel Package priced at Rs 19 each. In such a case, the tariff order says that the Star Sports Channel Package cannot be sold below a price of Rs 80.75, i.e., 85 per cent of the aggregate price of the five channels sold individually.

Tariff control requires care. Broadcasters already have to maintain a delicate balance between channel pricing and ad rates. Artificially depressing subscription fees can lead to market inefficiencies and make broadcasters disproportionately reliant on advertising revenue. This, in turn, has led to practices such as 'ball cutting' in cricket broadcasts where, to squeeze in more ads between overs, the broadcaster cuts away to ads before the ball is 'dead', and returns after the ball is already back in 'play', resulting in the television audience missing parts of the live action.

This issue was significant enough for it to be raised by the Lodha Committee, which went to the extent of recommending in its report to the Supreme Court that advertisements should not be permitted between the overs of a Test and One Day International match and should only be displayed in breaks in play like drinks, lunch and tea. The Supreme Court rejected this restriction on the BCCI's urging that such a limitation would destroy the commerce of the sport.

The Cable Television Network Rules, 1994 also include regulations restricting advertising time on television channels to twelve minutes per hour during the broadcast of a programme (of which only ten minutes can be commercial advertising and the other two can be the channel's self-promotional programming). The rules also state that all advertisements should be clearly distinguishable from the programme and should not in any manner interfere with the programme. TRAI is empowered to monitor and enforce these obligations.

As ad rates increase in response to subscription tariff control, the cost of viewership is also transferred from viewers to non-viewing consumers of the advertised products and services who—whether or not they watched the cricket—must share in the marketing costs, which are embedded in the purchase price of these products and services.

Regulation of channel tariffs and advertising standards aim to protect the rights of viewers to access content at reasonable prices, and to not have their viewing experience diluted by intrusive and excessive advertising. In competitive broadcast markets like India, regulation must interwoven carefully with the market forces of demand and supply.

Sharing is caring

As the airwaves opened up after the CAB case, a competitive market for sports broadcasting emerged. This also coincided with new modes of distribution like satellite television. Private broadcasters and foreign capital saw new opportunities. Multiple sports channels popped up. Doordarshan was unable to keep pace, and this meant that many matches were now available only to subscribers of the private sports channel. With the historic

India tour to Pakistan in the offing, the writ petition discussed earlier was filed by the consumer group.

In 2006, in the case of *Citizen, Consumer and Civic Action Group v. Prasar Bharati*,[3] the Madras High Court held that denying access to the live broadcast to non-subscribers affected the exercise of their freedom of speech and expression. In so doing, the court relied on the principles laid down in the CAB case recognizing the airwaves as public property.

The court held that primary rights over the Indian territory vest in the Indian public, labelling the broadcasting rights given to intermediaries as secondary rights. The High Court also recognized that the private broadcaster had acquired the rights for substantial consideration, and it sought to balance the private broadcaster's and its associates' commercial interests with the public's fundamental right to freedom of speech and expression.

Holding that the broadcaster's rights are subservient to the larger public interest, the court directed Ten Sports to share its broadcast feed for the series with Prasar Bharati for retransmission on Doordarshan. On appeal, this position was also affirmed by the Supreme Court. Identical petitions were filed for successive international cricket series that followed and similar judicial orders ensued.

In 2007, the Government of India decided to step in. It first promulgated an ordinance and then passed a law that was similar to 'listed events' and 'anti-siphoning' legislation in other jurisdictions. This is how The Sports Broadcasting Signals (Mandatory Sharing with Prasar Bharati) Act, 2007, came into being. This law and its rules cemented a 'mandatory sharing' obligation for 'sporting events of national importance' in India. It mandated all content rights owners to share 'clean', i.e., ad-free, broadcast signals of such events with Prasar Bharati to enable them to re-transmit the same on their free-to-air channels.

'Sporting events of national importance' have been defined as national or international sporting events, held in India or abroad, that may be notified by the Central government from time to time. The Ministry of Information and Broadcasting, in consultation with the Sports Ministry and Prasar Bharati, determines and notifies a list of such events. The criteria for compiling this list are left completely to its discretion.

The notified list includes all official One Day International and T20 matches played by the Indian Men's Cricket Team, any Test matches that are considered to be of 'high public interest' by the Central government, and the semi-finals and finals of the ICC Men's World Cup and the 'ICC Championship Trophy' (sic), regardless of whether the Indian team is participating in the match.

The list also includes international multisport events such as the Summer Olympic Games, the Commonwealth Games, the Asian Games, the Special Olympic World Games, the Paralympics and certain premier tennis, hockey and football events, whether or not the Indian team or an Indian is participating.

To compensate the rights holder for the sharing, the law provides for a 75:25 split between the rights holder and Prasar Bharati of the advertising revenue earned through the re-transmitted feed. The rules issued under the law describe how the feed is to be shared and how the marketing rights to commercial airtime on Prasar Bharati are to be managed.

Is this a fair balance between commerce and public interest? It depends on whom you ask.

The introduction of mandatory sharing obligations was frustrating for private sports broadcasters who were trying to find their way in a challenging regulatory environment. Their rights became non-exclusive and the business models for major events had to be recast. The law did provide a lifeline to Doordarshan, which could no longer compete in the market for sports rights.

If the proof of the pudding is in the eating, mandatory sharing has found a fair balance in cricket. Cricket media rights valuations have continued to soar during the era of mandatory sharing legislation. The public exchequer does not need to underwrite cricket rights, and private channels bid and transfer costs to advertisers and subscribers instead. Yet, every Indian can watch high-profile sporting events for free.

How does watching sports further free speech and expression? Before we get to that, let's look at another legal clash that ended differently.

Mandatory Sharing

What's news?

In 2011, India was playing co-host to the ICC Men's Cricket World Cup. Event promotions were everywhere you looked, and the nation stood transfixed as the Indian team blazed its way through the tournament and ended up champions. This was a cultural and commercial extravaganza, and India's private news broadcasters wanted a piece of the action. They covered the event with gusto, showing match footage on loop and running sponsored shows with highlights from the matches of the day.

Before the event, the International Cricket Council (ICC) had issued 'ICC Cricket World Cup 2011 News Access Guidelines for India', which it believed reflected appropriate fair dealing standards for recognized news broadcasters. The news channels were given parameters within which they could use audio-visual footage from the World Cup in a manner that did not infringe the broadcast rights of the tournament's official broadcaster and the ICC.

The guidelines placed limits on the amount of footage that could be used each day, the number of times it could be repeated, the minimum delay between the live match and the news broadcast of the footage, and prohibitions on commercialization of footage through use in sponsored shows or by the insertion of advertising overlays.

News channels ignored the ICC's guidelines, instead following what they considered appropriate standards, and continued to copy footage from the official broadcast and use it liberally in their news and analysis shows. Some of these segments and shows on the news channels had their own title sponsors and commercial partners, including sponsors that were direct competitors of the ICC's official partners.

Given what was at stake, something had to give. The ICC withdrew venue accreditation for journalists from the electronic news media. The electronic news media chose to boycott the final matches of the event, alleging a violation of their rights. Once the event was complete, and in preparation for the next ICC event, the ICC sued one of the prominent news broadcasters, NDTV, for copyright infringement.

Would the court draw a line in the sand?

SGBs recognize the important role journalists and the news media play in covering and communicating their events. The law also recognizes the importance of information flows, providing a fair dealing defence for news reporting of current events. However, when news coverage indulges in overuse and competing commercialization, it can start impinging on the commercial model of sport.

By the time the ICC sued NDTV, there had been a few cases in the courts that had dealt with the issue of 'news access', and some principles had been established. In the 2005 case of *Prasar Bharati v. Sahara TV Network Pvt. Ltd. and Ors.*,[4] the Delhi High Court tried to draw bright-line standards on such use. It recognized as reasonable Prasar Bharati's daily cap on a private news channel restricting their airing of match footage to no more than three repetitions of footage, with each individual clip not exceeding 120 seconds, and also imposed an overall limit of 7 minutes a day in aggregate. The judge stated that the use of the footage should only be for delivering cricket news without any commercial programming or advertisements immediately before, during and after such cricket news.

The court then reconsidered this approach in the 2008 case of *ESPN Star Sports v. Global Broadcast News Ltd.*,[5] stating that it was difficult to accept that temporal caps could apply 'across the board' and that one could ignore the context, the length of the original work borrowed and the purpose. As a result of these contrary holdings, ambiguity prevailed on what constituted 'fair dealing' in the context of journalistic usage of match play footage by the electronic media.

In September 2012, in *ICC Development (International) v. New Delhi Television Ltd.*,[6] the Delhi High Court delivered its judgment in ICC's suit against NDTV. The court upheld the restrictions imposed on live and archival footage laid down in the ICC's guidelines. It also held that NDTV could not use the name, image and logo of any advertiser in special sports news programmes, nor could it carry an advertisement immediately before, during or immediately at the end of a special programme using the footage belonging to the ICC. Such use was seen as inconsistent with the idea of fair dealing and prejudicial to the event organizer, the event's official broadcaster and the sponsors and partners of the event.

With the order having gone against it on most counts, NDTV took the matter back to the Delhi High Court in appeal, arguing that its use of broadcast footage was 'fair dealing'.

In *New Delhi Television Ltd. v. ICC Development (International) Ltd.*,[7] a Division Bench of the Delhi High Court relied on the test laid down in the New Zealand case of *Media Works NZ Ltd. v. Sky Television Network Ltd.*,[8] which differentiated coverage and reporting that is result-oriented from that which is primarily an analysis or review of a sporting event.

It held that a determination of fair use or fair dealing does not arise where the allegedly infringing activity is not 'reporting' that is undertaken 'currently'. The court proceeded to impose a time cap of twenty-four hours with regard to the currency of an event being news, holding that this mutates into history thereafter—meaning that any use after this point cannot be for 'news reporting' and will be treated as use for 'analysis'.

The court agreed that the time span or gestation period would vary from event to event. It also held that TV news channels would have two options—either display advertisements during special programmes and not use match footage, or choose to use the footage but not display any advertisements in respect of such programmes. On whether there should be a cap on the amount of footage used and the number of permissible repetitions, the court believed each case would have to be viewed on its facts.

After having moderated commercial and public interests using the mandatory sharing law to open up access to match broadcasts, the court's balancing act on the matter of news access brought about a different outcome. The delineation between news reporting and analysis programming was established. This brought clarity and order to TV news channels' use of match footage while recognizing the role news reporting plays in disseminating information.

Much has changed in the broadcasting world in the decade since this decision. We have seen democratized information production and consumption, the emergence of online streaming platforms, and innovation in the way that sport and news is produced and delivered.

When anyone can publish, broadcast and transmit content, who is a journalist and who isn't? With content cycles and lifespans growing shorter, is there a meaningful difference left between news and analysis?

Image management

'Pics or it didn't happen!' is a phrase that is part of today's pop culture. In a literal sense, it recognizes the ability of visuals to evidence, remember and give meaning to events.

Sports imagery is a form of cultural artefact, part of a commons of shared experiences from the past, meant to be shared with others in the future. We are influenced by the way imagery is created, controlled, used and reused, especially when we interpret and derive meaning from events of public relevance.

Private broadcasting has brought dynamism and innovation to sport. It has also powered its commerce. While it goes about doing its thing, vital public resources can end up behind private gates that control access. While the law incentivizes and protects broadcasters' rights, it must also prevent the stagnation that can result from exclusivity.

The sites of control in the broadcast of sports content are many—price, access, and the rights to reuse and remix. Every story is capable of being told differently by different people. Giving content owners too much control can lead to suboptimal outcomes in the marketplace of stories and meaning. The risks of giving air to only a single story are many. One-sidedness, a lack of criticality and an over-alignment with the powers of the day can result in a skew towards the recording of a moment and the memories it embeds in the social consciousness.

Sport can be a purveyor of national and collective identity. Its unique role in driving common and simultaneous mass viewership is increasing, with fragmented viewing behaviours becoming the norm in markets characterized by wide consumer choice, long-tail content and deep personalization. When even members of the same household are all watching different things, the fact that millions watch sport together is all the more remarkable.

Making key sporting events freely available to the largest possible audience promotes a wider public interest. From an economic perspective, this generates 'positive network externalities'—viewers not only enjoy the event, but their participation also adds value to the network for everyone else. Sport viewership promotes a form of 'cultural citizenship' that feeds into the creation and maintenance of a national culture, conversations, shared memories and national identity.[9]

Watching sport together, supporting the same team, having a common experience, discussing it threadbare—these are all ties that bind, giving us opportunities to experience our commonality and feel connectedness. These cultural interests are promoted by bringing into the fold those who may not have the means or the desire to pay for access.

Ever noticed that pretty much every Indian has an opinion on cricket? This brings together two favourite Indian pastimes—watching cricket and expressing opinions. This is the beauty of sport, and there's no better case to be made for keeping it open, accessible and thriving.

Chapter 14

On Influence

Will fans soon manage sports teams?

In its inaugural season, Formula E introduced an innovation intended to give the fan a more active role. In the lead-up to each race, members of the public could vote online for their favourite driver. On race day, the three (later increased to five) drivers who got the maximum votes were entitled to a 'Fanboost': a five-second burst of extra engine power that was stored and could be strategically deployed in the second half of the race.

With this move, Formula E converted the viewer into an active—albeit limited—participant in the race, and gave them agency. 'Interactivity' is the holy grail that both promoters and advertisers chase—the more engaged the fan is, the more likely they are to stay loyal to the sport. This, in turn, means a growing captive audience for both promoters and advertisers to exploit.

As has been discussed previously, TV viewership and public celebration of achievements are central to elite sports. Broadcasting and globalization have increased the pool of potential viewers.

More recently, leaps in consumer technology, communications and analytics have transformed the viewer from being incidental to the professional sports experience to being central to it. Engaging and keeping the attention of fans is now at the heart of the sports business model.

Attention can be monetized. But attention is limited, there is competition for it and, therefore, the fan is in the driver's seat. This power can play out in many interesting ways.

Fan drive

Audiences come to sports venues for the entertainment and thrill of watching live action. They buy match tickets or season passes. Once there, they are captive. A lot can be done with them, including making them watch advertisements and encouraging them to purchase merchandise and consume food and beverages.

Fans like to share the highs of the sports experience with their families, friends, colleagues, business partners and prospects. The social nature of sports engagement expands the fanbase. Live audiences create a spectacle in the stadium that is attractive to watch on television and create what commentators refer to as 'atmosphere'. This has become so central to the viewing experience that crowd noise from previous seasons was inserted into the broadcast of IPL matches played in empty stadiums during the COVID-19 pandemic.

Live broadcasts help sport reach larger audiences and find new fans. Viewers in different parts of India and across the world can simultaneously share a common experience. The fan interest magnifies the sphere of influence of athletes, teams, events and brands. Across the world, people know which shoes Lionel Messi and LeBron James wear, and that Heineken is the UEFA Champions League's official sponsor. As the size of the broadcast audience grows, the media rights, advertising rates and sponsorship fees increase in value.

New ways are constantly being added for sports viewers to engage with non-match content while watching a live match.

These include fantasy sports, prediction games, sports betting, social media contests and engagement, athlete interactions, polling and other feedback loops. Many of these are baked into the live broadcast. Gamification, connections and incentives provide new opportunities for fans to interact. They also create a stickiness, working to prevent viewer distraction or departure. Every ball of each match has salience and must be watched, followed and interacted with. Bums on seats (a popular term for spectators in the stadium) are supplemented by eyes on screens.

Data collection and analytics help promoters and broadcasters understand the fan and personalize the experience. Sports events provoke fans to be outspoken about opinions and interests, and this helps to profile them. This can sharpen targeting and recommendations, making the experience more meaningful for each fan and more valuable in commerce. For instance, a travel insurance brand would be willing to pay a premium to deliver marketing messages to fans who are known to travel abroad multiple times a year to watch the Indian cricket team in action.

Brands from small towns in Europe like Barilla pasta and Parmalat dairy (both from Parma, Italy), as well as large brands headquartered in Asia such as Samsung (from Korea) and Panasonic (from Japan), have promoted themselves through European football sponsorships. Indian brands like two-wheeler manufacturer Hero and tile-maker Kajaria have advertised in cricket stadiums in Australia, England, South Africa and the West Indies, though their target customers watch the telecast live a few thousand miles away from where the match is being played.

Despite the globalized market, not all sports action will immediately attract large audiences. In fact, the global nature of sport can make it challenging for some businesses to succeed. A case in point is Indian football, which struggles for viewership since it competes with top-flight football played in Europe.

Without a significant following, it is difficult to sustain the commerce of sport. Concerted efforts must be made to grow audiences and consolidate them. This is where innovative fan engagement methods are used to convert interest into following, following into fandom and fandom into commerce. The agency that such interactivity gives the sports fan is changing the game in other ways. Before we understand this evolution, let's explore more deeply the relationship brands have with sport, and the synergy between them.

Brand journey

Sponsorship is a key revenue source for the sports business. It allows the corporate world to invest in the sports ecosystem flexibly and with a light touch. There is no ownership or long-term commitment required. If things work out, the transaction can be repeated; if they don't, the sponsor can walk away.

Sponsors support an athlete, team, organization or event—in cash or in kind—for a particular event or over a period of time, and receive certain benefits in return. This could be a logo on clothing, a licence of image rights or a commitment to attend a corporate event.

Regardless of the motivations or size of sponsorship, every sponsor is looking for a return on their investment. While that return could be social or emotional—such as the satisfaction of being part of an athlete's journey and success or attending the event from an exclusive sponsor area alongside others—typically, commercial considerations are at the heart of a sponsor's motivations.

Most sponsors have either a product or service that they are offering to public consumers, other businesses, organizations or governments. The sponsor's objective is to achieve more adoption and consumption of its offering because that means greater sales and profits. For sponsors, sport can deliver exposure, association, experience and understanding. These are then meant to translate into sales and profits.

Sports events can attract and aggregate large viewership within a venue and on media broadcasts. The audience profile can overlap with a demographic that the sponsor is targeting. Typically, sponsors can get exposure through the application of logos within the event venue. Sponsor branding can be seen on advertising mats on the field, perimeter boards, large screens and other visible and camera-facing areas such as stands and concourses, press conference and interview areas, on team jerseys, umpires' clothing, player equipment and spectator seating. Anyone who has watched a cricket match at the Feroz Shah Kotla Stadium in Delhi (rechristened the Arun Jaitley Stadium in 2019), for instance, will have struggled to find an inch of stadium concrete that isn't covered by an advertisement.

Logos can also appear and brands can be mentioned on promotions outside the stadium, before, during and after the event—on television, radio, newspaper ads, outdoor hoardings, social media, letterheads and stationery. The sponsor looks to harness customer mind space at a time when a disproportionate amount of public attention is directed towards the sports event. The 1987 Cricket World Cup was sponsored by a relatively unknown company at the time. Three and a half decades later it is remembered—and referred to—as the Reliance World Cup, as the once obscure sponsoring company has become the largest business house in India.

There is a unique aura, brand value and goodwill attached to sports events. Many interest groups and varied types of people are aggregated on a common—often global—platform. Sponsors can get on board to make the public aware of their association with the event, team or player.

Prominent examples are the long associations Rolex has had with Roger Federer and Coca-Cola has sustained with the Olympic Games. In such cases, sponsors define their own brand through association with a celebrated athlete or event that the public is already aware of, interacts with and has a preconceived positive impression about. A sponsor wishes to receive the rub-off effect that comes from this association. To reinforce the association, it will try to amplify the commonality between the brand and the sports property in its communication, advertising and promotions: the style and timing of Federer's backhand is flawless, and so is the Rolex watch and its mechanism.

Those who attend sports events are given unique and valued personal experiences. These happen only once but can be talked about for a lifetime—you might have already heard from those who were there at the Wankhede Stadium to watch Dhoni finish off the ICC Cricket World Cup 2011 final with a six, or at the Melbourne Cricket Ground where Kohli hit a couple of his own in a tense group match against Pakistan at the ICC T20 World Cup 2022.

While such moments are special, they are also universal—available to everyone who was at the ground that day or was watching on television. What premium brands and sponsors might aim for is to go a step further and create memorable events that are unique, or limited to a special set of fans, giving them extra bragging rights.

Such special fan experiences could include attending a match from a dedicated stand, receiving hospitality benefits along with other prominent people, meeting players and former players, getting photographed with the trophy, receiving special merchandise and similar experiences.

As part of their sponsorship entitlements, sponsors often receive a number of these exclusive experiences from the event organizer. They offer these to people who are important to them, like key customers and distributors, clients, senior or high-performing employees and consumers selected through contests and promotions. Many Indian wealth management companies now regularly take their largest customers on fully paid trips to cricket, football and Formula 1 events. Sponsors hope that the recipients of these experiences might feel gratitude and respond favourably come the next opportunity to do business.

Sponsors also find it valuable to understand sports audiences. The gala environment and spirit of sport can encourage consumers to try new experiences and experiment beyond the sporting action. Sponsors can use this opening to present a sample of their product or service to those attending or watching. For instance, a new drink might be given away or sold at a sampling kiosk within the stadium and the consumers can be asked for their feedback. Sampling provides an opportunity for information to flow both ways—the consumer experiences the product or service, and this gives the sponsor a chance to receive feedback on consumer choice and decision-making. This might be through surveys, observation, market research and the like.

Sponsors are often given space to put up stalls in dedicated fan zones on the stadium premises where they can interact with the spectators before, during and after the matches. These provide sponsors the opportunity to build positive associations with a captive audience.

Brands aim to build awareness of their existence, command consumers' consideration, educate them about features and attributes and convince them to make purchasing decisions. Aided by its universality and the values it purveys, sport helps build and reinforce brand loyalty and affinity.

With the commercialization of sport, the fan journey has progressed, too. From being the beneficiaries of the largesse of sport governing bodies (SGBs) and event promoters to having their preferences become central to decisions on scheduling, formatting and packaging, the sports fan has come a long way. Today, no sports organization can afford to ignore fans and their preferences. Fans know this, and are making it clear that it isn't going to be one-way traffic. Their attention and interest aren't products to be sold to just anyone.

What does this mean for the market for advertising? How do fans influence decisions on and off the field? First, let's go to an ad break.

Ad block

All sports-related advertising must comply with public laws and self-regulatory codes that apply to general advertising. Regulations can differ across different sectors, forms of media and different products and services.

In India, advertising must not promote a product or service prohibited by law, such as betting or gambling. It may also not directly promote a product or service that is illegal to advertise, such as tobacco products or alcohol. More broadly, it must remain compliant with the self-regulatory principles set out in the Advertising Standards Council of India Code for Self-Regulation of Advertising Content in India (ASCI Code).

Among the objectives of the ASCI Code is to 'safeguard against the indiscriminate use of advertising for the promotion of products which are regarded as hazardous to society or to individuals to a degree or of a type which is unacceptable to society at large'. The Cable Television Networks (Regulation) Act, 1995 governs television advertising in India. The rules under this law contain an 'Advertising Code' that prohibits the carriage on television of any advertisement that violates the ASCI Code.

That is not the end of the story. The law permits the advertising of certain 'brand extension' products or services that share the brand names or logos with products that are illegal to advertise. This is subject to the condition that the brand extension is genuine. This is how (and why) we see advertising for drinking glasses, calendars, water, hot sauce and music CDs that use the same brand names as alcohol brands.

To be allowed to advertise like this, the advertiser must show that the brand extension product is distributed in reasonable quantity and is available in a substantial number of outlets where other products of the same category are available. This puts the onus on beer-makers Kingfisher to show that their Kingfisher calendar and Kingfisher water are genuine products, and Bira to show that their Bira hot sauce is actually being sold in the market.

The advertiser must also show that the proposed expenditure on such brand extension advertising is not disproportionate to the actual sales turnover of the product. Whisky-maker Royal Stag, thus, must show that the advertising of its Royal Stag music CDs is genuine and appropriate for the size of that product's market.

The ASCI Code also requires the brand extension product or service to be registered with the appropriate governmental authority, and to have independent certification that it has achieved certain minimum sales turnovers and has made investments in the manufacturing or procurement of the product. In certain cases, it may be required to provide evidence of turnover greater than 10 per cent of the turnover of the same brand in the restricted category.

In its advertising, it must also adequately differentiate the brand extension product being advertised from the prohibited products, and must not surreptitiously or clandestinely promote the prohibited products by using references, cues or imagery. It is no coincidence that packaged water and crystal glasses are used as brand extension products to overcome this restriction—they are suggestive of the act of drinking but not of the alcoholic product itself. The advertiser must also receive pre-certification from the Central Board of Film Certification as being suitable for unrestricted public exhibition.

This framework is designed to discourage advertisements aimed at circumventing the prohibition on the advertising of prohibited products. Despite the checks and balances, the exception for brand extensions opens the door for what is known as surrogate advertising, with product ranges of the same brand created with the sole objective of advertising the brand name that it shares with alcohol, betting or other products or services that are illegal to offer or illegal to advertise. Such surrogate advertising is commonly seen on sports broadcasts and within sports venues.

While it promotes the value of skill, fitness and health, does it make sense for sport to evangelize—albeit through surrogate advertising—brands that run counter to the ethos of sport? Should sport, without filters, accept funding from any brand that is compliant with the law? Fans are beginning to have their say on this.

Awash

Given the role of sport in society and the values we look to it for, public sentiment is shifting, expressing concern about the types of advertisers, products and services that are advertised within stadia, aired during sports broadcasts or associated with players, teams and sports events.

In India, there has not been an active public debate around the appropriateness of surrogate advertising through brand extensions. Elsewhere, tough questions are being asked about sports sponsorships. In the UK, even though it is legal to offer sports bets and advertise licensed betting services, a debate raged for many years on whether gambling advertising should be allowed in the Premier League given how widely football is followed by the youth. In Australia, despite it being legal to advertise alcohol products and gambling, SGBs are being pushed to revise their policies on advertising by alcohol brands and gambling companies during sports events.

The argument against such advertising is that early exposure to content promoting gambling and alcohol can normalize these activities and influence children, especially when they are at an age when their values, attitudes, behaviours and world views are still being formed. Similar questions are being asked about the appropriateness of athletes, teams and SGBs accepting sponsorships from makers of junk food and beverages that are high in salt or sugar, and from industries such as mining, petrochemicals and non-renewable energy. In the public consciousness, these are seen as having a negative impact on public health and environmental well-being.

In some cases, the sport itself has assessed the direction of the wind and decided to drop advertising for products deemed harmful. For instance, Formula 1 does not permit the advertising of tobacco products in any manner. Responding to public pressure, the Premier League and its twenty clubs announced in 2023 that they would no longer accept gambling sponsorship on their match day shirts following the end of the 2025–26 season.

All money entering sports through sponsorships theoretically helps promote sport. Can sport remain agnostic to the sources of its funding or does the business, history and conduct of the advertiser or sponsor matter? Should people or companies that have a record of behaviour running counter to the underlying values of sport, or products and services that have negative effects on physical or mental health or the environment, be permitted to receive the 'positive glow' of associating with the passion, goodwill, emotions and prestige that sport evokes?

The act of laundering or whitewashing reputations or brands through association with sports is now known by the umbrella term 'sportswashing'. Through sponsorship associations and advertising, a brand's reputation can be enhanced or normalized; sport can be used to divert attention from a sponsor's past and current activities through the power of association.

Arguably, these gains for the brand can only come at the cost of sport's reputation and goodwill. By allowing advertising that directly conflicts with its ethos, the values of sport risk being compromised and diluted. This has brought public morals—some would say, those that reflect Western standards—into SGBs' boardroom discussions.

The Beijing 2008 Summer Olympic and Paralympic Games and the Beijing 2022 Winter Olympic and Paralympic Games focused the world's attention on the Chinese state's treatment of Uyghur Muslims in Xinjiang province. Questions were also raised around Qatar's treatment of migrant workers in the lead-up to its hosting of the FIFA World Cup 2022. The Premier League has encountered public concern around the ownership and stewardship of multiple teams—often termed British cultural assets—by Saudi Arabian and other Gulf investors. In 2023, the

Professional Golfers' Association of America (PGA) faced strong criticism for partnering with promoters of former rival LIV Golf, after having spent a year painting them in poor light for Saudi Arabia's human rights record and its role in the 9/11 attacks.

In the past, sport's only focus was on how revenues could be maximized to benefit its own ecosystem. But now, it can no longer ignore larger societal concerns about the sources of its funding. The battle is imminent. Through its associations, organized sport affords a stamp of approval and a form of implicit social license to industries and organizations. It is going to face increasing public and governmental scrutiny and tougher questions on the associations it chooses and the connections it makes.

Cancel culture

As key sponsors and other intermediaries like broadcasters play more prominent roles in the professional sports ecosystem, they start exerting significant influence on matters of sports governance. These organizations have a ear to the ground about consumer and public sentiment. Brand perception and consumer response are vital currency for them, and this means they will generally act in ways that are respectful to and aligned with public views to ensure the sustainability of their businesses.

Sponsors and broadcasters remain wary of associating their brand with activities and conduct that are widely seen as immoral or inappropriate. Corruption in sports organizations, athletes found to be doping or cheating and tournaments that are rife with match-fixing can all set off alarm bells with sponsors who are concerned that they might be 'cancelled' by their consumers for supporting or associating with such activity.

In the aftermath of the 2013 IPL spot-fixing scandal, the title sponsor PepsiCo exited its sponsorship of the league. BT Sport, a UK-based broadcaster, ran a live 30-second piece on the human rights situation in Azerbaijan in its pre-match coverage of the 2019 UEFA Champions League final in Baku. In 2020, on the sidelines of the Sky Sports broadcast of the England v. West Indies Test series, former cricketer and commentator Michael Holding delivered a stirring address on the Black Lives Matter movement and the institutional racism black athletes face.

Sponsors will usually err on the side of caution and avoid controversy while making decisions to engage with events, SGBs, players and teams. When they do engage, they normally include 'morals clauses' that enable early termination of the relationship should there occur acts that result in disrepute or loss of goodwill. This puts the public sentiment—albeit expressed vicariously through intermediaries—squarely in the mix on the issue of ethics and accountability in sports governance.

An SGB that wants to attract and retain sponsors and broadcasters will also need to retain alignment with public mores. The pulls and pushes of commerce bring balance to decisions. This deters conduct and decisions that might not sit well with the public. Here, we see the fan begin to make the transition from being a grateful recipient of entertainment to taking a position of indirect influence.

Whether or not the SGBs themselves care about fans, they certainly do care about those who care about them—sponsors and broadcasters. They are now positioned to amplify the public sentiment. You might ignore the fan, at your own peril, but you simply cannot ignore your commercial partners.

On the menu

A fan's role does not end at being part of indirect pressure groups through sponsors and broadcasters. More recently, their position has progressed further—as a stakeholder with rights. Furthering sport's recognition as a quasi-public good, the law has brought additional levers of public accountability to SGBs. Among these are legal rights and remedies for fans.

With the fan increasingly seen as a primary stakeholder in sport, SGBs are being pushed towards greater transparency. With information comes understanding, and with rights come remedies.

Good governance principles include various affirmative public disclosure obligations of SGBs. The Sports Code requires national sports federations (NSFs) in India to publicly adopt proper accounting procedures at all levels and produce annual financial statements, adopt impartial and transparent selection procedures and maintain a website that provides and discloses important operational and financial details to the public.

Following the Lodha Committee Report, the Board of Control for Cricket in India (BCCI) updated its new constitution and listed among its objectives 'To . . . recogniz(e) that the primary stakeholders are the players and Cricket fans in India, and that accountability, transparency and purity of the Game are the core values'.[1] The BCCI constitution also provides that the constitutional documents, resolutions, orders and memoranda shall be made available on the BCCI website and also freely accessible to the public at a reasonable price.

The constitution requires the BCCI to upload to its website the quarterly financial and operational reports of the BCCI and all its committees, details of all payments and expenditures over Rs 25 lakh, auditors' financial and compliance reports and its notices and invitations to tender. The BCCI must also provide details of all cricket stadia and enable the booking of tickets for all matches from its website.

As part of the drive towards governance transparency, SGBs are also required to respond to information requests made by the public. The RTI Act provides the framework under which citizens can secure access to information that is under the control of public authorities. All NSFs are recognized as public authorities and their records are open to public scrutiny under the RTI Act.

Examining the issue on the Supreme Court's request, the Law Commission of India recommended that the BCCI (given that it is not recognized as an NSF) and all state cricket associations must also be brought under the purview of the RTI Act. However, this recommendation has not been acted on by the government.

The public's right to obtain extensive and granular information recognizes the public nature of an SGB's functions. As described by Justice Ravindra Bhat (then of the Delhi High Court) in *Indian Olympic Association v. Veeresh Malik*,[2] this 'furthers the process of empowerment, assures transparency, and makes democracy responsive and meaningful'.

Increasingly, legal frameworks provide access to institutional and legal remedies to members of the public. For example, the BCCI constitution now provides for the appointment of an ombudsman who, among other things, is to accept and examine complaints from any member of the public who is aggrieved concerning ticketing or access and facilities at stadia.

As the law has evolved, SGBs have gradually been exposed to the rigours of public law. Public interest litigation has opened the door to writ jurisdiction of the courts. This means that any aggrieved person—whether or not they are a member of the SGB—can challenge the arbitrary exercise of power by an SGB that impinges on their rights, or on the rights of the public at large. The availability of public legal remedies actualizes rights and expands the universe of stakeholders with the standing to challenge SGB decisions.

Other jurisdictions go further. In 2003, Brazil passed a Sports Fan Statute to actualize a rights framework for fans. It establishes a comprehensive catalogue of rights, including transparency, publicity and access to an independent ombudsman, just like the BCCI constitution. Uniquely, the statute also requires public disclosure of a match's gross revenue and the number of paying and non-paying spectators, disclosure of competition rules prior to a match, lotteries for choice of referees to ensure independence, rights of stadium-goers to adequate transportation options to reach stadia, rights to in-venue security and immediate public access to the referee's match report.

In some countries such as the UK and Australia, independent directors are finding their way on to sports boards based on legal requirements. Their role is to represent and advocate for the public interest. Board representation adds diversity to discussions, with everyone in attendance aware of the positionality and obligations of the board member. The public voice must now be heard before decisions are made.

Errant SGBs must be on high alert—here come passionate fans with a voice, equipped with ways to use it.

A seat at the table

The role of the sports fan has changed considerably. Once a mute spectator, today's fans have as much, if not more, say in the future of sport as competing athletes do. Is this where the fan's journey ends? Maybe not.

One day, fans could be managing and governing teams. There have already been initiatives by fans and fan groups to take legal ownership positions in football and rugby clubs in order to protect club heritage and traditions and to ensure that the club is run sustainably. Ownership and control take fan involvement to a whole new level.

The blockchain already enables Non-fungible Tokens (NFTs) that can act as fan tokens. The owners of these tokens get to vote on selected matters relating to the team. So far, these have been decisions such as which music will be played in the stadium when the team is announced, or the colour or design of the team jersey and such like. It takes little technological effort for these to expand to include fan-driven team selection or the ability to make in-match strategic choices on behalf of the team.

One day, in the not-too-distant future, we may see the creation of decentralized autonomous organizations (known as DAOs) that could administer teams and govern sport. Those bums on seats won't just be at the stadium, they'll also be in the boardroom.

Formula E eventually disbanded its 'Fanboost' feature at the end of the 2021–22 season. Nonetheless, it remains a pioneering example of fan engagement and is a sign of things to come. When (and it is probably no longer an 'if') fans start influencing their teams' field-of-play decisions, their remarkable evolution from incidental spectator to core participant will be complete.

Having the citizenry doling out the bread and organizing the circuses would be quite a reversal of ancient Roman fortunes. Content may be still king, but it is the fans who are jumping into the Colosseum of sport, girding for battle.

Chapter 15

On Rights

Should Anwar Ali be allowed to play football?

Hailing from a small village in Punjab, Anwar Ali was touted as the next big thing in Indian football. He was the prominent centre-back for the Indian team during the FIFA U-17 Men's World Cup in 2017, and was lapped up by Mumbai City FC soon after the tournament.

And then his world came crashing down. A routine medical test revealed hypertrophic cardiomyopathy, a rare heart condition. It did not impact Ali's on-field performance, but it increased the risk of him suffering a fatal stroke while playing.

The football system reacted swiftly to Ali's condition. His club determined that he should not continue to play and offered him a non-playing managerial position. Unsatisfied, Ali left Mumbai and signed up with the I-League 2nd division team Mohammedan Sporting. But this was only the beginning of his ordeal—the All India Football Federation (AIFF), the national sports federation (NSF) for football, also decided that he was not fit to play, citing a danger to his health.

Ali wouldn't give up. He petitioned the Delhi High Court to direct the AIFF to let him play. He argued that the ban violated his fundamental right to earn his livelihood and practise his profession.

Does Ali have the right to play? Does his condition justify restricting him from playing professional sport? Whose interests is the AIFF protecting by keeping him off the pitch?

Right flank

Fundamental human rights are standards of morally acceptable human behaviour that are embedded in our state of existence. We have rights because we exist. Human rights need not be granted by the state or any other body. Legal instruments only declare and recognize the existence of these human rights.

However, just because rights are inalienable does not mean that they are unlimited. They may be subject to reasonable and limited restrictions that are necessary in service of legitimate public objectives, or to permit the enjoyment of rights by others.

A right is meaningful when it is accompanied by a corresponding duty placed on another person. Together, rights and duties are our collective assertion of restraints on ourselves, each other and society. They require us to recognize the autonomy, liberty and freedom of others and our responsibilities to each other, especially when we are in positions of authority.

Duties can be positive (to ensure that rights are secured) or negative (to ensure that rights are not infringed). Who bears these duties? Generally, states have taken up the obligations and duties under international law to respect, protect and fulfil human rights. Increasingly, these obligations have been extended to transnational corporations and businesses through responsibility frameworks and guiding principles.

Do athletes enjoy fundamental human rights? Do national and international SGBs have to respect, protect and fulfil the rights of athletes? Does sport's special nature and role justify unique restrictions on rights?

Playing positions

A club might see athletes as financial assets. A coach will see them as talent assets. A fan will see them as performers, celebrities and perhaps even as role models. Sponsors see athletes as branding opportunities. Governments see them as professionals liable to be taxed. A judge might recognize that they are citizens entitled to enjoy constitutional rights like everyone else. A labour rights advocate will identify athletes as workers who ought to enjoy all the protections that follow. The rest of us might simply see athletes as fellow human beings.

These labels are useful and useless at the same time. All of them describe athletes, but none of these descriptions is either comprehensive or necessarily more useful than the other. Athletes can be humans, women, workers, users, consumers and minors, all at the same time. Yet, SGBs seem to want to recognize none of these, preferring to characterize them simply as 'athletes'—nothing more, nothing less. They then transact with them as a separate genus of people who must compete at their events on the terms of the competition rules presented to them.

Governing bodies have resisted adopting human rights standards in relation to athletes. They would like to retain the primacy of their decision-making powers. Ceding discretion to someone else would be a compromise. This approach stands on two limbs. The first is the assertion that SGBs are autonomous and not subject to international and domestic laws, as we have seen earlier. The other is that sport's nature and purpose mean that rights can be negated on the grounds of this higher purpose.

For instance, in a 2020 case,[1] the Court of Arbitration for Sport (CAS) dismissed a gender discrimination claim brought by a few athletes against the International Olympic Committee (IOC). It refused to hear the case on merits because the athletes apparently only had a 'sporting interest' in participating at the Olympic Games and no enforceable right.

More broadly, the cultural relativism of rights and restrictions has been used to suggest that the universal application of common human rights standards is impossible. The argument goes that each country has its own balance of rights, duties and obligations and it is not sport's job to upend these in its quest for uniformity.

Due to concerted pressure, some global SGBs such as the IOC, FIFA, Commonwealth Sport (formerly, the Commonwealth Games Federation) and Union of European Football Associations (UEFA) have adopted human rights policies and commitments, partially acknowledging their responsibilities in the international human rights framework. The IOC adopted the Athletes' Rights and Responsibilities Declaration, which has itself been criticized for not reflecting international standards or providing any remedies. Most other SGBs are even further behind, ignoring demands to adopt and implement meaningful rights frameworks. Calls have been made for the inclusion of an 'Eighth Fundamental Principle of Olympism' that would commit the Olympic Movement to respect and protect human rights.

When athletes enter the sports pyramid, they devote themselves to the cause of sport. Do we need to deny them their various human rights in the interest of sport achieving its purpose? For that matter, can sport achieve its social goals without a fundamental rights framework in place for its athletes?

There are four lenses through which the status, challenges and prospects of athlete rights can be seen—opportunity, safety, dignity and self-governance.

Opportunity

Organized sport seeks outcome differentiation through competition. It rewards the most skilled and best-performing competitors and, so, the most 'meritorious'. Contenders rise from the local to the national to the international events, until a champion is crowned and sits atop the sports pyramid.

Yet, are we finding the most skilled of the species? Are Usain Bolt and Florence Griffith-Joyner really the fastest man and woman to have lived? Has there never been a person who could jump further than Mike Powell?

Only a subset of humans has access to the knowledge and resources necessary to enter and progress through the organized sports pyramid. At the end of a championship, SGBs never stop and ask how many genuine contenders there were. As the concepts of merit and privilege are examined more closely across spheres, sport too must receive this scrutiny.

How should organized sport respond to the uneven social matrix it operates within? The South African experiment with sports transformation provides insight. Much like the rest of its society, South African sport was institutionally segregated during the apartheid era. With their sports teams comprised solely of members of the minority white settler community, South Africa faced a boycott from international sports.

Though the end of apartheid in the early 1990s brought the nation back to international sports, there were lasting scars from the long saga of segregation and discrimination. Non-white South Africans lacked equitable access to sporting infrastructure, resources, coaching, equipment and role models. This made it unlikely—if not impossible—for them to compete and rise through the ranks in sports teams.

With national SGBs not taking active steps to fix this, the South African government sprang into action. In 2012, the Transformation Charter for South African Sport was released, containing guidelines to address racial inequalities in sport. The aim of transformation was to ensure that teams represented the demographics of the country. It has taken various forms, ranging from investments in community sports development to quotas in domestic and national teams.

Transformation has radically changed the make-up of South African sports teams. Nowhere is this more evident than in the national rugby team. Ahead of hosting the Rugby World Cup in South Africa in 1995, President Nelson Mandela orchestrated a show of unity, calling all South Africans to back the white-dominated Springboks. The team—with just one black player in the squad—went on to win the World Cup, beating arch-rivals New Zealand's All Blacks in a close final in Johannesburg. Fast forward twenty-five years and Siya Kolisi captained the Springboks to another famous World Cup final win over pre-match favourites England in Yokohama, Japan. That 2019 squad included six black players, including Kolisi. The Springboks would go on to defend their crown four years later in a close final against the All Blacks in Paris, France, at the 2023 Rugby World Cup.

While successful in part, the transformation programme has also been controversial. Privilege does not lend itself to easy dismantling. Transformation became the punching bag when the national rugby or cricket team lost key matches, or when a promising (white) cricketer like Kyle Abbott migrated to play in the UK instead of committing to a future in South Africa.

The contestation is stark in cricket, a sport in which allegations of institutional racism have been raised vociferously. These voices compelled Cricket South Africa to appoint the Social Justice and Nation Building (SJN) ombudsman to investigate the allegations. The SJN ombudsman mechanism was aimed at truth, reconciliation and healing of cricket in South Africa. It is perhaps the first instance of such a process targeting restorative justice in sport. The focus is on victims, their stories, and reparations and remedies for those who have been adversely impacted. Has the SJN ombudsman been successful? It is early days yet, and the jury is still out. It could be a bellwether for other similar reckonings—for instance, how Indian sport responds to the historical inequalities engendered by caste identities, and the fair treatment of Aboriginal populations in the sports systems of Australia and New Zealand.

Today, most countries give SGBs a free pass to hold and organize their events by their own rules. They are not asked questions about who gets to their events, who doesn't and what can be done about it. At the end of the event, all we have is a result sheet. No data is collected or published on the contestants' backgrounds, their journeys, their social identity and the extent to which the talent pool is representative of different constituencies.

On the other hand, many people will go out of their way to highlight and glorify the anecdotal 'against the odds' stories of athletes who make it to the top having fought social and economic odds to compete, improve and excel. Mary Kom grew up in a mud house, skipped meals and became a World Champion in boxing. Rani Rampal, a cart-puller's daughter, captained the Indian women's hockey team at the Tokyo 2020 Olympic Games.

These 'feel good' stories make for catchy headlines but suffer from survivorship bias. They hide the existence of many other talented athletes who did not have the means or support to overcome the odds. Sporting competition is a test of athletic and strategic skills and aptitudes. Success at sport can also be an outcome of pre-existing privilege, or the ability or good fortune to find the means necessary to access it.

It is a long walk to transformation. Sport can, metaphorically, level the playing field, equalize starting lines, erase prejudices, and break barriers—all of this only if we want it to and allow it to. This requires thinking about a new balance where SGBs focus equally on organizing their events and competitions and on removing barriers to participation, providing funding and support for people from different places and backgrounds to start, progress within and succeed at sport.

Until this bargain is struck, large swathes of the population will remain excluded from contending. Winners will usually be from a pool that is itself a product of pre-existing structural and societal inequalities. Opportunity, like achievement, must be an end in itself.

Safety

All success comes at a cost—physical, financial, mental, social and more. This includes the opportunity cost of other things that could have been done instead with these resources and time. Elite sporting achievement requires athletes to push their limits. This has personal and systemic costs. Do the ends justify the means? Are there costs that athletes should not be expected to bear in their pursuit of excellence?

SGBs are being asked difficult questions on athlete welfare, safety and care. Sexual harassment, bullying, overtraining, psychological abuse by coaches, mental health trauma, risky manoeuvres, unsatisfactory equipment and inadequate injury management have always been part of the subculture of sport. Increasingly, athletes are speaking out about these, demanding safety and expecting responsibility, and they are receiving public support.

A right to 'safe sport' involves the creation and maintenance of a protective and healthy environment for athletes to train, compete and perform in. This may include the management of training loads to avoid injury, protection from abusive training methods, rule reviews to eliminate undue risks, and protection from psychological, physical and sexual harassment. The need for these mechanisms increases manifold when sport involves children and others vulnerable to abuse. A lack of safety not only imposes costs on athletes but keeps prospective participants away from sport.

Athlete welfare refers to athlete well-being and support, on and off the field. Many aspects feed into this, including measures to protect physical, mental and financial health, education and life skills, training for post-retirement opportunities, etc. This requires a rights-based approach where athletes are treated with respect and protected from injury and violence by imposing a duty of care on those in charge of their environments.

Pressure from the government, law, athletes and the public is pushing sports organizations at all levels to accept their duty of care to participants. They are being called upon to reduce the negative impact of sports participation. There is a greater recognition that harassment and abuse can be of different sorts, including psychological, physical and sexual. It can be episodic or systematic.

This means that an athlete welfare and safeguarding programme requires institutional checks and balances such as the appointment of a welfare officer, the formulation of policies, codes of conduct and protocols, regular monitoring and evaluation, and dispute resolution and escalation mechanisms. These measures also recognize the broader role of sport in human development beyond the 'win at all costs' hyper-competitive result-oriented environments that may have historically prevailed. In some countries, an organization's failure to put in place and implement adequate safety measures as part of its duty of care can lead to liability under principles of negligence and vicarious liability.

New challenges continue to abound, with athletes being required to play in unsafe and polluted environments and under severe weather conditions like heat. In 2017, India hosted Sri Lanka in a cricket Test match in Delhi with pollution at twelve times over the World Health Organization-prescribed safe limit. During the COVID-19 pandemic, international sport continued and players had to perform while living for extended periods in restrictive 'bubbles'. Athletes can find it difficult to speak out against their SGBs and clubs. There are inherent power disparities and complex interlinkages, including necessary trade-offs between their livelihoods and their well-being.

The involvement of children—a common phenomenon in sport—increases the responsibility for participant safety. Minors have limited ability to perceive, assess and respond to danger, risk and potential harm and fewer tools to protect themselves; they also lack legal agency to assume risks and consent to harm. As a result, sports training and competition involving minors requires the implementation of appropriate and specific child protection policies, protocols and actions to supplement and enhance the basic safeguarding policy.

For instance, it is essential for young cricketers to wear helmets at all times when batting, and young footballers are prohibited from heading the football to avoid injuries while their skull is still developing. Coaching academies prohibit interaction between an adult and a minor behind closed doors or without a second adult of the child's gender being present. All physical contact and touch in the course of coaching, physiotherapy, etc. is focused on essential touch and is to be undertaken in a transparent and monitorable manner. Official transportation arrangements may also factor in similar protections, such as requiring a guardian to travel with the team. Coaching feedback is to be given in a manner that is appropriate to the age and development of the child and should not use undue negativity as a source of motivation to succeed. These require a fine balance and may involve additional costs.

Sexual harassment is a species of abuse and harassment that athletes might encounter. This refers to any type of unwelcome behaviour that has a sexual element. Sexual harassment can not only bring concerns relating to personal safety but could also undermine performance, self-esteem and personal goals.

Athletes can be particularly vulnerable to harassment because the training and competition environment is characterized by close physical and emotional relationships. This gives perpetrators an opportunity for plausible deniability, and victims find it challenging to point out whether and when the line was crossed. There are also complex power dynamics between trainees and coaches, minors and adults. The matter has become the subject of workplace-related laws and laws in respect of minors that supplement existing criminal laws, including The Sexual Harassment of Women at Workplace (Prevention, Prohibition and Redressal) Act, 2013 and the Protection of Children from

Sexual Offences Act, 2012. While females might face these issues more often, both perpetrators and victims can come from any gender.

Over the years, the limitations of the law have been evident when attempting to apply it in informal or unorganized sectors such as sport. Abuse in sport is more prevalent than is reported. In India, most sports organizations are rarely alive to the need for clearly defined and carefully enforced sexual harassment policies despite this being a requirement of the Sports Code. Complaints are sat upon, and perpetrators get away with mere raps on the knuckles, leaving them free to unleash themselves on the next unsuspecting victim. In 2023, the matters relating to the Wrestling Federation of India—with prominent Olympian wrestlers taking to the streets to protest sexual abuse—laid bare these issues and brought them into the national limelight and consciousness.

Indian sport is not alone here. Nothing exemplifies the need for safe sport better than the USA Gymnastics sex abuse scandal. For over two decades, more than 500 gymnasts—mostly adolescent children—were sexually assaulted by gym owners, coaches and staff working for USA Gymnastics. The national team doctor was specifically identified as the abuser by more than 250 women.

Investigations revealed a lax system of oversight and systemic failures. USA Gymnastics had routinely dismissed sexual abuse allegations against coaches and failed to alert authorities. Several gymnasts have gone on record to state how the culture of abuse of USA Gymnastics impacted their physical as well as psychological health.

FIFA, too, has been uncovering sexual abuse in multiple places within the football world and has been trying to take an institutional approach to safeguarding and investigating misdeeds by its members, constituents and other participants.

The social context of sport involves adults who are looked up to as purveyors of knowledge, while trainees are encouraged to follow instructions and not challenge authority. The power dynamics and risks of retaliation mean that few offences are prosecuted or even reported. The informal nature of many training spaces and the lack of comprehensive information frameworks for background checks and police verification are additional challenges. This leaves many sports environments unsafe in ways they should never be. The costs of this reality are felt by many more people than the direct victims, creating a chilling effect on participation.

In generations past, the mental health of athletes was not talked about openly. It was stigmatized as an unwise display of weakness and vulnerability. This has changed in recent years, with many prominent athletes leading the way in talking openly about their mental health journeys. They have vocalized the unbearable mental and psychological toll that sporting life takes on them. Swimmer Michael Phelps, the most successful Olympian ever, has spoken out about his challenges with anxiety and depression. Gymnast Simone Biles, another legendary Olympian, withdrew from the Tokyo 2020 Olympics gymnastics team final due to concerns for her mental health. Former World No. 1 tennis player Naomi Osaka withdrew midway through the 2021 French Open after she was fined for not attending a post-match press conference on grounds of social anxiety. Indian cricketer Virat Kohli has been open about his challenges with mental health during periods when he had dips in form and performance. English cricketer Ben Stokes took a break from the sport, revealing that he was on anxiety medication to deal with panic attacks. These are no longer isolated cases, and they are coming from the top of sport. They signal that athletes—and all the rest of us—are not alone in dealing with mental health challenges.

SGBs are struggling to respond to these issues. Most of them try to put a lid on systemic crises, respond to authentic athlete concerns individually and keep the wheels of sports commerce turning. A combination of proactive, preventive and responsive measures is essential to create safe and wholesome environments for training and play. Violations and systemic weaknesses must be identified early, remedied quickly and affected persons must be treated with respect and care.

Safe sport and athlete welfare are where athlete rights meet the duty of care of SGBs. A lack of safety, undue risk and abuse should not be essential costs of sports participation and success. After all, sport is tasked with enhancing human development. The ends are important to sport, and so should be the means.

Dignity

Athletes compete voluntarily in sport. They often spend a significant part of their youth in training and competition. They may have fun and gain in multiple other ways. However, with the professionalization and competitiveness of sport, it is difficult to succeed unless you go 'all in'. Despite the sports industry maturing, athletes do not always enjoy the rights that other 'workers' would in exchange for their effort and labour. While they represent a particular country or a sport association, they most often do so as freelancers, neither enjoying current security nor future guarantees.

SGBs claim to share a regulatory rather than employment relationship with athletes. The special nature of sports is often used to justify commercial restrictions on athletes. A prominent example is Rule 40 of the Olympic Charter, under which athletes are restricted from monetizing their persona—their name, image or sports performances—before, during and around the period of the Olympic Games. In other words, athletes are constrained from benefiting financially from probably the biggest moment of their lives.

The IOC argues that it needs to impose this restriction to prevent ambush marketing and, thereby, ensure that it collectivizes the income from the Olympic Games and distributes it fairly to athletes in need under the principles of solidarity. It is noteworthy that athletes receive no prize money, appearance fees or compensation from the IOC for winning or participating in the Olympic Games—this, despite the Olympic Games being a highly commercialized environment with event sponsorships and broadcasting rights being sold for billions of dollars in the aggregate. In how many other professions would this be seen as a fair bargain for workers?

The power imbalance between SGBs and athletes leads to a collective action problem. Any attempt by an individual athlete to negotiate favourable participation terms or speak up on issues that concern them is laced with professional risk. The risk-reward equation rarely stacks up. Speak up and you risk isolation and exclusion. Take the case of quarterback Colin Kaepernick, who has not been selected by any NFL team after the 2016 season (when he knelt during the US national anthem to protest police brutality and racial inequality).

Given SGBs' monopoly and monopsony status, group action can act as an important counterweight. Player associations and unions try to establish common minimum standards applicable to all athletes, using the power of the collective as well as the participation of iconic and legendary athletes as part of their ranks.

These associations have been around since at least 1885, when the National Brotherhood of Professional Baseball Players was formed in the United States (notably, only for white baseball players). Athletes from all the significant professional sports leagues in North America have players' unions. The NFL, MLB, NBA and NHL have all had either player strikes or management lockouts or both in their storied histories. The relevant players' unions have always been there, negotiating on the other side of the table from the league.

India, especially Indian cricket, saw many failed attempts at establishing player associations until the Supreme Court mandated that the Board of Control for Cricket in India (BCCI) recognize one as per the Lodha Committee's recommendations. This enabled the creation of the Indian Cricketers' Association (ICA) in 2019, an association of ex-cricketers explicitly required not to act as a union but meant to advocate the interests of former and current players nonetheless. There is also the Football Players Association of India, which was formed in 2006.

The challenge many player associations face is balancing group interests with the divergent interests of the most elite athletes in their membership. Players each have individual needs, and not all may feel solidarity with their compatriots. Seniors like Rohit Sharma and Jasprit Bumrah may be more concerned about workload management and don't have to think about negotiating compensation, while younger players like Shubman Gill and Mohammed Siraj might want to play as much as possible and care about the category of their BCCI retainer contract. This type of divergence can pose a challenge for the leadership of the association and might limit the issues it explores, forcing it to focus its attention on common minimum standards and on core issues with adequate scope for individual variation.

Player associations can provide member support, including legal advice and representation, post-career training and counselling, group insurance, financial advice, injury and medical support, support in disciplinary hearings and grievance redressal, rehabilitation, sharing of financial and legal information with members and licensing of player agents.

One of their primary functions is to liaise and negotiate with players' employers, be they SGBs, clubs or other teams. In North American player unions, this generally culminates in the signing of a collective bargaining agreement (CBA) of minimum standards that emerge after detailed negotiations. Player unions can threaten and call strikes at various times as part of their negotiating strategy. Once collective bargaining commences, the parties must negotiate in good faith. Key terms that such an agreement might conclude are revenue sharing, salary caps, insurance policies, safety protocols, image rights, pension schemes and the like.

In the take-it-or-leave-it world of sport, player associations enable all athletes to enjoy basic standards that they might not have been able to negotiate on their own. The diversity of interests within the associations and unions is a source of power—if you can keep the flock together. It is also a source of challenge, given that not every member's interests will align.

Despite the important role they can—and should—play, athlete collectives remain on the fringes of governance in jurisdictions like India, and are intentionally denied a place at the table by incumbent administrators when key decisions are made. The attitude towards player associations and unions is emblematic of the view that athletes are not entitled to enjoy rights traditionally associated with employment and the delivery of labour. How much longer will SGBs be able to keep things this way?

Self-governance

Swaraj—self-governance or self-rule—is one of our fundamental aspirations as humans. Young people are quite capable of designing and managing their own sports events and competitions. Every neighbourhood playground shows that this is something they are adept at. Yet, right from grassroots sports organizations, adults step in to bring order and impose rules on participants.

Most of these self-appointed governors are non-participants: club secretaries, presidents, and the like. The chasm between participants and governors feeds upwards into every level of the sports pyramid. Non-participants represent the members of the superior organization and form the electoral college and potential leadership. Some of these governors might be former athletes, others might be sports parents or sports professionals. The majority will be none of the above.

The Basic Universal Principles of Good Governance of the Olympic and Sports Movement provide for the right of athletes to participate and involve themselves in the movement and in the SGBs. This is to enable their voice to be heard. As a consequence, athletes' commissions and athletes' committees have been created and recognized within international and national SGBs that are part of the Olympic movement. All participating athletes can stand for management posts and vote in elections to these bodies, which are meant to advocate for athletes' interests within the organization and the wider sporting ecosystem.

In cricket administration, the Lodha Committee identified the alienation of Indian cricketers from sports governance as a matter of concern. The Supreme Court endorsed the Lodha Committee's suggestion of establishing the ICA. It provided the members of the ICA the right to send their representatives to the BCCI's Apex Council (one male and one female representative), the BCCI's IPL Governing Council (one representative), and the Apex Councils/Executive Committees (one male and one female representative each) of every state cricket association. Although it is neither a typical player union nor an athletes' commission, the ICA has brought at least seventy-five former cricketers into the governance of the sport.

In respect of the national sports federations (NSFs), the Sports Code provides that, in order to be recognized as an NSF and eligible for assistance, the sports organization must include sportspersons (say 25 per cent) as members in the organization with voting rights and also in the executive committee structure.

For the longest time, this standard was not followed by NSFs, and such a provision was not enforced on them. As of 2021, the Olympic Charter has introduced a specific provision for the election of athlete representatives as members of NOCs and their boards. This involves the creation of federation-recognized athlete membership bodies that include both active and recently retired athletes with the right to vote their representatives into membership and governance posts. It sets a minimum requirement of two athletes as members and one as an executive committee member of the NOC, i.e., the Indian Olympic Association (IOA) in India, but has no upper limit for either.

In 2022, after a Supreme Court- and IOC-mandated reform process, the IOA adopted a new constitution that not only included two representatives (one male and one female) of the IOA Athletes Commission in the IOA membership structure (and electoral college) but also in the IOA Executive Council.[2]

It also went a step further and introduced IOA membership for eight 'Sportspersons of Outstanding Merit' (four male and four female), of which two would join the IOA Executive Council.[3] Earlier in 2022, on FIFA's demand, the AIFF had to amend its constitution to moderate and build protocols for the election of athletes to its membership and governance structures. The implementation of such standards across NSFs has been patchy, at best, but more of them can be expected to follow the IOA's lead, whether voluntarily or by mandate.

Where athletes' committees and commissions have been established, the entrenched leaders of SGBs have tried to limit their participation in governance to specific issues such as talent development, training and competition schedules, selection criteria, athlete grievance redressal and athlete support and welfare.

Is it appropriate to limit their roles to such matters? After all, there is no aspect of an SGB's decision-making that does not affect athletes. Any attempt to portray otherwise is simply a means to alienate participants from key aspects of governance oversight and defeats the very purpose of athlete representation in governance.

The difference between 'being heard' and 'having a vote' must not be missed. Many athletes' commissions struggle to change the course of decisions or have their perspectives count. Paradoxically, unless they are able to find independence and a voice, these commissions can also end up acting as gatekeepers. Their existence can be used as a fig leaf for the organization to demonstrate publicly that athletes and their interests are being heard. If they have derived power from proximity to power or otherwise remain unquestioning of authority, commissions can block rather than facilitate genuine athlete interests from counting.

The debate on whether athletes should be the ones governing sport has been a long and controversial one. On the one side, the levels of corruption, misrule and poor results have led to repeated public demands that only athletes must helm SGBs. In 2022, the Madras High Court went to the extent of ordering (and reaffirmed on appeal) that only sportspersons—and not politicians and others—should be office-bearers of sports associations and federations in the state of Tamil Nadu.[4]

As a counter to this approach, the argument is made that athletes who have been given a chance to lead have not shown any better results. It is suggested that athletes as a category are unqualified and unsuited to administer, bringing all the baggage of their playing days to their decisions.

The issue is more nuanced than this binary might reveal. As described earlier, the disconnect with self-governance happens at the base of the pyramid and cannot be reconnected at the top with the snap of a finger. Athletes are often called upon to lead when they mature and as they finish their playing careers. By this time, their alienation from administration throughout their careers means they have little relevant experience. P.T. Usha is expected to head the Indian Olympic Association—having been elected unopposed as its president—with the benefit of little, if any, prior governance experience. Any misstep by her will be used to argue that athletes do not make good administrators.

As we have seen, most attempts at athlete representation have targeted the top of the pyramid, but little is done to build the governance capabilities and experience of athletes. Making space for athletes to grow their professional and administrative capabilities within community and youth organizations during their careers is an idea that needs serious thought.

Given a chance, athletes are well-placed to become multiskilled professionals with experience, opinions and views, at least as capable of governing sport as anyone else.

Shots on target

Sports governance has had an uneasy relationship with athlete rights. Athletes have been given limited social licence to advocate for themselves or to object to wrongdoings. The underlying message to them is that they must 'stay in their lanes'. More and more state parties, sponsors, parents and athletes themselves are pushing back at this formulation, saying 'not in our game' and 'not in our name'.

In theory, global sport can be operated fairly and reasonably without a rights framework in place. However, when such a framework is missing, any systemic check on abuse of discretion and power will have limited success. After all, athletes playing within the sports pyramid also have social roles outside of it. While they aim to push the boundaries of human achievement, they play for themselves and they also represent the rest of us.

Will we treat these creators of our social and cultural capital as purely instrumental beings? Shouldn't we recognize that they are also humans, citizens, workers and much more? For state parties, SGBs and each one of us participating directly or indirectly in the world of sport, such recognition is a moral obligation. It should also be the basis of legal obligations.

What happened to Anwar Ali, the promising footballer who faced professional heartbreak? The AIFF had declared him ineligible to play without so much as a hearing, official communication or reasoned decision. The safe sport policy it used to restrict him was ostensibly oriented towards protecting him. It was also about making sure an untoward incident didn't occur on the AIFF's watch and have a negative effect on the organization, the sport, other players and viewers.

In 2020, Ali took his case against the AIFF to the courts. In its decision in *Anwar Ali v. All India Football Federation*,[5] the Delhi High Court expressed its sympathy for his situation and directed that Ali's medical evidence be heard by the AIFF medical committee. Once this was done, his ban was lifted. He was allowed to play at his own risk so long as there was emergency medical help available at the venue.

Ali not only resumed playing in the top-flight Indian Super League but was also selected for the Indian senior national men's football team. In June 2022, Ali sent a sharp left-footed kick into the roof of the Hong Kong net, scoring his maiden international goal for the Blue Tigers. If he hadn't battled the system, Ali might never again have taken the pitch, let alone scored for India.

Overlaying a fundamental rights framework on the disorganized yet hyper-commercialized, hyper-networked and hyper-competitive ecosystem of sport can seem like a complicated project. However, as Anwar Ali's case shows, with intent, commitment and effort, athletes' rights to livelihood can be recognized while also satisfying governors' duty of care to players, audiences and the public.

This does not need grand gestures. Little steps add up, and change happens.

The rights of athletes must not be seen as speed breakers to sporting progress and success. They can set important benchmarks on how far we go, how hard we push, the wholesomeness with which our athletes live their lives and the sustainability of the benefits we all derive from sport.

Chapter 16

On Individuality

Should the Olympic broadcast display Deepika Kumari's heart rate?

What's one of the first things every freshly minted Olympic champion does immediately after winning their event? You probably guessed wrong. Even before getting on the podium to collect their gold medal, they have to do this: pee into a cup.

In the immediate aftermath of their event, the athlete is relieved, emotionally spent after putting everything on the line, exhilarated and exhausted, usually dehydrated—and that is when they are whisked off to a secluded space and asked to provide a urine sample. Many athletes have spoken of the struggle to provide enough quantity of sample. Whoever said 'my cup runneth over' was probably not a professional athlete, at least not in the era of anti-doping tests.

The World Anti-Doping Agency (WADA) is responsible for monitoring the use of prohibited substances and methods in international sport, and it coordinates regular testing to ensure clean sports. To this end, athletes are required to provide urine samples and, more recently, blood samples. These samples are not only tested in the days that follow the event but will also be stored for many years for future analysis, should new testing methods and capabilities be developed.

The provision of samples is mandatory for all athletes wishing to compete. Athletes may not opt out of this testing programme—any attempt to do so would itself result in an anti-doping violation. At the time of giving their sample, athletes must sign a detailed 'consent' form under which they submit to the authority of WADA and its practices, and agree to the testing of their samples.

The collection and use of athlete samples produces data that is essential to conduct anti-doping testing as per the norms that exist today. Fair play and the integrity of sport depend on such rigorous testing, which ensures the athlete does not have an unfair advantage over their peers. There is no argument over whether WADA and every other sport governing body (SGB) has a legitimate interest in collecting and processing these samples. But anti-doping testing is just one purpose for which athlete data is collected today—and others can get more controversial.

During the Tokyo 2020 Olympic Games, the archery event integrated live heart rate data of athletes into television broadcasts. You could see the highs and lows as athletes won, lost, struggled, held their nerve and overcame. This was an unprecedented public display of the inner life of an athlete.

Deepika Kumari—ranked first in the world and India's medal hope—maintained a steady heart rate of 75 beats per minute during her first-round win against a Bhutanese opponent. Her next match against an American opponent was closely contested. Kumari's heart rate was 100 beats per minute during the first set and, as the match got close, went up to 175 beats per minute in the fifth set. Kumari went on to win that match and progress, but she was eliminated in the quarter-finals, losing 0-6 to her Korean opponent in just six minutes.

Returning empty-handed from a third successive Olympics, Kumari was immeasurably heartbroken, describing the elevated pressure she felt during the event. It was exactly this experience that World Archery was trying to convey through its display of athlete heart rate data. Its officials described the live heart rate broadcast as an attempt to give the television spectator the feeling of stress, which was not only felt by the athlete but was also palpable to those watching the event at the venue.

Archery was the first sport to use heart rate data in this way at the Olympics. It is unlikely to be the last. World Archery's use of athletes' biometric data to design a compelling broadcast is, however, not essential to sport in the manner WADA's sample collection is, and this raises key questions: Is such use necessary, fair and legitimate? Does it matter how the data was collected and used? Does the athlete get a say?

All of us are subjects of data collection, and it is easy to underappreciate how practices around data processing impact every aspect of our lives. The world of sport can show us what is at stake.

More than a statistic

There is a record of every run scored and every wicket taken in Test Cricket since the first match in 1877. Similarly, the results of every event ever held in the modern Olympics have been recorded. Statistical archives across most sports disciplines date back more than a century. Such collection and use of data has always been part of sport. These can show trends and help us compare performances across generations.

As the understanding of data became more statistical in nature, result analysis was used to improve performance. Training methods and game strategy improved on the back of these insights. Roger Bannister ran the first-ever mile in under four minutes at Oxford in 1954 after considerable scientific experimentation—after all, he was a medical student en route to becoming an eminent neurologist. He also used two pacemakers named Chris Chataway and Chris Brasher.

Much of the performance data that was being compiled and analysed was 'observable'. It could be collected by anyone who had the ability to watch the athlete in action, whether in private settings or public competitions. In this initial iteration, observable data was only the humanly visible and calculable manifestation of the performance of an athlete.

Scientific innovation and the medicalization of sport brought new methods and technologies to collect more data, analyse it more deeply and provide more insights—some that the athlete themselves or an expert observer might have otherwise remained unaware of. The pervasiveness of this collection and the varied uses of data have brought new elements to competition, training and fan engagement.

The next major advancement came with modern technologies like wearable trackers and scientific advances like genetic testing. These have changed the game. Athletes can be monitored and measured in granular detail. With this advancement, it is not merely the external manifestation of performance that can be collected, evaluated and analysed deeply; internal physiological data also becomes fair game.

The collection of 'invasive' data steadily became par for the course within organized sport. Football players wear vests with fibres that track their every move in training and match play. Blood and urine testing became a baseline standard for assessments. Again, this iteration of invasive data could only be collected with the consent of the athlete—a jab, a sample or agreement to wear a device was needed.

With the decoding of genetic sequences and the identification and linkage of specific gene markers with specific physical attributes, blood and saliva samples can also be employed to determine the individual's predisposition to certain illnesses and the propensity to bear certain physical and psychological characteristics. Genetic material, however, is innately personal and representative of the body composition of the host. Gene testing has already been used in countries like China for the purpose of early talent identification and to prioritize government funding by directing it to high-potential athletes.

Analytics has complemented the changes in how and what data is collected. Supercomputers and artificial intelligence are harnessed to convert the vast data sets that sports produce into actionable insights. This has blurred the lines between what is observable and what is invasive.

Beat it

In its decade-long quest to live broadcast the heart rate of its competitors, World Archery first experimented with wearables placed on the archer's leg. It was decided that this was inappropriate for elite athletes in competition, and the method was rejected. Instead, at the Tokyo 2020 Olympic Games, World Archery and its partners used high-frame-rate cameras that can detect changes in the skin colour of the athlete, the shape and colour of their face and the position of their pupils to determine their heart rate.

Thanks to a combination of artificial intelligence, behavioural data and image technology, what was previously in the category of invasive data became observable. No device to attach, no physical contact—and therefore, presumably, the athlete's consent was not required to determine their heart rate.

The collection and processing of athlete data by SGBs, teams and other organizations has been normalized. The focus has been on what data can be collected and how it can be used. The perceived benefits range from performance enhancement, team selection, strategizing and matchups to–like in the case of archery–fan engagement and marketing.

Data's expanded reach has happened in a creeping way, with hardly a pause to weigh the costs, benefits, ethics and long-term consequences. In each intended use case in sport, we must start by asking whether the data should be collected at all, how it should be used, and what role the athlete's consent must play in the process.

To World Archery's credit, it did put in guard rails at the Tokyo Games. Although the technology didn't require it, each archer's consent was sought to display heart rate data on the broadcast and they were given an opportunity to opt out. More than 90 per cent of the 128 archers in the competition consented. Reportedly, none of the raw data was retained by World Archery, the broadcaster or the data processor. Importantly, the data was only visible to television viewers and was not shared with the competitors or locally at the venue. This meant that it did not impact match play.

Data mine

The ability to make choices for oneself lies at the heart of human personality. This is the idea of individual autonomy. An autonomous person is able to develop their own thoughts, beliefs, ideologies and preferences. When the development of personality is free from external interference, the individual is best able to explore their uniqueness and exercise their right to be different, if they so wish. Self-determination promotes human dignity. In *Naz Foundation v. Government of NCT of Delhi*,[1] the Delhi High Court used a Socratic lens of the 'outer' man and the 'inner' man to describe the importance of protecting 'a private space in which man may become and remain himself'.

Information about a person's attributes, private choices, behaviour, preferences, associations, communications and decisions can provide a map of their personality and even predict their future conduct. While an individual is not just the sum total of their data and personal information, these reveal much more than trivia. Data is a vital asset in the hands of those who wish to understand, interact with and control others. This can range from governments to media platforms and marketing agencies. In the case of sport, this includes SGBs, teams and, of course, opponents.

As the Supreme Court remarked in *Justice K.S. Puttaswamy v. Union of India*,[2] while holding the right to privacy as a fundamental right, data privacy 'protects the individual from the searching glare of publicity in matters which are personal to his or her life . . . Privacy constitutes the foundation of all liberty because it is in privacy that the individual can decide how liberty is best exercised. Individual dignity and privacy are inextricably linked in a pattern woven out of a thread of diversity into the fabric of a plural culture'.

It is important to keep in mind that, today, analytics can find and reveal things about a person that they themselves do not wish to share or may not even wish to know. For instance, a 2015 study showed that by tracking just ten Facebook likes, big data analytics will know a person better than a colleague does; with seventy likes, it will know a person better than a friend or roommate does; with 150 likes, better than a family member does and with 300 likes, better than their spouse does. It can profile and predict attributes such as race, religion, sexual orientation and voting behaviour.[3]

These are 'just' social media likes. Imagine what always-on tracking of the physical and mental attributes of athletes, combined with further advances in analytics and artificial intelligence, can throw up. It is bound to find and reveal things that a person might not even know about themselves, and may never wish to know.

For instance, genetic testing combined with performance and behavioural data might soon be able to pinpoint the limits of their potential—a timing or distance that they are unlikely to better, for instance. It would be an ironic fate for our elite athletes—the outliers we celebrate for their individuality and willingness to push known boundaries—if we knew in advance the limits of their abilities. Watching Usain Bolt run is an adventure—we watch to see not whether he will win, but just how much further he can push the envelope of possibility. What if we knew, ahead of time, precisely how fast he was capable of running, and what his limits were? Would we watch with the same wonder and awe?

Despite the potential threats, the collection and use of personal data has achieved centrality in our lives. That 'data is the new oil' is already a tired cliché. Data has been monetized in many different ways, especially in the digital ecosystem, which is designed for wide collection. Social media, search engines, online shopping, email and other digital services are offered for 'free'. The hidden cost is that they collect and use consumer data on an unprecedented scale and manner. This data is then used for product development, sales, marketing, advertising and risk management. The proliferation of digital devices that are almost always connected to the Internet means that every person is constantly generating data points based on their individual behaviour.

The march of technology and, more recently, machine learning has prompted concerns over the unhindered use of data and its impact on society and the rights of individuals. Many governments across the world have responded by enacting or proposing data protection legislation. Among the most prominent interventions is the EU's General Data Protection Regulation 2018 (GDPR). The GDPR imposes obligations on organizations anywhere that target or collect data related to people in the EU.

These laws require the processing of data to be legal, fair, transparent, for a lawful purpose, minimal, accurate and secure. Collection and processing of data must be either with the consent of the subject or on the basis of a legitimate interest (such as fraud prevention, security or threats to public safety). It must be stored for a limited period and the processor must be accountable for compliance.

The data protection law moves beyond the simpler consent-based frameworks that were appropriate when invasions of privacy were necessarily spatial and physical in nature, such as entry into a dwelling unit or providing a DNA sample. The site of the potential invasion is now metaphysical. It is a way of life, a theoretical space and bodily and mental autonomy—and the law tries to keep up with that tectonic shift.

The conflicts over rights and interests in data continue in jurisdictions with established data protection laws. They are equally ripe in a country like India, which lacked a data protection framework until the enactment of the Personal Data Protection Act, 2023.

Testing times

At the beginning of this chapter, we described the in-competition tests an athlete must submit to for anti-doping purposes. Other methods employed go further. For a small set of the elite athletes in each discipline, known as the Registered Testing Pool, WADA has instituted a programme to collect 'whereabouts' data.

Athletes in the Registered Testing Pool are expected to provide their daily expected location during out-of-competition periods. This involves providing self-declared locational data of a place they will be at on every given day during the period, while providing a sixty-minute band for each day of the exact place they can be found for testing without prior notice.

This became a bone of contention for India's top cricketers, who argued that this constituted an invasion of their privacy. They held out for as long as they could, until 2017, when the BCCI had to commit to the ICC that the players would comply with WADA rules without any exception.

With the medicalization of sports preparation and the various efforts used by cheating athletes to not get found out, out-of-competition 'surprise' testing plays an important role in maintaining and protecting the integrity of competition. All 'clean' athletes have an interest in a strong and foolproof anti-doping programme.

However, a legitimate interest is not a blank cheque to collect unlimited athlete data through whatever means possible. Athletes may generally be willing to cede the expectation of locational privacy in the interest of the system's workings. However, there is a point beyond which the liberties of the clean athlete are made hostage to the cheats' agenda. The balance is similar to the one faced with mass surveillance programmes by various governments that justify these measures in the name of anti-terrorism and national security. In the bargain, everyone receives the same degree of liberty as a suspect—which is to say, none at all.

Legitimacy of data processing is not an absolute concept. It depends on the purpose, necessity and extent of data processing, and must balance the legitimate interest and lawful purpose being promoted with the data subject's rights. That said, protecting the best interests of the athlete in data use is no easy task. The interests of athletes and data processors are sometimes aligned and at other times not. As we shall see, these alignments and misalignments are transient, dynamic and context-specific.

Changing positions

Every athlete and sports team wishes to perform at their best and succeed in competition. Various types of data can bring insights to training and preparation, and provide the edge that makes the difference on the field. It can allow for more incisive and personalized training and fitness management. This helps with injury prevention and monitoring, talent identification, strategy planning, stress and fatigue level measurement and in determining the impact of training methodologies.

Athletes eager for a first break might willingly submit themselves to testing and performance trials for the purpose of selection. Data also drives the fan engagement and commercial model of sport, of which athletes are beneficiaries. The archers who consented to the display of their heart rate data on the broadcast did so because they thought it would help the popularity of their sport.

In such cases, where data is being collected by a team or an SGB, the interests of the data subject (the athlete) and the data processor (the team or SGB) are largely aligned. There is mutual benefit, and the willingness of the athlete, as a joint beneficiary, to part with data is high.

The broad principles that have emerged across general data protection laws require, among other things, that data is processed in a fair and reasonable manner and pursuant to a clearly identified, specific and lawful purpose. However, when data collected for one purpose is sought to be used for another purpose or for the same purpose in a changed context, the interests of the athlete and the SGB may not remain aligned. Would the archers consent to the display of their heart rate data at the next event if they felt that their opponents were using this information to analyse their behaviour for strategic purposes?

As Lionel Messi's career moves into the sunset phase, the data collected by his club during training could be used to suggest—to his detriment—that he is ageing, and this will then factor into contract renewal and trading negotiations.

Similarly, there have been cricketers who have played for multiple—in some cases, even four or five—IPL teams over the years. They will inevitably come up against a team they played for previously. For instance, Hardik Pandya and Shubman Gill moved to the Gujarat Titans after multiyear careers in the Mumbai Indians and Kolkata Knight Riders franchises, respectively. Let's say the Mumbai Indians have Pandya's data—collected during his stint with them—suggesting that his heart rate goes up when facing a fast bowler consistently bowling over 140 kilometres per hour. Meanwhile, Kolkata Knight Riders have tracked Gill while he played for them, and know that he gets flustered when he has to face a left-arm spinner when the ball is still new.

This data insight was gathered to help the players. They may have worked on addressing these issues once their teams brought the insight to their attention. Be that as it may, can it now be used against them by their former teams in a competitive context? Should players have the right to ensure their former teams delete all the performance data they have collected? Can they carry a copy of this data to their new team?

Clear boundaries have not yet been drawn in Indian sport. However, there are other countries where the battle lines are better defined and therefore can show the way.

Collect and bargain

The dynamic tension between the interests of the athlete and the SGB provokes an examination of who owns and controls the data, what consent means and whether the data given can have use limitations.

Beyond requiring a lawful purpose for processing data, legal principles also require the data subject to receive notice of the modes and purpose of collection, the intended use and recipients of the data, the consequences of non-provision of data and the term of data storage. Additionally, some frameworks grant the data subject the rights of access, the right to correct errors, the ability to make data portable and to walk away with it, and the right to demand that data collection and processing cease at some point and even be deleted.

A system that adopts the principle of 'privacy by design' would prioritize compliance with these principles and the concept of data minimization. This involves limiting data collection to the bare essential elements required to serve the stated purpose.

Sport is some distance away from adopting this concept of privacy by design. Data collection and processing is everywhere, with barely a thought given to whether there are such things as too much collection and over-processing. Technological tools are engaged in agnostic data collection without purpose or nature limitation. Urine and blood samples are retained by regulators for years, if not decades. With each bit of non-essential data collected or held beyond the time required for its purpose, the risks of reuse beyond the original purpose increase. Without principled limitation and tests of proportionality, this will remain a one-sided game with potential consequences for the autonomy of tens of thousands of participants.

There is very little that a single athlete can do to reset an unfair balance. The power resident in SGBs and teams places them in an unequal bargain with athletes. Athletes are presented with take-it-or-leave-it terms that they must sign to be eligible for participation. These often include open-ended consent terms for the collection and processing of data that do not circumscribe the purpose, term or nature of use.

An individual athlete cannot object unless they are influential or vital to the sport's commerce. An individual objector bears the disproportionate financial and social costs of fighting for the cause. For most athletes, sitting out of all competition is the only way to avoid agreeing to unfair terms. They also have nowhere else to go. This is a binary and disproportionate consequence of opting out, and is far removed from the graded privacy 'opt-out' agreements we see online, which might result in no longer receiving personalized content or advertising, or would encourage one to use another service offering fairer terms. Player unions try to solve the collective action problem and, wherever in place, have played the vital role of pushing back on data overreach.

Collective bargaining means that athletes stand as a single block rather than as lone fighters. Negotiated terms then find their way into collective bargaining agreements (CBAs) that apply to all players uniformly. In the US, the Major League Baseball (MLB) and National Basketball Association (NBA) CBAs have led the way on fair use of athlete data. They do not concern themselves with determining ownership over the data. Instead, they ensure that the athlete's access and information rights are respected, and prevent the use of collection methods and data that are adverse to the athlete's interests.

Wearable devices such as smartwatches are approved by player unions after determining that they are safe and secure to use, that they only collect what they are claiming to collect, and that they are scientifically rigorous in their measurement. The NBA CBA obligates teams to provide athletes with information about what the device will measure, what such measurement means, and the benefits to the player in obtaining and processing such data.

The CBAs also restrict teams from using the data in contractual negotiations or for strategic outcomes adverse to the athlete. These arrangements mandate that all wearables must be approved by the player association after determination of the data being collected on them. The athlete must be provided full access to all data collected from their use of approved wearables.

In 2022, the worldwide representative organization for professional footballers, FIFPRO, launched a Charter of Player Data Rights with a view to implementing global industry standards that protect the privacy of professional footballers and allow them to benefit from personal rights to manage and access information about their performance and health. The charter has been developed in collaboration with FIFA.

These CBAs and the charter start from the position that athletes have rights in—and to—their data. However, where player unions are barred or not recognized, there is little to counter-balance the SGBs' and teams' seemingly insatiable hunger for data.

Offside

In open systems like India with no CBAs in place, boundaries will continue to be pushed. SGBs will collect more, use more and publish more athlete data. How much is too much? As SGBs come under increasing pressure to commercialize fan engagement through new media, they will increasingly deal with athlete publicity rights and data rights. After all, audiences are there for the human connection. Will athletes get a fair share of the pie? That battle has begun.

Over the years, many prominent professional football clubs and SGBs entered into commercial partnerships with data-driven businesses, including those involved in sports betting, gaming and data processing. The data partners pay fees for preferential access to basic player statistics such as goals scored, appearances made, assists, tackles and yellow cards; advanced statistics such as average shots per match, shooting accuracy, pass success percentage, distance run, average positioning and expected goals/assists/tackles per match, and player personal statistics such as cardiovascular metrics, body composition and medical history collected by the clubs. The players receive no direct compensation from these deals, despite being subjects and providers of the data. They are now fighting back.

More than 850 football players across various leagues in the UK have collectivized under the banner of 'Project Red Card'. They have threatened legal action against the clubs, SGBs and their partner companies, demanding compensation worth millions of pounds for what they call the 'unlawful trade' of their personal information, statistics and data in the past. They are also demanding the right to continued licensing income from these deals.

While the basic—and some advanced—statistics are largely in the public domain (and so could be collected by these companies or anyone else watching the matches), the partnerships also provide access to data, including some non-public advanced statistics such as shooting accuracy in training and player personal statistics like body composition and medical history. The footballers' allegations are that, as a package, this infringes their rights, uses the data beyond the purpose for which it was legitimately collected, and unjustly enriches their employers and other companies to the players' detriment.

This is not just a claim for compensation but one that understands the importance of ownership and control.

As virtualizations, digital identities, fan tokens and the metaverse add to the digital realms of sport, this is a fight for far more than commercial territory. At stake is control over the digital personas that will increasingly come to represent each of us in our interactions, and which can feed back into our own conceptions of our inherent selves.

Creep

All individuals, including athletes, enjoy a right to privacy. This includes a right to protect their personal information and a right to decide how to use and divulge it. There are several instances where athletes interact with the public sphere. These interactions should not be seen as a licence to extract, analyse and commercialize every ounce of personal information from them.

Sport must recognize that data is a form of property, and that athletes are the true owners of their personal information. This recognition does not need to upend the business models of sport and its stakeholders. It will merely ensure that the flow and use of data is both lawful and fair.

Sport is only a representative site of the contest between control and autonomy. The dangers ahead are familiar to anyone who has followed the national biometric identity scheme such as Aadhaar in India. In 2019, in *Justice K.S. Puttaswamy vs. Union of India*[4] (known as the Puttaswamy II case), the Supreme Court pushed back on the use of Aadhaar, permitting its mandatory collection only in limited cases where there was a legitimate state interest such as the provision of subsidies. It held that mandatory linking to bank accounts was unconstitutional as it did not meet the test of proportionality. Yet, it is impractical—if not impossible—to open a bank account or operate a corporate organization today without either disclosing one's Aadhaar number or providing other documents to which it is mandatorily linked. This makes it available for seamless cross-purposing by the state, leaving the citizen with little control or remedy.

Ensuring lawful and fair processing of data can go a long way towards building a sustainable relationship between athletes and others in the ecosystem of sport, as much as it can do the same for citizens and their governments. It is possible to recognize the legitimate interests of governors while also respecting the boundaries of individual privacy and the rights of individuals to their autonomy. How we treat the most talented athletes can establish a blueprint for the healthier relationships we all need—with those who collect, use and process our data.

As an individual loses control over their data, they can begin to lose their individuality. People's behaviour can be altered and controlled by presenting them with algorithmically targeted and limited sets of information and experiences. These can influence the individual to adopt a certain perspective or mindset. People will start becoming who they are told to be, not just who they intrinsically are or, free of these influences, could have become. In aggregate, the dilution of individuality can lead to a society that loses its heterogenous texture, one with a reduced ability to adapt to change and remain bound together as a collective.

One day, perhaps, organized sport will have outlived its current purpose. Driven by data, all of us will be tuned and automated to perform flawlessly in a battle of processors. All T20 bowlers will be leg spinners, everyone will play the double-handed backhand, and a goalkeeper will always predict the penalty taker's chosen direction—even the odd Panenka when it is attempted. Until that time, individuality will remain at the heart of the human experience of sport, and we must value and care for it.

Chapter 17

On Risk

How does Mary Kom not have a criminal record?

Mangte Chungneijang Mary Kom is a household name in India. An Olympic medallist and a world boxing champion six times over, her life has been chronicled in the eponymous Bollywood biopic. She has successfully juggled parenthood and a sports career with elan, and even holds public office as a nominated member of the upper house of Parliament, the Rajya Sabha. Despite having landed thousands of successful punches, this lawmaker isn't treated as a lawbreaker.

Eric Cantona famously went legs-first at a fan who taunted him after he had already received a red card for kicking a Crystal Palace player. But it is opponents—not spectators—who are the second most commonly kicked subjects during a professional football match.

During Lionel Messi's heyday at Barcelona, arch-rivals Real Madrid used deliberately incapacitating fouls to counter him. At the FIFA World Cup 2014 in Brazil, the home team's pacy striker Neymar was repeatedly taken down by opponents as he approached the penalty box; a deliberate push from behind in the quarter-finals against Colombia gave him cracked vertebrae and he took no further part in the tournament.

During a Premier League match in Manchester in 2001, Roy Keane tackled Alfie Haaland in a way that was clearly designed to hurt the player rather than to wrest control of the ball. Haaland was carried off the field and was unable to regain full match fitness, resulting in a premature end to his career. Keane wrote in his autobiography that the tackle was a deliberate act spurred on by the acrimonious history between the two. Keane himself had missed much of the 1997–98 season with an anterior cruciate ligament (ACL) injury after tripping up during a skirmish with Haaland.

Are all football tackles fair game? The case of the misdirected kick—accidental or intentional—connects four concepts embedded in our legal system: risk, liability, consent and context.

In everyday life, a perpetrator is responsible for the harm or injury caused to others, and becomes liable to be sued and/or punished. But sport isn't everyday life. Injury is part of the game, and every athlete acknowledges the risks that come with their sport. A tackle in rugby could lead to a fractured shoulder, a hard punch in boxing could result in a broken nose. What if there are bitten ears involved? The last is not just a hypothetical question, as Evander Holyfield can attest. Surely we must draw the line somewhere.

How does the law apply to on-field harm? When does it intervene? Let's take a stab—or a bite, if you prefer—at exploring sport's culture, and the legal principles around incidents like these.

Saved by the bell

Sport gives its competitors many returns; personal accomplishment, fame and money are some of them. There are costs to most things that give a return. Competitive sport comes with risks. Injury is not only possible but—in combat sports like boxing—is a likely outcome. Competitors go in knowing this, and balance the known risks against the benefits they hope to derive.

Consent evokes the spirit of an individual making a well-reasoned decision, using all the information available to them, and weighing the pros and cons. An athlete assumes and consents to the inherent risks and uncertainties that come with their sport. To what extent does the law recognize and permit this assumption of risk and consent? Can an athlete assume the risk of grievous harm or even death?

Generally, when it comes to attributing liability to a perpetrator for violence and harm, there are two types of law that come into play—tort law and criminal law. While tort law provides a victim civil remedies like monetary damages, criminal law might look at the act as a public offence and can impose punishments such as imprisonment and fines.

A tort is a civil wrong. Negligence is a common example. Remedies for torts are usually in the form of monetary compensation from the perpetrator—known as damages—for the injured party to be made 'whole' again from the damage they have suffered. For instance, if you cause a motor vehicle accident, you will have to pay for the other person's car to be fixed and perhaps also cover their medical expenses. A claim like this arises when a person has a legal duty of care towards another person and breaches that duty through their action or inaction, and causes injury or harm to such other person or their property. The nature and extent of liability depends on the type of breach and the extent of damage.

Can athletes claim tort law damages for on-field injuries? Can a hockey player who suffered a tibial fracture claim damages from the opponent whose stick made contact with his leg? Enter *volunti non fit injuria*, a Latin phrase that means 'to a willing person, no injury is done'. It recognizes the autonomy of the individual to expose themselves to—and assume—the risks of their actions.

A person capable of comprehension is presumed to appreciate the known risks associated with an activity they voluntarily participate in. They may not later seek compensation for any injuries that occur in the normal course of things.

In sport, the level and duty of care varies by context. A claim for compensation for injuries occurring in the regular course of a game is unlikely to succeed. This is because the participant is aware of the existence of risk, understands the nature of the risk, and voluntarily accepts it. Where any of the elements is missing, tort remedies may be available. What is in the regular course of play differs by sport, being shaped by its environment, rules and culture. An act that is the subject of a tort claim can also give rise to an action under criminal law.

Where there is a meeting of a criminal act and a criminal intent, ordinary criminal law (such as the Indian Penal Code, 1860 or IPC) imposes responsibility and penalty on the individual who causes harm to another. For instance, if A hits B with a stone, and A intended to cause harm to B, criminal law will spring into action. Depending on the gravity of the harm that results, this would amount to either hurt or grievous hurt under Indian criminal law. The action, the intent and the harm are all elements of the offence.

Assault and battery are other criminal offences to the body that may be relevant in the sporting context. Assault involves intentionally putting another person in reasonable apprehension of imminent harm. Battery is knowingly using force such that it is likely to cause harm to another. Punch someone on the street and you will be punished for the offence of battery. Do it in the course of a boxing bout and you won't.

The law provides for exceptions to liability even when an act has occurred. These are commonly referred to as defences. Consent is one such defence. This defence can be claimed when the other party had consented to the activity or series of events that resulted in the harm. It is implied that the person had consented not only to be at the receiving end of the act but also to the natural consequences of the act, which can include injury and harm. While consent is an exception from the imposition of liability, it operates in a specific context and within the bounds of reasonableness.

Criminal law recognizes that consent can be used as a defence to the most common acts causing harm on a sporting field, in both contact and combat sports, even where death or grievous harm may result. For instance, Section 87 of the IPC states that it is not an offence for a person to cause death or grievous hurt if they do not intend to cause such harm and do not know that such harm is likely, in cases where the other person, aged over eighteen, has consented to be the subject of the act. The illustration it provides is of participants in a fencing match who are playing for amusement. It describes how they are not responsible for any harm that ensues in the course of a fencing match that is played fairly and without foul play.

This example clarifies that consent does not act as an open permit to cause harm. It only extends to harm occurring in the ordinary course of play, within the established rules and norms of fair play. There are also limits to consent. The law does not permit anyone to agree to intentionally or knowingly suffer grievous hurt or death. That is against public policy.

Consent can be explicit or could arise—and be implied—from the circumstances. A football club may require all players participating in the game to sign a consent form that states that they know and assume the risks of participation. This is explicit consent. An athlete participating in a city-level boxing competition without signing any paperwork would be said to have implicitly consented to the potential harm inherent to amateur boxing competitions.

In addition to the legal test and the remedy sought, there is another fundamental difference between claims under tort law and criminal law. This is known as the standard of proof. It is the degree to which a claimant must prove their case, using evidence, to succeed. As criminal law imposes graver consequences, including the taking away of personal liberty through imprisonment, it imposes a higher standard of proof. In tort cases, the standard of proof is 'balance of probabilities' while in criminal cases, it is 'beyond reasonable doubt'. What does this mean in practice?

To succeed in a tort case, the claimant must merely present evidence that it is more probable than not that the elements of the tort were made out. This makes tort law a more likely contender for providing remedies when lines are crossed on the sports field.

In criminal cases, where the state usually acts against the accused, it must present evidence of the offence sufficient to remove any reasonable doubt in the minds of the judges. This furthers the principle of presumption of innocence of the accused, and the principle 'let a hundred guilty be acquitted but one innocent should not be convicted'. With the high standard of proof and the difficulty of proving intent in relation to on-field incidents, it is rare to see criminal law being resorted to in sports injury cases.

Questions remain. Where do we draw the lines when assessing the 'ordinary course of play' and play that is 'unfair'? Is it wise to keep criminal law entirely off the sports field?

Ringside view

Extending consent and assumption of risk to on-field actions serves an important policy and sporting function. Legal immunity supports the autonomy of sport governing bodies (SGBs) to deal with events occurring on the field of play as internal disciplinary matters, without the consequences spilling over beyond the sporting arena. Keeping the machinery of the general legal system outside the stadium gates is every sports governor's preferred option.

Most SGBs have rules and panels of experts who can make an informed assessment of an incident before determining whether disciplinary action is necessary. Playing bans and fines from disciplinary proceedings can adversely impact opportunities to play, compensation and livelihoods. Recognizing the penal nature of some of these sanctions, SGBs tend to use an intermediate standard of proof known as 'comfortable satisfaction' that is positioned somewhere between the civil (balance of probabilities) and criminal (beyond reasonable doubt) standards. The in-sport penalties can have a significant—some would argue sufficient—deterrent effect on participants' excessive conduct.

Sport can lose meaning if caught in a legal maze. Imagine a Mary Kom only sparring, not punching. Athletes can push themselves further when they don't need to think about any liability that could flow from their actions on the field.

That said, immunity from legal liability is available only when the harm is caused during the ordinary course of play or due to the inherent risks of participating in a particular sport that is played in accordance with its rules. Participants can also be exposed to risks that are not natural or inherent to the sport or its circumstances. The athlete is not expected to assume or consent to these risks, or accept the injuries and damage that might ensue.

When Neymar consented to the risks associated with professional football, did that consent extend to deliberate off-the-ball acts that could result in critical, potentially career-ending, injuries?

Below the belt

So then, does an athlete enjoy legal immunity for the harm they cause? There's hardly a better set-up question for a lawyer's favourite answer: it depends. It depends on the context and culture within which a particular sport is played, the circumstances and facts surrounding the occurrence of harm, and the knowledge and understanding of the risks.

You should expect to get punched on your ear in boxing, but wouldn't ever imagine that someone might bite off a piece of it, as Mike Tyson did to Evander Holyfield. Similarly, a cricketer doesn't expect to receive an ACL tear from being kicked by an opponent. What is par for the course for a sport like football is outside the course of normal play for cricket.

Although the law makes space for sport, there will be cases where the legal machinery will intervene. Sports injuries can be serious, even fatal. Immunity is not absolute for all on-field conduct. Serious aggressions not usually associated with the game, such as abnormal, unreasonable, reckless and intentionally violent behaviour, are not enveloped in the assumption of risk or consent and will not receive cover. In these cases, tort and criminal law will intervene, as it must.

The context in which a sport is played, its culture, and the nature of a sport are vital to the understanding of risk. Broadly, sports can be classified as non-contact and contact-based depending on the extent and nature of interaction between and among participants. Contact sports are sports like rugby, wrestling, kabaddi and boxing that witness physical contact between the players or with their equipment. There is also limited contact in sports such as football, handball, volleyball, basketball, squash and hockey. Non-contact sports are sports like athletics, swimming, lawn bowls, weightlifting and shooting, where players participate in separate lanes or turns. In sports like cricket, golf, tennis, table tennis or badminton, play is structured such that there should be no occasion for contact.

The distinction between contact and non-contact sports is vital to understanding the inherent risk of participation in the sport. Naturally, contact sports involve a greater likelihood and risk of physical injury. Rugby injuries are common. Even within contact sports, combat sports are likely to be the riskiest. In sports like boxing, wrestling and mixed martial arts, the rules require participants to engage in a one-to-one fight.

The lines between contact and non-contact sports can be porous. Cricket, which is largely a non-contact sport, involves its share of on-field injuries. Batters (like Phil Hughes) and fielders (like Raman Lamba) have died when hit on the head by the ball. Collisions can happen between fielders and batters and sometimes between fielders chasing a ball or trying for a catch.

Each sport and its inherent risk has to be assessed individually. This means that the notions of assumption of risk and consent are closely linked to the context of each individual sport, its rules, style of play and culture. Rugby and kabaddi are similar in the skills required and some of the movements, but the gameplay and culture make the likelihood of injury far higher in rugby than in kabaddi. While a punch to the face is not inherent to a cricket match, it would be common in a boxing ring. Even in a boxing contest, there is a fine—perhaps even invisible—line between landing a punch with the intention of gaining points and one aimed at attacking an opponent. An intentional kidney punch is delivered with knowledge of its ability to cause the opponent harm or injury. Boxers must tread that fine line, metaphorically separating what is above board from what is below the belt. Referees have the unenviable task of policing this line.

Other factors that impact the assumption of risk and consent are the physical attributes and skills of the participants, the conditions in which the event was played and whether safety measures were in place.

On the mat

While context and culture lay the groundwork for assessing risk in sport, the circumstances and facts of the particular incident are equally important. If participants play according to the rules and regulations, the conventions and the spirit of the sport, they are said to be acting in the ordinary course of play.

Injuries can occur during the ordinary course of play. Perfectly legitimate play in squash might result in an eye injury to the co-participant due to the speed at which the ball travels and the relative location of the players. Here, the participants can be said to have assumed the risk of such harm and consented to it, and no action for liability for any such injury would lie under tort or criminal law.

Do the concepts of assumption of risk and consent also envelop contact beyond the rules, when a foul could be called under the rules of the sport?

A foul tackle in football can result in an opponent fracturing an ankle. While it is a breach of the rules, ordinary fouls are unlikely to invite legal liability as the possibility of being fouled is contemplated by the athletes. Footballers know and accept that such fouls and harm can occur during play. The foul may not involve a breach of duty of care or an intention to cause harm, and neither tort nor criminal law would be invoked. Penalties and deterrents are also available within the rules of the game, including yellow and red cards and disciplinary bans. These are, generally, seen as proportional punishment for the harm caused.

Negligent fouls are a degree up from ordinary fouls. These occur when a player is not taking proper and reasonable care as would be expected of them in a particular situation. A Formula 1 driver might, for instance, continue to drive on dry-surface tyres even after it starts raining heavily, causing an accident involving multiple cars and resulting in injury to other drivers. Here, the driver (and their team) should have changed to wet-surface tyres for better grip and safety.

In professional racing, drivers rely on their competitors' due care and competence. The driver and the team owe a duty of care to their fellow participants. Yet, drivers and their teams usually escape with sporting penalties and fines. For a breach of duty of care, a claim under tort law could well succeed. A criminal law action would be tougher to prosecute given that negligence might not meet the standards of intent that such offences may require.

Reckless fouls are another degree up from negligent fouls. An individual or a team could be said to be reckless when they play in a manner, or adopt tactics, while knowing that such play may cause harm to opponents. A prominent example is the 'Bodyline' Test cricket series played between England and Australia in 1932–33. The English cricket team devised a tactic to bowl the cricket ball, at pace, at the body (head and shoulder) of the batter such that the batter is forced to duck or play defensively. The resulting deflection could be caught by fielders who were standing close by for that purpose.

In that era, cricket was played without any of the protective equipment and headgear that is commonplace today. Such bowling was uncommon and batters neither expected it, nor developed the skills to play such bowling. While several players suffered injuries due to 'Bodyline' bowling, fortunately, none were serious. Realistically, the injured players could have brought a tort claim for recklessness against the English team as they could not be said to have assumed the risk of such harm in that day, age and context. This is the case even though the bowling (and related field-placing) was not prohibited by the rules of cricket at the time. Given the intentionality along with the knowledge involved, the breach of duty of care was graver, thus inviting greater liability. An action in criminal law could also, possibly, have been sustained in this case as the elements of assault and battery may have been satisfied.

Intentional and malicious conduct is the highest degree on the 'intention–injury' continuum. In the Keane-Haaland example mentioned earlier, Haaland and his club considered legal action against Keane. They eventually did not move forward, and Keane escaped legal liability after it turned out that the proximate cause of Haaland's career-ending troubles was a separate, pre-existing injury. Otherwise, Keane's tackle could have been an appropriate case for the invocation of the harshest liability under tort law due to the clear and intentional breach of duty of care resulting in harm. Criminal law could have also stepped in to punish Keane as there was action as well as intention to cause harm. Keane's claims in his autobiography would have been handy in supporting the prosecution on the key element of intention.

The degree of assumption of risk reduces along a sliding scale as we move from ordinary course of play to ordinary foul to negligent and reckless foul to malice (such as the Tyson-Holyfield incident). As the intentionality of the act causing the harm increases, the likelihood of an action in tort and criminal law also increases. In cases where a participant has disregarded the rules of the game, and indulges in unacceptable behaviour and conduct (by sporting standards), liability is more likely to attach. The required standard of proof also plays a role in determining the actions—either criminal or tort—that are likely to succeed.

Injury on the field can also be emotional or mental. Steve Waugh's 'mental disintegration' tactics of grinding down opponents' spirit with sledging come to mind. Athletes are not automatons. They, too, respond to emotional stimuli and these can trigger physical responses, sometimes even violent ones.

If the sledging proves too personal—say, it is about a family member or has a racist undertone—this might be recognized as a mitigating circumstance for any physical retaliation that ensues. Such a provocative trigger is unlikely to absolve a perpetrator of liability but it can result in a less severe punishment. Zinedine Zidane's headbutt of Marco Materazzi could fall in this category, with Materazzi allegedly having abused Zidane's family members. The same leeway was not extended to Eric Cantona and his kung-fu-style kick of the spectator. He was found guilty of assault and sentenced to two weeks in prison. On appeal, this was reduced to 120 hours of community service.

While these context-based standards promote the sporting interests of participating players and teams, they can tend to leave players to their own devices to define the boundaries of acceptable conduct. This is not easy in hyper-competitive environments that do not reward nuance or moderation. Others must play their part.

Majority decision

Athletes cannot be the only ones who bear responsibility for everything that happens on the field. SGBs have crucial roles to play. They have the power and the resources to change the landscape on safety, and also bear the responsibility and the duty to make sport safer.

The legal concepts of vicarious liability and contributory liability clarify SGBs' responsibilities. Vicarious liability arises when one person is held liable for the offending acts of another. Such a claim can succeed if there is an employment relationship between the parties, a wrong is committed by the employee, and it occurs during the course of employment. In sporting contexts, an SGB or a club that employs a player could be liable for the wrongful acts of the player, including intentional acts such as assault. A football club may be held responsible for an intentional act of violence by a player, considering the employment relationship it shares with the player. Contributory liability arises when the actions or inactions of multiple parties cumulate to contribute to the harm. It does not require an employment relationship and applies where more than one person or entity is negligent or participates in a wrong.

The context and nature of each sport are determined not only by its culture but also by its rules and architecture. These are squarely in control of the SGB. An intervention can transform the nature and extent of the risk borne by participants. The rules that mandated the use of a halo safety device in open-wheel racing are a good example.

Open-wheel car racing has seen several injuries and a few deaths in accidents. The halo is a driver crash-protection system, which consists of a curved bar placed to protect the driver's head in case of an accident. In 2018, the Fédération Internationale de l'Automobile (FIA) made the halo mandatory in some racing series, and it has been credited with saving the lives of multiple drivers. By intervening in the rules and architecture of the sport, the FIA helped reduce the degree of inherent risk. Had it not taken steps to improve safety, the FIA could have been held vicariously and contributorily liable for the injuries and deaths occurring on the racetrack.

The nature and level of officiating, how the rules of the game are applied and its conventions can also contribute to the environment in which harm can occur or be prevented. Stricter officiating with a low tolerance for negligent or reckless play can nudge the behaviour of participants away from risky conduct. A change in rules can also play a part in preventing certain events from occurring. A good example is the prohibition on dangerous play in hockey that prevents raised shots in the field.

The perception, knowledge and understanding of risk is one area where SGBs have both responsibility and potential for research and intervention. In the Olympic boxing event, female boxers like Mary Kom must compulsorily wear headgear. Headgear used to be compulsory for male boxers too, but this was discontinued in 2016. These decisions were supported by studies that showed that women are far more susceptible to concussions as a result of combat sport head trauma. Specific education programmes can also make participants at all levels, skills and ages aware of the risks involved in the sport. Enhanced research in understanding risk, disseminating information about it and mitigating risks can help bridge knowledge gaps.

SGBs' duty of care has come into sharp focus in the last few years with the revelation that the lives of several former athletes have been adversely affected due to previously unknown (or unrevealed) risks of long-term brain injury and dementia—Muhammad Ali is the best-known example—in sports such as rugby, boxing, football, ice hockey, racing and skeleton.

Several rugby players have initiated legal proceedings against the international and British SGBs for rugby. They argue that the SGBs were negligent as they failed to take reasonable action to protect players from permanent injury caused by repetitive concussive and sub-concussive blows. A similar lawsuit against the National Football League (NFL) in the United States led to a settlement, with the league paying out more than a billion dollars. These concussion litigations illustrate the application of the concepts of vicarious and contributory liability, and the responsibility SGBs bear for the environment in which athletes play.

SGBs have the moral responsibility and legal duty to ensure safe sport for anyone who enters the sporting pyramid. Besides being proactive with research, they must enforce and revise equipment guidelines, safety guidelines, operating procedures, training of staff and officials, codes of conduct, disciplinary proceedings and other pre-emptive measures and protocols backed by the results.

For instance, all sports must follow concussion testing protocols when a player suffers a head injury. Cricket has this protocol in place whenever a batter is hit on the helmet. It has also modernized its rules to include a 'concussion substitute' who can replace a concussed player. This ensures that there is no undue pressure on a player to sacrifice personal safety at the altar of their team's interests.

Bout last night

Many sports events require participants to expressly assume the risks of participation through contracts. Consent and waiver forms cover the negligence of other participants as one of the assumed risks. Are there limits to the risks one can assume and consent to? What happens in unofficial and inherently dangerous sports where there are no SGBs?

Take a local mixed martial arts club, where participants fight both for sport and for money. Organized in informal settings, fights can be held in environments with poor safety measures and skeletal rule structures. Participants might not wear protective headgear while fighting, and the range of permissible moves can be far greater than permitted in official boxing or wrestling. A study done in Alberta, Canada, showed that 59.4 per cent of mixed martial artists sustained some sort of injury during their bout.[1] To what extent can a participant be said to have consented to the risks involved in such an event? Can the state intervene? Indeed, does it have a duty to do so?

This is an issue that has come up in boxing. It prompted the US to pass the 1996 Professional Boxing Safety Act, which was then amended in 2000 by the Muhammad Ali Boxing Reform Act. This law protects the rights and welfare of boxers through state oversight, prevention of exploitation and limitation of conflict of interest. It recognizes that professional boxing is not governed by any league, association or any form of an established organization. Its enactment was in response to the widespread abuse of boxers within this environment.

Among other things, the law requires boxing promoters to maintain safety standards. Boxing commissions are urged to make appropriate health and safety disclosures to registered boxers. This includes making them aware of the risks associated with boxing, particularly the risk and frequency of brain injury and the advisability of periodically undergoing medical procedures designed to detect such injuries. There is a movement in the US to extend this law to all combat sports, including mixed martial arts. This is an example of a proactive approach to athlete safety in unregulated environments.

Some sports are extremely dangerous, for instance, bullfighting and *jallikattu*. It is not uncommon for participants to die in such competitions due to the involvement of an innately uncontrollable bull. Do participants in such competitions assume the risk of death? Can a human ever consent to death? It might be natural to respond with a 'no' to that question. Public policy does not allow anyone to consent to their own death. We have already seen that the IPC does not permit an individual to consent to acts that they know would result, or are likely to result, in them suffering grievous hurt or death.

Context can complicate matters. These events are often held in the form of community gatherings organized by small clubs or other local organizations on shoestring budgets. They can lack the resources to formalize their events and focus on matters like safety. Practices such as bullfighting and *jallikattu* also have deep cultural roots and traditional or religious significance. Attempts to prohibit or regulate them are fiercely opposed, and courts have baulked at stopping these practices.[2] Instead, meaningful interventions in such cases might involve the provision of funding, resources and support to modify existing practices that are unsafe and risky. This could be done in a manner acceptable to the participating communities, retaining their meaning while enhancing participant safety. It requires a genuine engagement with the community and a joint commitment to finding solutions.

Similarly, knowledge of actual risk is another aspect of the assumption of risk and consent. Can children consent to the risks involved in youth sports? Those under the age of eighteen are not considered eligible under law to have the capacity to contract or consent. It is their guardians or parents who can agree on their behalf. Do the guardians know and understand the risks properly? Do they comprehend and appreciate the heightened and unique risks that children may face while participating in sports?

Knowledge of the actual risks is equally important for adults. Merely because a person has crossed the age of majority does not mean that they will know all the actual risks inherent to a sport. Are athletes explicitly made aware of these risks through education and training resources? Don't athletes have a right to know all the risks inherent to their sport? These are questions SGBs must answer.

Pulling the punches

Participation in sporting activity involves the risk of injury and potential harm. The nature and degree of risk and injury vary by discipline and circumstances. While all efforts should be made to eliminate or reduce fatal and serious risks, efforts to completely remove all risk would take away from the essence of sport itself. Participants recognize this truth. They accept this bargain, and are willing to run the risk of some harm in return for all that sport offers them.

Primarily, the rules, regulations, conventions, practices and officiating, safety, equipment and disciplinary protocols and procedures of sport can police the boundaries of these risks. In egregious cases, the compensation of tort law and/or the punishment of criminal law can play an important part in shaping behaviours.

Athletes involved in organized sport should not be exposed to an unbounded range of risks, especially those that are avoidable or beyond the ordinary course of play. This is not part of the sports compact. Athletes should not have to sacrifice their safety for the prospect of sporting glory. A clear understanding and fair apportionment of the rights and duties of various actors is a first step. Each SGB must take the reins of its sport and drive it with an eye on safety. Avoidable and excessive harms that occur on the field in the name of sport can be limited.

While athletes, SGBs and event organizers have rights, responsibilities and duties, there are some harms and injuries for which no one can be held responsible. When humans are pushing the limits of achievement, unusual and unfortunate accidents can occur despite all the precautions and good intentions. Such accidents should be made as rare as possible and instruments such as event, health, accident and liability insurance must be used to soften the blow of such cases.

Mary Kom has thrown many punches and broken innumerable stereotypes in the course of her boxing career. The only 'Hands Up' commands she ever heard were from the referees during her bouts. Playing by the book has allowed her to stay out of legal trouble. She thus joins 70 per cent of her colleagues in the Rajya Sabha and 57 per cent of the Lok Sabha members in the list of members of Parliament who do not have a criminal record.[3] In boxing—as in life—the means are just as important as the ends.

Chapter 18

On Justice

Was Azharuddin cleared of all match-fixing charges?

On 2 November 2000, Mihir Bose wrote a piece for British daily the *Telegraph* titled 'Azharuddin confesses all'. It began thus: 'For the first time in the near decade-long corruption scandal, one of the world's leading cricketers, Mohammad Azharuddin, has confessed that he took money to throw matches.'[1]

Azharuddin eventually retracted the confession he had made to the Central Bureau of Investigation (CBI). Many legal challenges later, the Andhra Pradesh High Court in 2012 lifted the life ban imposed by the Board of Control for Cricket in India (BCCI) on the former Indian captain. Azharuddin immediately claimed that the court's decision was proof of his innocence.

Was it a 'clean chit', as he claimed? The sequence of events makes for interesting reading.

On the completion of the CBI's investigation in October 2000, the BCCI had appointed former CBI joint director K. Madhavan as commissioner. He was tasked with inquiring into the alleged sports fraud. Relying on the commissioner's report, a BCCI committee concluded that Azharuddin was involved in match-fixing. It handed him a life ban, prohibiting him from playing official cricket and holding any position in the

International Cricket Council (ICC), the BCCI or any of their affiliate organizations.

In August 2003, the City Civil Court in Hyderabad rejected Azharuddin's plea to overturn the ban on the grounds that the constitution and operation of the BCCI committee contravened the rules of the governing body. Azharuddin filed an appeal before the High Court against the City Civil Court's order, alleging that BCCI had violated the principles of natural justice during its disciplinary proceedings.

What are the mechanisms used to deliver justice? What is the role of the principles of natural justice?

Pitched battles

Conflicts and disputes are natural features of the high-stakes, competitive world of sport where boundaries are constantly being pushed. Conflicts need management; disputes require resolution. These are essential for the sports ecosystem to serve its purpose.

Dispute resolution's role is to bring clarity, consistency and certainty to interactions and transactions. Every sport has rules and regulations for participants. They guide appropriate conduct on and off the field of play and describe the consequences of rule violations. These rules must be interpreted and applied. Violations need to be called out. This usually needs human intervention, though non-humans are increasingly playing a role here.

The emergence of new technological capabilities presents opportunities for refereeing and dispute resolution. Today, video assistance supports on-field refereeing and umpiring, especially with respect to binary decision-making, such as whether a ball or foot has crossed a line. When combined with machine learning and artificial intelligence, it is inevitably going to be entrusted with more decisions both on and off the field. But, for now, the final call usually remains with the human adjudicator.

With this being the case, how do we ensure that disputes are resolved fairly and justly by these human adjudicators?

The answer lies in using the appropriate fora, mechanisms and procedures for each type of dispute.

First, it is important to understand that fairness and justice are not absolute terms. They have to be understood contextually and with an eye on priorities and objectives. Some disputes—like those on the field of play—require immediate or real-time resolution. Others are not as time-sensitive. All disputes are important to the disputing parties, but some of these have consequences for others as well—fellow competitors and organizations, and in some cases the public at large. Whatever the context of the dispute, the participation of competent and unbiased people following the proper process increases the likelihood of a fair result.

On-field rule violations are typically resolved by referees and technical officials in real time. These may relate to the application of rules, the calling of fouls, the awarding of points and the like. Once these decisions are made, they generally will not be overruled unless corruption, fraud or malpractice by officials can be shown, or where a decision results in a grave miscarriage of justice. Such situations are rare. So, in-game and technical decisions are left to those who are trained and knowledgeable, and who understand the game. Swift, efficient and final resolution is a key requirement of such disputes.

Regulatory disputes, such as disciplinary matters relating to on-field and off-field conduct, are usually resolved by sport governing bodies (SGBs) using their own internal dispute resolution mechanisms. These could involve a disciplinary committee, dispute resolution panel or the office of ombudsman. The SGB might embed such fora into its constitution and grant them exclusive dispute resolution powers. Submission to their jurisdiction becomes mandatory for all participants as a condition of participation. In these cases, appeals would usually be heard by a national sports-specific dispute resolution body, if it exists.

Prominent examples of such bodies include the National Sports Tribunal of Australia, the Sports Tribunal of New Zealand, the Sport Dispute Resolution Centre of Canada, the Japan Sport Arbitration Agency, the Portugal Arbitration Court for Sport and Sport Dispute Solutions Ireland. In most other cases, any appeal will only lie to the Court of Arbitration for Sports (CAS) in Lausanne, Switzerland (if such an appeal is also provided for in the constitution).

Many disputes might be of high public significance. The matter of match-fixing in Indian cricket is a good example. Whether Azharuddin and his colleagues would face consequences for their acts was not just a matter for sport—the question involved a distinctly public element. Everyone who follows cricket and invests emotion and sentiment in the fortunes of the Indian team is a stakeholder in the quest for truth in such a case. Should the BCCI have the sole prerogative to attribute responsibility and culpability for the manipulation of these matches?

Such matters cry out for independent external parties to participate in the resolution processes. However, even in such cases, SGBs have tried their best to maintain control over disputes. This furthers their claims of autonomy and supremacy over the sport they govern. Perhaps equally important to them is to manage costs—financial and reputational—and control the outcome and the narrative that will follow.

The constitutional courts, however, have not let things lie. In cases where public rights and interests are in contention, or where internal or internally organized mechanisms have acted arbitrarily or improperly, the public justice delivery system has come into play.

The case of Azharuddin again provides a good example. Match-fixing, whether or not criminal law sees it as a crime, is a scam on the cricket-watching public. In the first place, the matter was not uncovered by the BCCI but was stumbled upon by the police during a phone tap while investigating organized crime. The BCCI showed itself to be ill-equipped institutionally to investigate the matter. It outsourced the investigation to the commissioner. The processes it followed were not equipped to withstand judicial scrutiny.

In *Mohammed Azharuddin v. The Board of Control for Cricket in India*,[2] a division bench of the Andhra Pradesh High Court upheld the former captain's appeal against the BCCI's life ban. The court found that the BCCI rules required a committee to be constituted in cases of player misconduct, and did not contemplate the appointment of a commissioner. This meant that the appointment of the commissioner by the BCCI exceeded the authority granted by the BCCI rules.

The court also held that the commissioner had failed to respect the principles of natural justice. It found that the commissioner had relied on a preliminary inquiry report prepared by the CBI that had not yet been finalized. He had also failed to re-examine any evidence or adduce additional material, and had not provided Azharuddin with the opportunity to cross-examine witnesses or rebut witness testimony.

Good judgement

Whatever the forum—on the field, internal to a sport body or in a courtroom—fairness has a procedural element. The Bangalore Principles on Judicial Conduct identify the seven core values of a fair adjudicatory process: independence, impartiality, integrity, propriety, equality, competence and diligence. These focus on ensuring a neutral, consistent and effective structure with substantive, procedural and institutional safeguards.

Not only do the appropriate rules have to be applied correctly, the process followed must be visibly fair and appropriate. This brings legitimacy to the process. Enter the three principles of natural justice: impartiality, fair hearing and a reasoned decision. Together, they recognize human fallibility and try to build multilayered structural defences against it.

Impartiality requires that no person shall be a judge in their own cause or in a cause in which they are interested. This is also known as the 'doctrine of bias'. Bias can be caused by pecuniary interests (commercial stakes), personal interests (familial, relational or social) or official interests (positional duties).

To invalidate the standing of the adjudicator, there is no need to show actual bias; a possibility of bias is usually enough. Not only must justice be done, it must also be seen to be done.

A question to ask here: Is a sports body like the BCCI—with its obvious internal conflicts around publicizing the muck within its own game—adequately impartial to deliver justice in a serious matter of match-fixing involving many of its own players, including the national captain?

Fair hearing, the second principle, involves the right of disputing parties to be heard and have their arguments considered. It recognizes that the different perspectives of a dispute must all be considered before a decision is made. A hearing should not be reduced to a mere formality. Notice must be issued to the parties; each must have the right to make representations and adduce evidence to support arguments. They must also be provided reasonable time to file replies, the opportunity of a personal hearing and the opportunity to cross-examine the other side's witnesses.

The right to legal representation can also be asserted as part of this principle of fair hearing. While the right to appeal and to be heard by a superior authority is not always available, it will add to the fairness of the overall process where it is. Appeal and review processes act as checks on the adjudicator in cases where an error may have been made.

As we have seen in Azharuddin's case, the commissioner had failed to give him a fair hearing, having limited his ability to bring new evidence or cross-examine witnesses or rebut other witnesses' testimony. The BCCI and its appointees were in a hurry to make a public statement and put the matter to rest, and the life ban was meant to be a lightning conductor for public anger. In the quest, due process was bypassed. This again raises a question on the appropriateness of the internal forum for such matters of public importance.

The third principle, a reasoned decision, needs the adjudicator to explain the background, the evidence relied on and facts considered, the rules and laws found applicable and the basis on which the final determination was made. This provides a degree of closure and understanding and helps move parties towards respecting an unfavourable decision rather than just accepting it.

A written, reasoned decision also gives a dissatisfied party the opportunity to take it to another authority or forum in appeal or review, where available, and also gives parties something to rely on when documentary proof of the outcome is sought or required.

Natural justice principles act as checks and balances on the adjudicator's conflicts of interest, and on implicit and explicit biases. Adjudicators are human and come with the baggage of histories, relationships and opinions. The principles force these to be brought to light.

The adjudicator must go through certain motions and not rely on shortcuts or predetermination. Faith is placed in the belief that a reasonable person will gravitate towards the better argument once they hear it and then reach the just decision on that basis. Similarly, the natural justice principles reduce the opportunity to make whimsical, unaccountable and binary decisions. The adjudicator's own reputational concerns come into the picture. Adjudicators are taken through a journey of shedding their known and unknown biases.

Independence, impartiality, integrity and propriety are at the heart of fair adjudication. Yet, with sport's desire to control all dispute resolution processes, these principles can run into rough weather when disputes arise.

The Andhra Pradesh High Court did not determine whether or not Azharuddin engaged in match-fixing. It only found that the procedures adopted by the BCCI in imposing the administrative life ban did not pass procedural muster. It ruled that any product of such procedures is automatically vitiated. As a result, the court held that the life ban imposed on Azharuddin was no longer in effect.

Had justice been delivered? To whom?

Neutral umpires

The SGB, its office-bearers or its members are parties in most disputes handled by an SGB's dispute resolution panel. To make matters more challenging, office-bearers and members often populate these panels. Even in the Azharuddin case, the BCCI rules of the time required the creation of a committee to investigate the matter.

Where panels include one or more 'independent' members, these are usually appointed either by the general body or the office-bearers and serve at their discretion. Their financial terms and tenures, which may include the possibility of renewal, can be determined by those making the appointments. Can such panels be genuinely independent and neutral? The identity of the adjudicators, how they are appointed, the terms on which they operate and their conflicted incentives take on relevance.

For instance, a retired judge with no other known sources of income might be appointed as an adjudicator to resolve the internal disputes of an SGB. If they are appointed by the general body or are externally nominated—say by reference of a court—they might have fewer allegiances or dependencies than if they are appointed or nominated by the body's office-bearers, at whose discretion they will then serve.

If they receive a predetermined, standardized compensation, this might create incentives towards independence, as opposed to a negotiated and dynamic compensation, which can be modified at the whims and fancies of the SGB's leaders and be implicitly tied to the nature of their decisions. Similarly, a fixed term of a reasonable number of years with security of tenure and without the prospect of renewal tends towards greater independence than a tenure that can be prematurely terminated or a shorter term that needs to be renewed regularly.

These structural elements consciously and subconsciously influence decision-making. Adjudicators may owe their allegiance to the SGB, or might not have the right incentives to displease those who appoint them. This impacts the genuine independence of such internal dispute-resolution mechanisms.

These challenges in sports dispute resolution are illustrative of the challenges of independence and neutrality in every sphere. In India, for instance, the government and the judges are locked in combat over the right to select and appoint judges, and the meaning of independence. Like SGBs in sport, the government remains a party in the vast majority of disputes in the courts. For the government to appoint judges, therefore, violates the first principle–impartiality–of natural justice, since a judge appointed by the government would have to sit in judgment in a matter involving the government.

On the other hand, what guarantees do we have that judges will appoint other judges who are independent-minded? Judges are not democratically accountable and, given a free hand, they can reinforce existing power structures and display nepotism. The lessons from dispute resolution in sport are revelatory of the fault lines and challenges on both sides of the ongoing judge appointment and independence debate.

In fact, global sport's dispute resolution mechanisms have witnessed similar controversies and challenges.

Courting controversy

The CAS presents itself as an independent and specialized authority to resolve sports-related disputes. As most international federations and other SGBs have adopted its jurisdiction into their constitutions and statutes, it has jurisdiction over a wide range of sports disputes.

Having operated since 1984, the CAS members were originally appointed by the International Olympic Committee (IOC), the international federations, the National Olympic Committees (NOCs) and the IOC President. All the operating costs of the CAS were borne by the IOC, and the CAS statute could be modified only at the IOC session on the proposal of the IOC executive board. Given its heavy reliance on the institutions of sport for its formation, existence and sustenance, the CAS has had to deal with multiple questions about its structural neutrality.

In 1992, horse rider Elmar Gundel brought a case that would result in a restructuring of the CAS.[3] It related to penalties imposed on him for horse doping, which were approved by the CAS. Gundel filed a public law appeal with the Swiss Federal Tribunal (the Swiss Supreme Court) against the CAS decision, arguing that the CAS did not meet the conditions of impartiality and independence needed to be considered a proper arbitration court.

The Swiss Federal Tribunal pointed out the various links between CAS and the IOC, and held that these were sufficiently serious to call into question the independence of the CAS in cases where the IOC was a party to the proceedings before it.[4] This forced the CAS to try and become more operationally and financially independent of the IOC.

Thus, the International Council of Arbitration for Sport (ICAS) was created to safeguard the independence of the CAS. It is constituted by twenty members, each a highly regarded jurist required to sign a declaration that they undertake to exercise their function in a personal capacity, with total objectivity and independence. The ICAS must decide upon any changes to CAS codes or procedures. It elects its own president and office-bearers as well as the CAS arbitrators, and also approves the CAS budget and accounts.

This structure was tested in 2018 in *Mutu and Pechstein v. Switzerland*[5] in the European Court of Human Rights (ECtHR). The applicants in these cases were Adrian Mutu, a professional footballer who had been ordered to pay a very high sum to his club for a unilateral breach of contract, and Claudia Pechstein, a speed skater on whom sanctions had been imposed for doping.

These two athletes had raised questions concerning the fairness of the procedures before the CAS. The ECtHR decided in favour of ICAS that 'the system of the list of arbitrators meets the constitutional requirements of independence and impartiality applicable to arbitral tribunals, and that the CAS, when operating as an appellate body external to international federations, is similar to a judicial authority independent of the parties.'

The CAS, albeit restructured, remains the subject of examination and critique. Is it truly a neutral and independent forum extending no advantage to the SGBs that may be parties to a dispute? Is the involvement of ICAS a genuine layer of independence, or does it simply provide plausible deniability of bias?

ICAS members are appointed by SGBs. The terms of ICAS members are renewable, and the criteria for selection remain opaque. There is little room for public accountability. ICAS does not publish its annual reports or financial statements, and only a handful of the CAS awards are published. The message these bodies send out is that they are independent and neutral simply because they say so.

As for the arbitrators at the CAS, the ICAS chooses a closed list of a few hundred arbitrators. A small number of these are empanelled repeatedly in key cases. Appointment procedures are not clearly specified and the qualification criteria are unclear. There is no obligation on arbitrators to publicly disclose their other associations or official positions that may make them potentially interested or conflicted parties in disputes they handle.

This is particularly worrisome because several CAS arbitrators are elected officials and sports officers, holding positions in SGBs. Many others are in private practice with SGBs as their and their firms' significant clients. The fact that arbitrators are predominantly Western, white, male, middle-aged, private-practice lawyers has also not gone unnoticed, with over half coming from Europe and 10 per cent from the US.[6] The lack of diversity results in a structural imbalance limiting the breadth of life experiences of those deciding on sports matters that come to CAS from across the world.

Athletes are forced to accept the jurisdiction of CAS as part of the terms of entry into various national and international competitions, with no opt-out or alternative. Arbitrators must be chosen from the closed list of candidates specified by ICAS. Except for disciplinary matters challenging the decisions of an international federation that are adjudicated for free, the costs of a CAS matter are considerable and can run into tens of thousands of dollars for each party.

The specific procedures and filing requirements can also mean that athletes have to engage a lawyer and pay their fees—which are often quite significant—to stand a chance of success. This puts athletes, especially those with limited means, at a significant disadvantage in accessing remedies, since the odds are stacked against them in many ways.

Autonomy is generally seen as supportive of and promoting independence. Sports dispute resolution shows that this is not always the case. When an institution is rife with conflicts of interest, then the notional independence of the institutional mechanisms becomes a dangerous smokescreen that shields wrongdoings rather than uncovering them. There could be no better example than the case of Azharuddin. If you thought the story ended with his life ban lifted, think again. Worse was to come.

Decision review system

National courts generally defer to the decisions of SGBs on sports-related disputes. They refuse to get involved in general and transactional matters unless the disputant has tried to access the internal mechanisms for dispute resolution within the body and has failed to get a hearing.

Once internal remedies have been exhausted by the disputant, courts have been more willing to intervene, but on limited matters. On private, civil, sporting and technical matters, they prefer not to substitute their own judgments for those already made but might intervene if they feel that the principles of natural justice have not been followed. They have also stepped in where decisions have been taken arbitrarily, with bias on display, where the body has ignored its own rules and regulations—as we saw the BCCI do in the Azharuddin case—or where the constitutional rights of a party might be in jeopardy.

The controversy over the selection of the Indian wrestling team for the 2016 Rio Olympic Games provides an excellent example of these dynamics. In the case of *Sushil Kumar v. Union of India*,[7] the Delhi High Court rejected Olympian wrestler Sushil Kumar's plea to intervene in a selection dispute, observing that 'a writ court will not interfere in the exercise of discretion of the National Sports Federation and substitute its own judgement except where the discretion is shown to have been exercised in an arbitrary or capricious or perverse manner or contrary to settled principles or practices.'

In selection disputes like these, courts recognize that this is a technical sporting matter best handled by the body itself. Typically, it will hold the body to its own standards and also determine whether these were fair and reasonable in the first place. It will go into matters such as whether a process of fair notice of criteria, opportunity and decision-making was undertaken for the selection of a team.

If it finds that there was an arbitrary or incorrect application of process, it will require the SGB to undertake the process again in a fair and transparent manner. This may happen under the court's own, or an appointed committee's, supervision and oversight.

Recognizing their public relevance, courts have also been ready to intervene in sports election matters, disputes between factions of SGBs claiming official status, and in cases of alleged fraud and corruption. From the Indian Olympic Association and the All India Football Federation to the hockey, table tennis, equestrian and other SGBs, almost every election is disputed, challenged and made the matter of a case before the courts. Not to be left behind, disputes between warring factions of NSFs have resulted in avoidable situations like two teams arriving at the venue of a tournament claiming to represent the same federation. Courts do not take kindly to such situations and pierce the veil of autonomy of these bodies in the public interest.

In 2016, the Sports Ministry issued guidelines, called 'Safeguarding the interests of sportspersons and provision of effective Grievance Redressal System in the Constitution of National Sports Federations', through which it advised every NSF to consider having an effective, transparent and fair grievance redressal mechanism in its constitution for the expeditious settlement of any disputes, and also a specific provision invoking the jurisdiction of the CAS if a party was aggrieved by the outcome of the NSF's redressal process.

Most NSFs in India have not followed these directions, and most sports disputes in India end up in the courts. CAS jurisdiction is rarely invoked and courts readily accept cases challenging the decisions of SGBs.

However, the progressive recognition of the public functions of SGBs—and their impact on the public rights of individuals—expands the scope of judicial review to potentially include reference to human rights issues and other matters of public law. The amenability of sports disputes to judicial review, and the ability of members of the public to approach courts directly where their rights are violated, recognizes the public interest in ensuring that sport is run fairly and not arbitrarily. This is particularly so because of the monopolistic and monopsonistic nature of SGBs—a suspension and disqualification, for example, leaves an athlete with no options to exercise a trade or profession.

The extent to which courts intervene in sports disputes impacts how decisions are made within sports organizations. The prospect of court intervention can act as a strong deterrent against corruption, bias and mala fide conduct. When courts choose to intervene only after disputants have exhausted internal remedies, they push SGBs to establish and operate such internal remedies.

Courts acknowledge their own limitations when they intervene cautiously, but the fact that they do intervene increases the pressure on SGBs to operate internal resolution mechanisms fairly and transparently, following natural justice principles. When they intervene, the courts do so with the legal and moral authority of advancing the public interest, which the SGB was meant to promote in the first place. The need for their intervention serves as a rap on the knuckles at the very least.

The umpire strikes back

The resolution of disputes is the foundation and the scaffolding of the sports system. The commercialization and medicalization of sport has put significant pressure on the rules of sport and their enforcement. Every loophole is exploited and every possible advantage taken. Dispute resolution has to hold the line and not only police behaviour but also maintain a level playing field.

Whether decisions are made by referees, arbitrators, judges, technologies or algorithms, questions must always be asked about their neutrality and independence from influence. Where there is human choice, there is room for discretion and the possibility of bias creeping in. Conscious effort is needed to remove bias. Whether in matters of rule enforcement or dispute resolution, the quest for unbiased and fair decision-making is a search for justice.

Was justice done in the Azharuddin case? It depends on who you ask. Azharuddin claimed he had finally received a well-deserved clean chit from the court. This claim was debunked by Justice G. Krishna Mohan Reddy of the Andhra Pradesh High Court, who in his short concurring judgment observed: 'This case is one best example (sic) of a player wriggling out of the serious allegations of match-fixing, betting, etc. made against him mainly because of the inaction of the Board (BCCI) to take appropriate action as per the procedure established by law. Non-proving of the allegations does not amount to whether (the person is) guilty or not guilty of the charges whereas it only amounts to non-proving of the charges.'[8]

As a reminder, impartiality, fair hearing and a reasoned decision are the three principles of natural justice. What purpose did these principles serve here? They helped show the system a mirror.

Justice Reddy concluded his observations by stating that the inaction of the BCCI 'may cause more damage than a player who involves (sic) in such serious activities can do to the game'. Prescient words, expressed pithily.

By the time the ban was lifted by the court, it was 2012 and Azharuddin was a sitting member of Parliament, having been elected from Moradabad, Uttar Pradesh, in 2009. Many years had passed since he had been dropped from the national team. The BCCI neither appealed the Andhra Pradesh High Court decision nor reconstituted the committee in accordance with its rules. Its work was done, and there was nothing more for it to gain. Did it have the mechanisms in place, the incentives or the intent to pursue the truth? Clearly not.

Thus, one of Indian cricket's murkiest episodes was seemingly buried forever. The public wound remained open. As if to exemplify all that was wrong with this situation, there was a pound of salt at hand.

As a player and captain, Sourav Ganguly had been credited with rebuilding the Indian team after the sordid era of match-fixing under his predecessor, Azharuddin. In 2018, Ganguly was serving as the president of the Cricket Association of Bengal. He invited the same Azharuddin to ring the ceremonial bell at the Eden Gardens before the start of an international match being hosted at the venue.[9] This was meant to be a signal honour and is bestowed only on a select few. Salt, meet open wound.

In 2019, Azharuddin was elected as the president of the Hyderabad Cricket Association (HCA) and also became the association's representative to the BCCI—the very organization that had once banned him for life. Ganguly was elected president of the BCCI around the same time. Then, a stand was named in Azharuddin's honour at the Rajiv Gandhi International Cricket Stadium in Hyderabad, a stadium operated by the HCA, which he was now running.[10]

At the time of writing, the HCA's administration lies in disarray under Azharuddin's leadership.[11] It has not held its elections on time, is being overseen by an administrator appointed by the Supreme Court of India, and its men's senior team has been relegated to the lower (Plate) division of the Ranji Trophy after ending the 2022–23 season without a single win over seven matches.

Any fan who followed the Indian men's cricket team in the 1990s will feel the lack of closure and a sense of injustice in relation to the match-fixing saga. No law, no prosecution, no penalties, not even social reprobation. Add to that, salt rubbed into that wound again and again. Justice not done, justice not seen to be done.

The late 1990s will go down as a particularly dark era of Indian cricket. Meanwhile, Azharuddin remains the only player in the game to end a career with ninety-nine Test appearances. Sometimes, the only justice available may be of the poetic variety.

Chapter 19

On Collaboration

Why do so many of our prime stadiums lie unused?

In 2010, a refurbished Jawaharlal Nehru Stadium in Delhi played glittering host to the Commonwealth Games. Much was made of how the stadium upgrade—completed at an enormous cost—would serve Indian athletes for years to come.

Just over a decade later, any mention of the stadium evokes a sinking feeling. Literally. Despite its world-class credentials, it hasn't hosted a track and field event in several years. The reason? A mismanaged track relaying project that led to the entire track caving in, leaving it totally unusable.

This story is no outlier. Many a state-of-the-art sports stadium sits in a prime location in one of India's cities or towns. The premises house offices and administrative blocks that are leased to government departments. Some stadia are used for weddings and political rallies while others are overgrown, with weeds competing with blades of wild grass. The silent stands and concourses tell the sorry tale of what could have been.

This picture stands in stark contrast to the carefully tended dreams of thousands of talented aspirants, each looking for a small patch of track to train on. Why isn't this infrastructure maintained well and used extensively? Is there anything we can do about this state of affairs?

Organized sport relies on physical infrastructure like these stadia, and on training venues, playing fields and high-performance centres. It also relies on knowledge and human infrastructure such as coaches, physiotherapists and sports scientists. Creating and sustaining this infrastructure requires funds. The classical means of production must come together: land, labour and capital. The Indian state has been called on to build, operate and fund sport.

Sports infrastructure in India has not kept up with the talent potential or the national demand for facilities. Mobilizing public funds to build infrastructure is no easy task. The opportunity cost is high when one considers other national priorities and potential uses of the funds.

In many cases, it is the obligations associated with hosting international and national events that drive Indian public spending on sports infrastructure. To organize an event of scale, the hosting government is responsible for financing, constructing, operating and maintaining the infrastructure. Event budgets are tight, and construction costs tend to exceed projections. These budgets will rarely factor in post-event maintenance and upkeep, and this can cause government-controlled stadia to move into disrepair and disuse.

In a country as vast and heterogeneous as India, this is not a sustainable approach for the systematic development of sports infrastructure. Where can we find a solution?

State of play

Historically, Indian sport relied on the patronage of wealthy individuals and royalty. Under British rule, the colonial government had no formal policy on sport. At the 1920 Antwerp Olympic Games, the first-ever Indian Olympic contingent of six athletes was personally sponsored by Dorab Tata, chairman of the Tata Group and the first president of the Indian Olympic Association (IOA). Various royal houses with a long history of martial sports took an interest in organized sport and promoted the spread of sports like cricket and polo. This helped in the wider adoption of sport and the creation of basic institutions and systems.

In independent India, the state—somewhat reluctantly—took on the responsibility for leading sports policy and development. Despite hosting the First Asian Games in New Delhi in 1951, sport was—quite understandably—not high on the priority list for a young democracy and its government. Yet, the centralized planning system did make forays into building sports infrastructure and supporting national sports federations (NSFs) and national teams.

In a resource-starved environment, athletes like Ramanathan Krishnan, Prakash Padukone, P.T. Usha, Vijay Amritraj and Ramesh Krishnan made giant strides in individual disciplines. The Indian hockey team carried on its pre-Independence legacy through the first three decades of independent India. The Indian football team reached the semi-finals of the 1956 Olympics, ending fourth. For each sporting success, the government gave out minor cash awards, at best.

Athletes were given job opportunities through government-mandated sports recruitment drives by public sector undertakings. The Railways, the Services (representing the Indian Armed Forces), and the government-owned banks and oil marketing companies remain the largest employers of India's athletes to this day. Government-driven efforts like these were rudimentary, yet valuable, when there was little other support available.*

* Over the 1970s and 1980s, some private companies such as the Tatas, Nirlon, ACC and Mafatlal operated private teams and employed several prominent cricketers and footballers.

In the Indian Constitution, 'sports' was included as Entry 33 in the state list. Here, it was placed alongside theatre and dramatic performances, cinemas, entertainment and amusements. This meant that only state governments had the competence to legislate on matters relating to sports. Nonetheless, the Union Government began notifying guidelines and regulations for NSFs that were selecting Indian national teams. This was endorsed by the courts as an exercise of powers under various entries of the union list (such as Entries 10, 13 and 97) relating to foreign affairs, participation in international associations and bodies, and other residuary powers.

Today, the Department of Sports under the Sports Ministry bears the responsibility for establishing, regulating and monitoring India's institutional sports structures. Every state also has its own department of sports. In 1984, the Sports Ministry created the Sports Authority of India (SAI) as its field arm. It was tasked with broad-basing and promoting excellence in sports across the country through its multiple training centres and academic institutions.

The SAI runs academic programmes like coaching, physical education awareness programmes and talent development programmes. It also provides infrastructure, equipment, coaching facilities and competition exposure to athletes. Many states have similar sports authorities to play these roles at the state level. In recent years, the Union Government has built National Centres of Excellence, launched the Khelo India Scheme under which it hosts the Khelo India Youth Games and Khelo India University Games, set up dozens of Khelo India Centres across the country, and operated National Sports Talent Contests.

NSFs are recognized by the Sports Ministry and receive most of their funding from the government. The Sports Ministry recognition is undertaken on an annual basis, based on the criteria laid out in the Sports Code. The funding is through direct support to NSFs or funding towards the NSF's Annual

Calendar for Training and Competition. The degree and amount of funding can vary by sport.

In recent years, the Sports Ministry has also funded Olympic and Paralympic aspirant athletes directly through schemes such as the Target Olympic Podium Scheme, a more structured version of the National Sports Development Fund. This is done while keeping the NSFs informed and receiving their inputs on the process relating to athlete preparation and performance management.

Not all NSFs are equal; we frequently read about governance lapses and administrative high-handedness in many of these bodies. Almost all the NSFs have remained entirely reliant on Sports Ministry funding. This has limited both the organic and inorganic growth of the sports they govern. At least some of the challenges with Indian sport can be attributed to how the NSFs have functioned over the years.

In more recent decades, as the country awoke to the possibilities of sport, the Indian government has taken it upon itself to solve for and deliver most of the requirements of the sports system. This approach is a product of the stage of the nation's development, the public expectations that the state must deliver public goods, the prerogative of universal access and a general scepticism about the private sector and its profit motives.

In contrast, many mature sports ecosystems like the US, UK, Australia and countries in Europe have businesses, educational institutions, non-profits and private enterprises leading the sports movement while also helping the ecosystem achieve its broader objectives. The time is ripe for India to reconsider its heavily statist support structures for sport.

The opportunity

As we have seen in previous chapters, the governance of organized sport embodies elements of public functions. Openness, fairness, level playing fields and due process are important elements of such a role. Often, it is presumed that the state is best placed to exercise such functions, and the government has taken on the mantle of solving every problem in Indian sport, including those that should have fallen to the NSFs. Despite the country's economic progress after liberalization, it is unclear why this thinking has not been revised and the approach updated.

Infrastructure, talent identification, coaching, events, athlete development, rewards—all these are considered to be in the ambit of the government. While it may take these tasks seriously, state capacity, competing priorities and the opportunity cost of public funding will always be considerations in decision-making. These can limit the growth and sustainability of Indian sport.

Every public function need not be performed by the state alone. In fact, the state can often be less capable than private entities in terms of resource availability and programme delivery. The capacity of the state is always being called towards other priorities like health, education and urban and rural development. Each rupee spent on sport is a rupee not spent on something else. Public finance is also an expensive form of funding, with the costs of tax collection and tax administration raising the cost of such funds. Private enterprise can potentially bring talented people and new skills, innovation and efficient capital to sport. These can be luxuries that the state does not have in-house.

Here lies an opportunity for Indian sport. Indeed, the Indian state is uniquely positioned with respect to its ability to access and use land, public resources and public funds. The line between public and private enterprise is increasingly being blurred, and numerous private institutions and citizens take on public duties and carry out public functions. As the Supreme Court of India explained, the Board of Control for Cricket in India (BCCI) is a prime example: it is unique among Indian sports bodies insofar as it relies entirely on the private markets for its funding.

The growth of the private media industry in India provides an equally good example. After they stepped into what was a state monopoly, private operators now far outstrip state capacity in disseminating diverse sources of information to the public. This industry has developed under a self-regulatory model, with the state playing a limited role. The media industry may be broken in other ways, but it doesn't suffer from a lack of opportunity, imagination or potential.

Indian sport, too, can invite more producers and funders to the table. SGBs, businesses and social enterprises, including universities, schools, sports academies and sports clubs, can play key roles alongside Union, state and local governments in building public infrastructure, support structures, competitions and institutions.

The options

The American domestic sports system revolves around private professional sports leagues (some of which host their own, entirely domestic, 'World Series') and a thriving amateur college sport circuit under the banner of the National Collegiate Athletic Association (NCAA). The United States Olympic & Paralympic Committee (USOPC) is an independent body that was created by the Ted Stevens Act, a carefully structured law that details its obligations and the procedures it must follow.

The USOPC partners with, and raises multimillion-dollar sponsorships from, private enterprise. This frees it from reliance on government funding. Youth leagues, school sport and the NCAA system actively feed talent into the minor and major leagues. The government has little to do with running sport. The state is not entirely missing. Strong regulatory structures and effective enforcement mechanisms–including on matters such as corruption, consumer protection and safety–support these frameworks. Parks, open spaces and public sports infrastructure are abundant and maintained by municipal and local bodies.

On the other hand, Europe displays considerable variation in terms of national sports systems. VOCASPORT Research Group undertook a classification of the European national sports systems, using four parameters to place them in one of four buckets.[1] These four parameters included the role of public authorities, the level of coordination within the system, the roles of the voluntary, public and private sectors in the delivery of sporting provision, and the adaptability of the system to changes in demand.

Using these criteria, VOCASPORT categorized national systems as 'bureaucratic', 'entrepreneurial', 'missionary' and 'social'. In each of these, there is a varying degree of centralization and decentralization of power. In some, it is the government setting and controlling the agenda, while in others, the government plays more of a supporting role.

In Spain, Belgium and most Eastern European countries, public and governmental authorities are the primary drivers of the 'bureaucratic' model. Their regulatory role tends to be supported by a sports-specific legislative framework unilaterally imposed by the government on other actors. SGBs act through government delegation, and there is a limited role or opportunity for social partners, users, consumers and private entrepreneurs.

In contrast, the 'entrepreneurial' model found in the UK and Ireland relies on markets and the discipline they bring. Not only do private players find market solutions themselves, but the government also outsources the management of publicly owned facilities. Public authorities facilitate a framework that is oriented towards enabling market logic to express itself.

The 'missionary' model is found in countries like Germany, Austria, Italy, Denmark and Sweden. This is characterized by the dominant presence of SGBs enjoying a high degree of autonomy. They take on most of the responsibility for guiding sports policy.

Social partners have little presence, and users and private entrepreneurs act on the fringes of the federation-driven system.

The Netherlands is unique in purveying the 'social' model. This builds on the involvement of civil society through interactions with social partners such as trade unions, and on voluntary and commercial sector providers. Without a dominant player, this type of system relies on collaboration among public, voluntary and commercial players. Social sports clubs are known to play important roles in the Dutch sports system.

Although the Indian sports model does not fit neatly into any of these categories, it most closely tracks the 'bureaucratic' model. The BCCI stands alone in its financial independence from the government. It has built a thriving economy around cricket, including through a professional league structure in the form of the IPL. In that sense, cricket in India is a rare example of the 'missionary' approach in play, with the BCCI tapping private and social enterprise in the IPL and club cricket at the grassroots. Other professional leagues in various sports have been much less successful.

As we have seen in earlier chapters, while private leagues in these other sports might not have used effective business models, they have also faced regulatory limitations. The overarching sanctioning powers of SGBs when trying to recruit players, officials and infrastructure have given them limited freedom to operate and created a high-risk, low-reward environment. In multiple instances, the SGBs have used their sanctioning powers to outsource risk and costs to private operators but have been quick to intervene and try to expropriate the league at the first indication of success or profits.

As the growth of the private sports broadcasting, sponsorship and advertising markets have shown, the appetite for private investment in sport is high where a return on investment is possible. However, in sports other than cricket, the opportunities to participate are limited to the fringes of a centralized and government-driven system. With learnings from the 'entrepreneurial', 'missionary' and 'social' models, a range of avenues emerge for growth in scale, impact and diversity of outcomes. A hybrid model could borrow from these and contextualize them to Indian socio-economic conditions.

A handful of new leagues in sports like volleyball and basketball have begun challenging the existing paradigm, launching their initiatives without SGB sanction. With support from the competition law framework, these leagues can spur new ownership models, stronger incentive structures and stable professional avenues for athletes.

The system

Using a software analogy, in Indian non-cricket sport, there is only one developer—the government. It designs, develops and controls the operating system. It also codes all the applications that bring functionality. Why aren't other stakeholders writing the programmes and applications?

The operating system and all the applications that sit atop it can become outdated quickly in a single developer model. An absence of collaboration limits innovation and the expansion of opportunities. In all probability, this state of play is a product of circumstance, as detailed earlier in this chapter, rather than any deliberate attempt by the government to 'own' Indian sport. Other stakeholders have not found ways in which to contribute or participate. Even where private funding is at hand, it doesn't flow into the government and the SGBs. The trust factor is low. Will the money be used efficiently and honestly? Will the SGBs govern sport fairly? History has not thrown up too many case studies that would help us answer these questions in the affirmative. A low-trust environment risks stagnation.

It is time to proactively change this, while continuing to protect sport's values and spirit. In a reformed model, the state would open the sports pyramid to other developers by providing them interfaces, much like the application programming interfaces (APIs) of the software world. A participative model would give organizations and individuals ways (the said interfaces) to easily connect to the sports pyramid, and to make targeted and modular contributions to address the specific needs of the system. Organized sport would then have access to innovation, scale, pecuniary positive externalities, and self-motivated pools of people, resources and capital that were previously inaccessible.

To shepherd this change—and we will get to ways in which it can play out—the government must have a new mindset and develop different muscles. The state need not intervene in the sports ecosystem only in 'do' or 'fund' mode. It can also enable, make space for others and then 'regulate' and 'reward' them. It has the power to pass and enforce laws and regulations that are backed by the coercive power of the state and its institutions.

In the state's toolkit are potential regulatory instruments that allow it to get out of the way while enabling the 'public' function to be carried out by others. Once these are in place, there are also partnership models available to create opportunities for non-state actors to collaborate and contribute.

Regulator

To move from operational to regulatory mode, the government must be able to exercise broad oversight of the ecosystem. The current constitutional scheme that places sport squarely in the realm of the states can be limiting for information flows and coordination. There have been repeated calls to move sport to the concurrent list. This would give concurrent legislative capacity to the Union and state governments and enable a uniform and common national-level framework that could be implemented with local nuance.

The Constitution (61st Amendment) Bill, 1988 first made the recommendation, but it was withdrawn in 2009 due to a lack of consensus. The Draft Comprehensive Sports Policy, 2007 reiterated the need for sport to be moved to the concurrent list. However, this met the same fate and was withdrawn in 2015.

The sports framework remains scattered and needlessly heterogeneous in many aspects. As a simple example, an athlete who wins an Olympic medal is entitled to pre-declared cash awards from the Union and state governments, with the quantum of the latter depending on which state they are domiciled in. The amount might vary from tens of lakhs to many crores.

State sports budgets also vary widely. States like Odisha spend amounts comparable to the Union sports budget and take on national-scale sports projects like sponsoring the national hockey teams and hosting prominent international events. All this, while many other states do not even prioritize the sporting needs of local athletes. The need for a coordinated Union and state government framework is real, and such reform can enable a system that 'thinks nationally and acts locally'.

In its role as an enabling regulator, the state's first task is to bring greater accountability and transparency in the administration of SGBs at the national and state levels. Only a handful of the NSFs are professionally governed. The others face little consequences for lapses.

As a reminder, save for the BCCI, NSFs survive almost entirely on government funding. While the law limits the use of funding as a carrot or stick to intervene in governance, the government has not used this reality to refresh, or systematically enforce, the Sports Code. Accountability frameworks for SGBs have been driven primarily by judicial interventions based on public interest litigation driven by activists such as lawyer Rahul Mehra.[2] The government remains a—seemingly reluctant—respondent in these cases. A few recent cases have also asserted the importance of bringing governance reforms and standards down to the state and district levels. This is a clarion call that must not be ignored. It finally presents an opportunity for bottom-up change.

In a refreshed governance framework for SGBs at all levels of the pyramid, the focus can be on the responsibilities of these bodies as the flip side of respecting their autonomy. The private sector has expressed an interest and willingness to participate in the growth of the ecosystem. Private capital can be demanding. It will expect accountability and transparency from SGBs.

Budgets, utilization certificates, project reports and audited financials must be published and available for inspection.

Apart from the BCCI, Indian SGBs remain unattractive partners for private sponsors and donors. However, this is not a one-way street. With profit motive and private capital come new risks to the integrity of the sports movement. While welcoming private interests, moderating them is also a crucial role for sports governance. Without strong ethics codes and scrupulously implemented conflict of interest policies, we could go from the unused frying pan into the fire.

As mentioned earlier, implementing a carefully outlined competition law framework—as it applies to sport—can also lead change. Moderating the role of SGBs and their core regulatory functions involves decoupling these from their commercial activities. The natural monopoly in the regulatory function must be carefully protected while competition is promoted in the commercial sphere. This can focus the attention of SGBs and better define the exclusive powers they wield within the pyramid.

Delineating the extent of an SGB's regulatory powers also presents opportunities. One should not need the sanction of an SGB to hold an event that is not connected to the sports pyramid and does not attempt to send winning competitors upwards into superior competitions. This can create a permission-less environment for community, youth and social sport initiatives and competitions, thereby inviting civil society and private interventions and contributions.

Counter-intuitively, more self-driven initiatives outside the pyramid can strengthen the sports pyramid's role and core function by increasing participation rates and driving talent into the official funnel. We have already seen how state-level cricket leagues such as the Tamil Nadu Premier League have helped unearth talent that would have otherwise never had a chance to shine. Similar talent abounds across sports, waiting for platforms and opportunities for expression.

A maturing sports ecosystem might also need fundamental developmental interventions that businesses might not find attractive—at least not at first. Here, non-profit organizations, civil society initiatives and corporate social responsibility (CSR) programmes can contribute to creating the social infrastructure. Private philanthropy and corporate donations must be encouraged and enabled. A broadly framed and enabling CSR policy and tax credit structure can drive social change and impact through sport.

The current formulation of CSR in sport under the Companies Act, 2013 includes support for building and maintaining sports infrastructure and the training of athletes. CSR spending is mandatory for companies of a certain designated scale and profit. A regulatory environment that uses tax credits and incentives to promote and encourage CSR is likely to be more sustainable and effective in the long run than one that enforces corporate philanthropy. Just as the UK has used the public lottery for sport and culture funding, India must find its own innovative solutions.

The legal, regulatory and tax structures also determine how easy it is to begin and operate a venture and to organize or sponsor national as well as international events. Many aspects of a sports event require licences and government permissions, including holding matches (which might require security and public management), broadcasting (which may require licences to operate and carry live content), sponsorship (which involves foreign exchange flows), an intellectual property registration system that works efficiently and protects key rights, copyright and trademarks on which sports brands and sports content rely, tax breaks, the flow of people and equipment required temporarily for the event, and other similar aspects. Laws and policies that increase the 'ease of doing business' will naturally promote private enterprise and encourage entrepreneurship in sport and allied fields.

In each of these cases, the role of the state is to establish a regulatory environment that brings other players into the game through open access and incentives. It must simultaneously set and enforce standards and protocols that will reinforce the quasi-public nature and function of organized sport and the importance of maintaining its values. While this approach can unlock market forces and bring them into play for growth, the state needs to build capacity for its regulatory role and function.

The oversight, monitoring and enforcement of the regulatory environment requires skilled professionals of integrity and institutions that are adequately resourced, well-trained and make good decisions. This is a different type of muscle and needs a sophisticated understanding of the various interests and how they can be balanced.

There is private capital waiting on the sidelines of Indian sport. In the wings is also a cadre of professional talent that is ready and eager to add expertise to professional sports environments. Sport has the unique ability to attract passion-driven management talent that wants to make a difference. If you build it, they will come.

Partner

Across the country, we will have to deploy thousands of crores of rupees to build new sport infrastructure to respond to demand, and we must also maintain, update and renovate existing facilities to make them fit for use. Despite the government's best possible intent, expecting the state to deliver on these requirements puts immense pressure on an already stretched public exchequer.

Achieving this objective, therefore, needs the government to move beyond 'do' and 'fund' modes and to find new, effective and inclusive models of partnership with private enterprise. In infrastructure projects, this takes the form of public-private partnerships (PPP). The use of PPP models in India is quite common in infrastructure projects such as highways, tunnels, bridges and airports. The use of the model for building sports infrastructure has been limited, even though it has the potential to provide access to capital and scale that the ecosystem desperately needs.

How can PPP projects be structured to make them attractive for partners, and yet accountable to the public?

PPP models can differ significantly. In the US, many stadiums in which private franchises play their 'home games' are publicly funded. Cities and municipalities compete to host teams in the hope that the economic benefits will accrue to the locality and to businesses in the area. As league culture and broadcasting grow, stadium branding and naming rights are another area to unlock value. Across the US and the UK, businesses from across the spectrum have paid for naming and branding rights of prominent stadia and arenas. These include airlines like Etihad and Emirates, energy companies like Enron, financial services majors like Citi and Invesco, telecom companies like Vodafone, O2 and British Telecom, insurance companies like Allianz, soft drink brands like Pepsi and Minute Maid, computer software and hardware companies like Qualcomm, HP, Wanda, Monster and Dell, consumer goods companies like Wrigley, Heinz and Gillette, courier companies like FedEx and DHL and many more. What's in a name? Many million dollars, clearly.

In India, much of the leading sports infrastructure—including some of the best-known cricket stadia—have been built on public land rented on long lease or sold at subsidized rates. In certain cases, the construction has been funded by public authorities which continue to own the facilities. In other cases, SGBs might finance the facility and take over operating rights or even ownership. There are a few privately built sports infrastructure projects, but they are the exceptions. Most prominent stadia, old and new, are named and renamed after administrators or politicians.

The next phase of growth is likely to come from partnerships led by governments that bring land to new projects. They might also bring already built projects that need maintenance and operational support as their contribution to a partnership. Private enterprises can add funding and managerial expertise to such projects. For new projects, the government is likely to enter long-term design, build, finance and operate contracts. For existing projects, operating contracts would have private enterprises maintain and run the facility on specific terms.

In PPP projects, the private partners take on obligations and enjoy rights and concessions. In theory, these models are apt for sports infrastructure. They can align public and private incentives and provide commercial runway and control for private parties to realize returns on their investment. In reality, there are many potential points of failure when these projects are designed and executed.

There is a delicate balance between making these projects attractive to private investors and prioritizing the original intent of the project, i.e., public benefit. The governance mechanism must ensure transparent processes for the choice of partner and commercial terms. This includes a thorough check of credentials and expertise in executing projects. Commercial terms must be structured to ensure adequate private incentives but should not be skewed so as to be detrimental to the public.

Is the availability of the facility itself the public benefit? The case has often been made that the access to a high-quality facility and the ensuing economic development and growth around it are themselves the project's public contribution. While this is true to an extent, the mutual concessions and rights structure and the revenue-sharing obligation can ensure a fairer balance.

Price controls for certain categories of users or during certain times of day can be a part of the operating terms. For instance, the management of municipal swimming pools in Bengaluru is contracted out to private management agencies through a tender process. However, the terms of the contract require the pool operator to run public batches. During these hours, anyone willing to pay a fixed, nominal fee has access to the pool. Outside these hours, the pool operator has the freedom to operate. The operator can then be given relative freedom to test the market on pricing for other periods and through other means such as events, partnerships, rent from approved sub-leases, food and beverages, and retail.

Getting models like PPP to work effectively can be an iterative learning process. Managing partnerships requires time, care and attention. Governments must transact professionally and allow the legal and institutional structures to play their part in the trust-building process. To build confidence in the partnership mechanism, it will be important to prevent corruption and rent-seeking, respect the sanctity of the contract and facilitate independent dispute resolution. Just as we have seen with the private sports leagues and SGBs, fears must be allayed around the potential appropriation by the public sector of successful private projects that were just beginning to bear fruit. It is the same with concerns around the potential orphaning of unsuccessful ones. Meaningful change and strong partnerships demand time and patience on both sides. Not everything will work on the first go or will sustain itself without constant innovation.

As with the government in 'regulator' mode, the government in 'partner' mode requires managerial capacity. Perhaps even more importantly, it also needs changes in intent, behaviour and attitudes that reflect in transacting and governance protocols.

Together

We have all become used to the mindset that when it comes to organized sport, the buck stops with the Indian government. Its exercise of iron control is taken for granted. So is its responsibility to fix anything that goes wrong.

The transition from a bureaucratic, government-centric system to a collaborative one needs a change of mindset and of approach for all of us. This won't be easy. Yet, for a country of India's size and appetite, with a massive talent pool waiting to be tapped, it might be the only sustainable path ahead.

Here, a word of caution. Private capital and enterprise can assist growth. In theory, this will expand opportunity sets for everyone. In practice, markets can also be unforgiving and prop up inequality, reinforce privilege and exclude those already marginalized. Private players' profit motives can dilute the public function and social role of sport. New barriers to access can result. The transition must, therefore, be tracked with care and managed with caution.

Building at scale requires cohesion, shared common interests and awareness among the state, SGBs, civil society and private enterprise. Benefits can flow to the system, including greater investment and innovation, better facilities and more capacity. Long-standing gaps can be bridged, and initiatives can be scaled up in new and exciting ways. Every sports venue, new or old, should be buzzing with sporting activity every day of the year. It is an essential aspect of keeping Indian sport on track.

Sport can be an engine of social mobility and societal change, and this makes systematic growth models not only an opportunity but also a moral obligation. There is much to be gained from getting sport to work for everyone.

Faster, higher, stronger—together.

Chapter 20

On Legacy

Should India bid to host the Olympic Games?

Are the benefits of hosting the Olympic Games worth the expense? This is truly a multibillion-dollar question.

Some might see playing host to the Games as a statement, and an expression of soft power. It can put the host city and country on the global map. Events like the Olympic Games are also seen as distinctive opportunities to catalyse economies, improve public infrastructure, upgrade sports facilities and stimulate social development.

Once chosen as host to the Games, there is only one way to go—'all in'. The apparent public consensus to play host is used to make large and targeted investments with, arguably, less friction than otherwise might have been the case. These spends can conceivably be justified on various grounds—that the global profile and coverage can bring attention and opportunities; that direct economic benefits will come from increased tourism, hospitality, food and beverages, transportation, retail shopping and entertainment; and that the attention of the global community can convert into foreign investments, partnerships, jobs and local economic opportunities.

The host must put on its best face. It is encouraged to build or upgrade roads, airports and public transportation, and make other improvements to public infrastructure and urban facilities. Investments in Games-ready sports infrastructure will be made. These are expected to contribute to greater public access to world-class infrastructure, the nurturing of champions, and increased sports participation, activity levels and general health and wellness in the population.

Indirect and intangible benefits are also projected: for instance, a boost to the host city or country's image, more efficient local governance, and an improved sense of community and pride among citizens and residents.

All of this comes at a cost. Hosting a major sporting event is an expensive proposition. Submitting a bid itself involves significant expenditure—some estimates suggest that, on average, bidders for the 2012 Olympic Games spent nearly 200 million Euros each. The urban infrastructural changes and retrofitting of venues to event standards can also cost hundreds of millions of dollars. Cost overruns are a feature of every Olympic Games, only varying by degree. While the average cost of hosting the last eight editions of the Summer Olympic Games was approximately $9 billion, the last three editions in London, Rio and Tokyo averaged $15 billion in hosting cost.[1] In such a scenario, public funds are inevitably used to plug the gaps between expenditure and event revenue.

Not all countries will spend the estimated $220 billion that Qatar spent on and around the 2022 FIFA World Cup, but whatever the final bill, justifying the costs incurred is important for any host. This puts the focus on the legacy impact of the event, which includes both tangible and intangible elements.

While there is no agreed definition of what legacy means or includes, Chappelet and Junod describe an event's legacy as including sporting, urban, infrastructural, economic, social, environmental and political elements.[2] These could include improved public transportation, upgrades in telecommunications systems, Games villages that are converted into housing for students or lower-income families and local pride and positive sentiment among citizens of the host city and country.

Paying host

All the original BRICS countries except India have hosted either the Olympic Games or the FIFA World Cup in this millennium. India will likely be tempted to host such a mega sporting event to show it stands shoulder-to-shoulder with its peers. In October 2023, the Indian government expressed its intent to bid for the 2036 Olympic Games.

In the enthusiasm to host an event like the Olympic Games, the benefits can often be overstated and the true costs underplayed. A cost-to-revenue analysis of the hosting proposition is not a straightforward calculation. Spending comes in different forms and can be from both public and private sources. Public expenditure can be in the form of land grants, tax cuts, public lending at low-interest rates and other instruments. Private persons and entities may make investments they otherwise would not have made. On the other side of the balance sheet, tabulating revenues and returns is no easy task. Many of them are prospective and intangible.

Recent experience shows that, at the best of times, hosting the Games can put serious stress on the public exchequer. Except for Los Angeles 1984 and Barcelona 1992, virtually every Olympic Games (and FIFA World Cup) host over the last many decades has been left with a heavy debt burden. The citizens of Montreal continued to pay a special tax for four decades after hosting the 1976 Games to pay off the city's debt. Greek taxpayers bore the brunt of hosting the 2004 Athens Olympic

Games. The country faced a grave debt crisis, further deepened by the global financial crisis.

The prospect of economic growth is a popular driver of the decision to make a bid to host the Games. However, independent economic and social science research has demonstrated that massive public expenditures do not bring commensurate local economic and developmental benefits.

India's experience with hosting the 1982 Delhi Asian Games showed that many of the projected benefits that were used to justify the expenditure on the event did not actually fructify. The real economic benefits, such as increased foreign investments, did not meet pre-event projections. There was also little evidence of a bump in international tourism during the event or in its wake.

Also, not all event legacies are positive. While a major sporting event may attract new visitors, it may put off others who will avoid visiting an over-stressed and expensive location. For example, South Korea's tourism market shrank in the year it co-hosted the FIFA World Cup 2002. Local residents bear many hidden costs.

Hosting the event can also bring net negative goodwill. When the bright lights of the world shine on the host city and country, there is increased scrutiny and amplified media coverage. The hosting of the 2010 Commonwealth Games in New Delhi brought elements of both pride and embarrassment to India, with the construction delays and the corruption making international headlines. The report of the Comptroller and Auditor General of India found that the event cost India $4.1 billion instead of the $270 million initially estimated. Whether intentional or not, the under-budgeting of costs skews any possible cost-benefit analysis undertaken before the hosting decision is made.

Sports infrastructure is expensive to build. According to the World Stadium Index, it costs on average $269 million to build an Olympic main stadium. Venues like these are used for their original purpose only for a few days during the mega event. Once the Olympic Games are done, they can be expensive to maintain. Regular activity levels may be unable to make full use of such elite, high-capacity facilities. It can be difficult to adapt them to the daily training needs of athletes and smaller competitions and events. Without regular events in the venue, stadiums quickly become a financial burden and increase the legacy costs of the event. Many Olympic venues lie unexploited and abandoned soon after the Games, with Athens and Rio providing relatively recent examples.

More pertinently, an event like the Olympic Games is unlikely to create a long-lasting interest and a sports culture on its own steam. The indirect positive impact of hosting the Olympic Games on fitness, activity levels and health of the local population also tends to be overstated.

A core element of the London 2012 Olympic Games legacy was the commitment to increase participation in sport and levels of physical activity in the national population in the UK. This was to be supported by upgrading local facilities, protecting playing fields from development, training local sports leaders and encouraging 1,00,000 adults to try Olympic and Paralympic sports in a charity challenge. A few years after the Games, the evidence was inconclusive on whether these legacy initiatives had a positive impact on activity levels. There had been an increase in participation numbers immediately after the event, but these fell in the years that followed.[3]

Other studies have shown that significant differences can be observed between different socio-demographic groups, with the legacy effects tending to be localized within certain communities—close to where Olympic events are staged—and among particular segments of the population. Already marginalized groups did not gain the same legacy benefits from major sporting events.[4]

Major sporting events tend to have positive 'demonstration effects' on people who are already active, but the 'trickle-down' effects of inspiration do not necessarily have similar gains for others. In fact, sporting achievements at the Olympic Games can discourage the average person from physical activity due to the gap they perceive—and the Games demonstrate—between their level of ability and the capabilities of elite athletes. They remain spectators.

Besides underachievement on projected economic, sporting and health benefits, social costs and environmental damage are also common. Populations and communities—again, those already marginalized—are regularly displaced from the location of new sports venues and other infrastructure. Labour rights violations and other human rights compromises might occur during the construction of venues and other preparations for the event.

Rapid, unsustainable and unchecked development can also occur. The demands of the event can put stress on local administrations as well as the political class. This diverts focus from their primary responsibilities and can lead to governance dysfunction. Other important social schemes can end up deprioritized and underfunded. Sport-for-development programmes and community support undertaken in the host country before and during the Games can end up raising hopes without leaving a lasting mark. Particularly when an emerging economy is in the hot seat, the budgets get magnified and the local capabilities are limited. This increases costs all around. Lack of strong governance frameworks can also result in opportunities for rent-seeking and corruption. The most vulnerable sections of society often face the brunt of the negative impacts.

All told, deciding to host—or even bid for—the Olympic Games needs thoughtful analysis and public debate. This must involve a careful weighing of the costs, the revenues, the gaps, the societal, human rights and environmental impacts and the legacy benefits. The corruption scandals relating to multiple FIFA World Cup bids involving the top officials in the sport, the human rights challenges surrounding so many of the recent Olympic Games, Paralympic Games and FIFA Men's World Cup hosts (Brazil 2014 and 2016, Russia 2018, China 2008 and 2022 and Qatar 2022 come to mind), the ballooning costs of hosting the Olympic and Paralympic Games (ask Tokyo 2020, which faced enormous challenges with a postponed Games during a pandemic), and the large gaps between the projected legacy and the real impact (as we have seen with London 2012) show just how challenging it is to achieve a net positive outcome from pulling off an event like this, even one that appears to be successful.

The experience of other recent hosts provides a cautionary tale and lesson for India. From asking whether India is ready to host the Olympic Games, the question could well change to whether the Olympic Games and other mega sporting events are worth hosting at all.

Moving the needle

The Olympic Games hosting question prompts a deeper reckoning for Indian sport and its future. Intrinsically, sport can be about so much more than just large stadiums and glitzy events.

However, our focus on elite sport pursuits has positioned sport as a pursuit of the few on behalf of the many in the common consciousness. Athletes participating inside the sports pyramid are creator-suppliers, and everyone else outside the pyramid is a spectator-recipient.

Inspiration, learning, entertainment and even identity—these represent the vocabulary of engagement and the commodification of meaning. Major events like the Olympic Games shine a light on this binary. They celebrate the participants as the best of the species, with everyone else left to passively enjoy the afterglow, values and spirit of their performances. There are insiders and outsiders, and the twain shall meet only on carefully curated terms.

For reasons that are not immediately apparent, the health of Indian sport is measured solely by the national contingent's standing on medal tables at major events like the Olympic Games, Commonwealth Games and Asian Games. Over recent years, the government has been proactive in rewarding medal success with cash awards and national honours. While successes in these events remind us of the power of sport and give us joy and entertainment, they also give pause for thought. What is sport's role in our society? What is its potential? Can we do more with it?

Sport has more than just a single story to tell. It is intrinsically a 'quasi-public good', paid for by the collective and available for all members of society to enjoy. Theoretically, the sports pyramid is open to everyone—but only theoretically. Not only are the access gates controlled by private organizations, but sport is administered more like a 'club good'. All of us pay for it but only a few—those found to be deserving—can use the opportunities to progress and excel. Moreover, in this notion of the 'deserving' are embedded pre-existing privilege, unequal starting points and disparate access. There are other ways to administer and use sport in a more inclusive manner.

Globally, the 'sport-for-development' and 'sport for social impact' movements have used sport as a powerful instrument of socio-economic change for individuals, communities and regions. Sport has addressed issues such as inequality, social and economic exclusion, rehabilitation and community development, among many others. The movement is still nascent in India, and

The Private XI

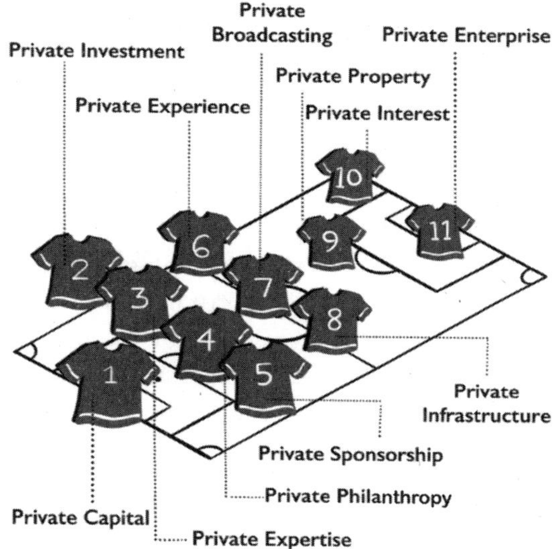

The Public XI

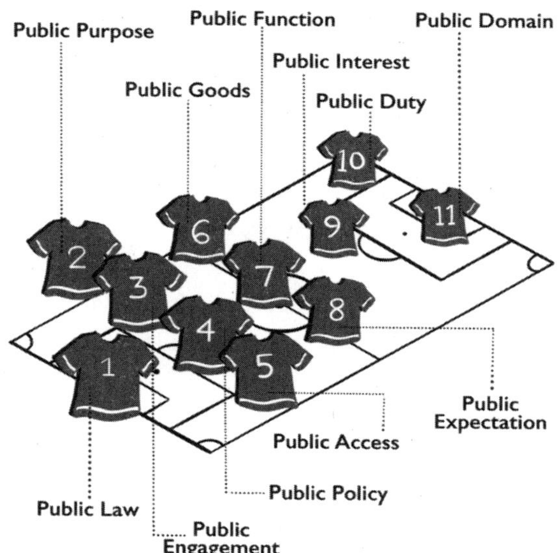

the country has an untapped opportunity to build on sport's inherent power.

Across the world, the winds of change are beginning to blow over the cultural commons called sport. It is a commons that must be opened up, tended to and cared for. Everyone can then enjoy it together. This needs new perspectives, activities and forms of regulation and oversight.

Can we enable every Indian to make their own meaning through sport, not just as spectator but also as participant? Acknowledging sport as a public cultural commons brings into focus the goals of universal access, universal participation and universal benefit. This trifecta—the goals of universal play—can drive a national agenda to make sports work for everyone. This can drive India forward across many dimensions, including health, productivity and comity, leaving a longer-lasting legacy than hosting an Olympic Games ever will.

Universal play

The goals of universal play make us take a closer and deeper look within our system. How widely are the benefits of sport enjoyed in the country? How do we address the existing fault lines limiting access to sport and physical activity for most of our population?

Every so often, we shine a spotlight on our successful elite athletes. Many have had challenging childhoods and have overcome obstacles along the way. Their victories bring public attention to their life stories, and they can often be put on a pedestal. They are presented as evidence that the system is working well, that it is not only allowing but also actively enabling the best talent to shine through.

However, these individual journeys are usually the product of the athlete's bloody-mindedness and their careful navigation of a faulty system. They can paint an overly rosy picture of the 'system'. It masks the reality that a vast swathe of the population will never experience sport, enjoy its benefits or explore their talents.

Aiming for universality makes the system undertake an honest assessment of the barriers to participation across various demographics. Mapping the status of access, adoption and activity data from across the country periodically can help us understand the state of play better. This will help us identify system gaps and enable the monitoring of progress and the success—or lack thereof—of initiatives that try to bridge access gaps.

Delivering universality of opportunity, experience and benefit also gives elite sport the chance to find its public purpose. Without it, the public expenditure on elite sport becomes difficult to justify beyond a point. With the goals of universal play as Indian sport's North Star, international success can play a supporting ambassadorial role in the campaigns for physical literacy, adequate physical activity and sport for all. As the gates of access open to a wider population, the talent pool of elite athletes also gets wider and deeper. Increasing opportunity sets within sport will generally have that result.

Ultimately, only an approach that encompasses the whole system can bridge the yawning gap between elite sport and universal play. When contemplating this, it is critical to recognize that mass participation is not just a by-product of elite sporting success. These are interdependent but different goals that might need conceptually similar and interconnected inputs but distinct approaches.

To build a sustainable, thriving ecosystem, we must look at a model that simultaneously focuses on the dual goals of elite success and mass participation. Continuing with the technology-systems analogy used in the previous chapter, this can be visualized in the form of a 'Sports Stack' with multiple distinct layers that form part of the ecosystem. The goals of excellence and universality can be achieved through concerted measures across the various layers that focus on serving these co-dependent goals. As we will see, each layer is critical to a self-sustaining and participative sports ecosystem. Much can be accomplished if every layer is monitored regularly and strengthened consistently.

Social wins

Sport can be used to drive physical activity levels and promote interactivity and teamwork among diverse groups. This can produce healthier, happier, more productive and well-rounded individuals and communities. Sport is a unique 'social glue' that can keep societies together. It needs public and private participation, supportive policy frameworks, regulation, and financial and human resources and capacity to come together. The quests for excellence, friendship and respect need not be one at the cost of another.

As we have seen with other hosts, it is unlikely that hosting the Olympic Games alone can lead to an increase in sports participation levels in a country. This must be independently driven by making infrastructure across the country accessible and responsive to local needs, integrating physical literacy into education systems, increasing availability of qualified coaches and trainers from community-level to high-performance, driving the spirit of volunteerism, providing access to equipment adapted to various needs, promoting social enterprises that work in communities, and implementing policy frameworks that bring all this together. Where there are other contributing factors in place, elite sport can play a part in promoting mass participation and increased activity levels.

The physical activity levels in India are concerning. The World Health Organization Physical Activity Profile of India in 2022 suggests that over 70 per cent of adolescents, 25 per cent of adult males and 44 per cent of adult females in the country do not get adequate physical activity.[5] With a large youth population, and also a rapidly ageing one, this has significant consequences on health, productivity and other outcomes.

One day, we may all be able to benefit from hosting the Olympic Games. But not quite yet. First, we must take measures to ensure that every child is playing and that our adult population is physically active—walking, yoga, cycling, dancing, it all counts. We have all heard of the 'trickle-down' effect from elite sport. How about putting in play a 'bubble-up' approach using the power of universal play?

Whether excellence or participation is the sporting objective, the basic inputs remain the same.

Physical infrastructure, equipment, coaching and knowledge resources are obvious needs. In addition, elite sporting achievement forms a library and resource for impact and legacy within the community. Through accurate documentation and thoughtful communication of achievements to new groups, the capabilities, potential, learnings and value of these can be increased manifold. The beauty of Olympic gold medals won by Abhinav Bindra and Neeraj Chopra, and Paralympic golds won by Avani Lekhara and Pramod Bhagat, is that Indians from across the socio-economic spectrum have people like themselves to emulate. We must provide young people with accessible ways to convert their interest into action.

As more Indians from more diverse backgrounds play, the base of athletes is broadened, and more benefits from sport will be enjoyed in ways that are meaningful to a wider range of participants. World-class athletes will almost certainly be produced in the bargain.

This social feedback loop allows for awareness, encouragement, enhancement and expansion of sport's imprint on society. A successful legacy impact also pushes more people to demand access to sport. This can increase demand and drive entrepreneurship in local markets. Academies, training camps and gyms begin to spring up. Businesses and social enterprises then have the incentive to find solutions that are responsive to the community's needs. Innovation and changemaking can ensue.

We must now expend much of our attention and resources on bringing every Indian to sport and physical activity as a way of life. The policy structure can target physical literacy and adequate physical activity with a concerted focus on ensuring inclusivity for under-represented segments of society. This must include a primary focus on addressing disadvantages faced due to gender, disability and other identities.

Sports that are easy to play with limited resources and equipment can be promoted. Football has shown us the power of simple formats—one ball is all it takes to bring the world together.

Removing barriers to access also requires a broader approach. It needs an investment in knowledge and information dissemination and policy frameworks that purvey inclusion and fairness. Developing human capacity creates more opportunities to sample and progress in sport, with a focus on the safety and sustainability of the sporting experience. Innovations—in technologies, development methodologies and business models—help keep the system dynamic, while accountable governance maintains the balance of the ecosystem. All these aspects play into the issue of participation in their own ways. This is not unlike the roles they play within organized sport in ways we have seen throughout this book. Here, the 'Sports Stack' approach demonstrates an integrated approach. Each layer matters, whether you are an Olympic or Paralympic athlete or someone just looking to make a start.

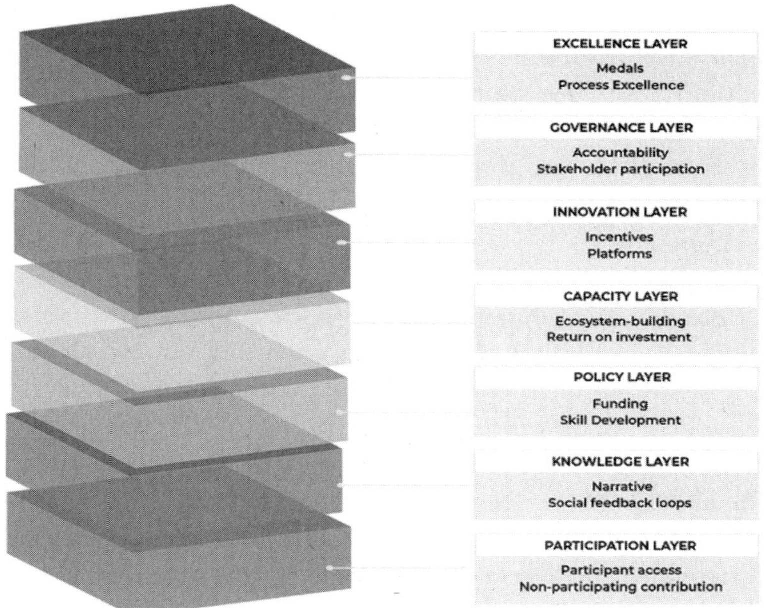

Being able to access opportunities and progress purely on the basis of one's talent can act as a significant incentive to participate. The inability to do so can be a barrier to starting or staying in sport. A progression pathway needs proactive knowledge dissemination about sport coupled with enabling policy frameworks. Funding models and institutional mechanisms must support athletes at different ages and stages of development, recognizing the diversity of their starting points. Skill development among coaches and facilitators and similar capacity-building initiatives address and support these needs as they arise.

Sport can be a source of livelihood for a diverse array of people. Sustaining athletes becomes vital for the ecosystem. If there are no social protections and risk mitigation tools, sports careers and upward mobility will be limited to a few. More broadly, sport survives on social licence and it is important that it continues to give more than it takes, from people and from the environment. Sport cannot afford to sit on the sidelines on the issue of climate change—it must find ways to lead. Urban and rural planning can support universal play by creating environments and systems that are inclusive, welcoming and promoting of physically active lifestyles.

Safety is an underappreciated barrier to access. Any risks to the physical and psychological safety of participants can also act as a significant disincentive to getting started. Stories of sexual abuse and assault of minors, toxic training environments and the like will put both young athletes and their parents on guard. The allegations of systemic sexual harassment in the Wrestling Federation of India made by elite wrestlers in 2023 reportedly led to an immediate drop in enrolment rates in the wrestling *akhadas* of Haryana.[6] Rights-based frameworks and sport safeguarding mechanisms can support participation rates as much as they do elite performance.

As we have seen in the previous chapter, innovation, entrepreneurship and collaboration are essential elements of the ecosystem. A dynamic ecosystem must remain open and welcoming to genuine contributors while protecting the core values of sport.

Of course, in all of this, governance has a major part to play. There will be many diverse interests that need a careful balancing act. Investing in governance infrastructure is a critical need for continued growth. Delivering on the promise of universality will require support, investments and thoughtful decision-making and these will bring the expectations of accountability and transparency.

With a strong 'Sports Stack' we can—and we must—get every child playing and every Indian physically active. It is a winning proposition for India.

Sports and society

The idea that sport can contribute to a society's growth and affect social change is not a new one. It dates all the way back to ancient Greece. Yet, in a country like India, sport has not been seen as a front-line instrument or approach for social development.

Much of the focus of this book is on institutional and rule-based frameworks for organized and elite sport. However, India's national sporting priorities do not necessarily have to remain in the realms of excellence, competition and performance alone. Using sport to improve the lives of one-sixth of humanity is as worthwhile a quest as any.

When people find ways to participate in sport and live active lives, they learn to create their own social meaning. Sport can contribute to the values of inclusion, empowerment and equality with its inherent tilt towards fair play, excellence, comity and respect. It also takes each participant through a journey that can result in personal growth and engaged citizenship.

Hosting the Olympic Games can be an emotive issue. In the case of the 1982 Delhi Asian Games, critics—and anyone else raising questions about the merits of hosting the event—were, reportedly, labelled as traitors.[7] When patriotic fervour cuts through more than red tape, it is difficult to use logic and data to make the best decision. Irreversible decisions can be made in haste in these situations.

Cold, hard analysis of costs and benefits should drive this decision. That there are public funds involved must be at the front and centre of the evaluation. Rather than benefit a small minority, their use must benefit society at large, or at least a large portion of it.

Once we set up the social and institutional infrastructure that can deliver the benefit of sport and physical activity to all Indians, we may be able to meaningfully host the Olympic Games. We may even find that we have achieved more meaningful goals by then. After all, achieving universal play would be a national accomplishment of Olympic proportions.

Awakening India to the full potential of sport and physical activity, and the role it can play in building a healthier, fitter, more productive, inclusive and empowered society, is a matter that affects us all. It is a project we must all get behind.

Ready, set, go!

After the Whistle

Growing up, I believed that there were only two types of people—those who start reading a newspaper from its last page, and everyone else. Earl Warren, the former Chief Justice of the United States of America, was clear that he belonged to the former tribe: 'I always turn to the sports pages first, which records people's accomplishments,' he famously said. 'The front page has nothing but man's failures.'

The last page of the newspaper had everything I needed to know. It told me stories I cared about, of history as it was being made. Every article and report revealed new possibilities. The scorecards and records called out to me like personalized invitations to new adventures. While playing representative cricket at the junior level, I took a few wickets here and scored a few centuries there. This meant that my name occasionally made it to the sports pages, extending the glow of success for another few days, the ego waiting to be punctured by the next low score. One article proclaimed that I was the 'Times Star of the Week'. It referred to me, my childhood idol Kapil Dev and the term 'all-rounder' all in the same sentence. It was surreal to share real estate on the sports page with my sporting heroes. After all those hours of solitary role-play in front of the mirror, there were now others watching me.

I made my way through the roller coaster of representative cricket, even captaining the Karnataka junior team. Then, the demands of studying law at the National Law School of India University seemed to have put paid to my dreams of playing first-class cricket. I did score a memorable century as our university team—representing 400 aspiring lawyers—found its first-ever success in the Inter-University tournament, beating a university that had tens of thousands of students.

Winning the Rhodes Scholarship seemed like a reward for my sporting pursuits of the past, as much as it was an endorsement of my academic achievements. This took me to Oxford, where I took out my kit again and was selected for the University of Oxford team. An unfortunate pre-season back injury in my first year dashed my hopes of playing the Varsity match against Cambridge, which would have been my first-class debut. My year at Harvard Law School exposed me to the professional world of US sport. I played in the local cricket league while working as a lawyer in California, making many friends along the way.

Eventually, the demands and realities of adulthood took over, and a life in the law became inevitable. But sport continued to fill its crevices. That was until my work as a lawyer started addressing the gaps that abounded in Indian sport. This turned my profession into a calling. I was a lawyer, yes, but I was consumed by sport again.

Time has not been kind to my binary classification of people by their newspaper-reading habits. Fewer folks I know read newspapers today, and I am not yet a crazy billionaire who owns a social media site that is tracking and profiling people's web browsing behaviour. Every so often, the sports news moves up in the newspaper, shaking the very foundation of my people-filter. Front-page stories have celebrated India's rare Olympic gold medals, a Thomas Cup win and a Cricket World Cup triumph.

Happily for the Indian sports fan, such stories involve Indian athletes and teams with increasing frequency. To balance the euphoria, front pages have also featured sports corruption, match-fixing, conflict of interest, controversy, Supreme Court cases and a rainbow of dramatis personae—administrators, ministers, bureaucrats, former athletes, judges and retired judges.

A relationship with sport can be deeply personal. It can also be much more. The essence of sport's role in society may not feature in the headlines. Sometimes, it is hidden in paragraph three or four. Most often, it is not written about at all. Away from the bright floodlights and the digitized scoreboards, however, it plays a role in mediating our experiences and shaping our world.

One of sport's special gifts is to give each of us a chance to reflect on who we are. What can we do with our bodies? What do we hold dear? How far will we go to get it? What are we capable of when we collaborate? What stands in our way?

Sport presents uncensored, unfiltered, even uncomfortable feedback. It gives us a chance to take a good, hard look at ourselves, as people, as societies and even as a species. Our best, our worst, our excesses, our shortcuts, our emotions, our manipulations—all there, intimately visible. Sport knows, and makes sure we know, too. Here, sport acts as a mirror. It tells it like it is.

We are all different but, wherever and however we live, we are also alike. How so? How much? With its universal vocabulary, sport helps us navigate our diverse worlds on our own terms. It allows us to educate ourselves, observe others' attitudes, skills, approaches and practices, and recognize our common interests, goals and sense of purpose.

Sport also gives us the chance to open ourselves up to others, to share, to be observed, to educate and to inspire. Geographies, accents, appearances, skills, rituals. A vocabulary of difference, using a common language. The world is one large, diverse but common playground, with each of us better off for it. Here, sport acts as a window. It allows us to look out into the world and expand our understanding. And, if we allow the world a look in, it gives us a chance to be seen.

Authenticity and integrity are about being real, true and fair. They are also about remaining open, receptive and responsive to evolution. Of ideas, opinions, habits, attitudes and behaviours. Sport shepherds us through change, sometimes gently and at other times not. In its quest for the same rules and level playing fields for everyone, competitive sport is forced to be on the front lines of some of the most complex social, political and economic issues of our times. On gender, ethics, safety, mental health, inclusion, independence, consent, diversity, representation, migration, worker rights, governance, disruptive businesses, monopolies, climate change and so much more. A concern of one of us is a challenge for all of us.

The sports movement confronts these challenges head-on, with a bias towards resolving them using experimentation, deliberation and balance. The autonomy enjoyed by the bodies that govern sport provides a degree of protection from the politics of the time and the differences in national legal systems and social contexts. In sport, fairness claims primacy as a filter, barometer and guide. Here, sport acts as a catalyst. It shows us that change is constant, inevitable and necessary for us all. By taking the reins, it helps us encounter, engage with and navigate the difficult conversations we must have and the decisions we must make.

Many might view sport as a marginal curiosity. Some describe it as a distraction and a meaningless, fabricated pursuit. This encourages them to sit on the sidelines rather than engage in the most heated debates in sport: on the governance of sport institutions, the fairness of rules, the inclusions and exclusions, the politicization, the corruption and the greed. As with any powerful agent, sport can be misused. It can divide us, it can provoke the worst in us. Enjoy sport or not, follow it or not, we are all influenced and impacted by decisions made in sport.

As sport continues to shape our globalized world, we cannot just wish away its relevance. We can all choose to care, to engage and to participate. More often than not, sport will make that investment worthwhile.

We should not, however, take for granted that sport will remain a force for good in our world. For sport to deliver on its social potential, it must be widely recognized for what it is—a quasi-public good and a cultural commons. This commons is controlled by an autonomous network of private organizations that often act like they own sport. We can place the public interest and fair play at the centre of sports governance only when we recognize that these governors are simply custodians and trustees of sport, acting on behalf of all of us.

While nothing is ever perfect, the quality of governance is a factor of the leadership, talent, diversity, intent and integrity of the people who make it happen. Yes, the independence and autonomy of SGBs must be vigorously protected from governments, political agendas and commercial capture, but we must also regularly monitor, appropriately limit and carefully regulate these bodies that control our sport.

Former Indian cricket captain Rahul Dravid had this to say when speaking of successful teams: 'It is like a pot of energy. You are either putting into the pot or taking away from the pot. You are in charge of the pot of energy and it's your responsibility what sort of environment you want to create. Everything that you say and do has a consequence on the team and on the people. At times, you need to take from the pot. If you filled up the pot with energy when you have the opportunity, when you have a tough time you have that energy to fall back on.'

This is the language of the 'commons'. We all gain from the pot of energy that is sport. For it to serve us all, we need to constantly replenish it. In the good times and in times of change and growth, its essence must be protected. Then, in times of need, it will be able to give back. On the other hand, a depleted pot cannot serve us all, and an empty one can serve no one—not even its minders.

Is Mr India a sportsman? Should chess tournaments be segregated by gender? Should M.S. Dhoni be able to patent his helicopter shot? Can Anwar Ali play football for India? Why is sports betting illegal? Which types of injury does an athlete consent to in the course of play? Is there a right to watch cricket for free? Should athletes be able to control all uses of their personal data? Should India bid to host the Olympic Games? This book has waded through these, and other, seemingly random questions. In the answers lie common themes that reveal the purpose of sport, the meaning of fair play, the choices we make, how we see ourselves and each other, the way we organize our affairs and the type of world we want to create.

More than half of humanity tunes in to the football World Cup. For some minutes, distance, time difference, nationality, allegiance, all fade into irrelevance. In today's world, what else can give us anything like that?

Organized sport is one of the few remaining global projects. It is designed to contribute to our societies and our world. Delivering on that promise isn't always simple. It needs a careful balancing of various interests—private and public, individual and communitarian—and a unique combination of freedoms, constraints, concessions and protections.

Time, interest, attention and care. When we give these to sport, sport will always give back.

Reflection, learning, change.

That's sport.

Acknowledgements

Numerous games of Uno and Scrabble, movie nights and dinners were missed during the writing of this book. Now that it's done, there are at least as many people I owe apologies to as I must thank. In the interests of brevity, I'll stick to the acknowledgements here.

I owe a massive debt of gratitude to my colleagues R. Seshank Shekar and Shubham Jain for their tireless and matchless research assistance throughout. My thanks also to my former colleague and visual communicator Kruthika N.S. for illustrating the cartoons that pepper—and spice up—the chapters.

When I mooted the idea of this book, there was one person who believed in it more than I did. Fortunately, this turned out to be my editor, Karthik Venkatesh, at Penguin Random House. He saw something in it when I had little to show, and his confidence and guidance have shaped this book in ways tangible and intangible.

Working through this book gave me the privilege of many wonderful conversations with the inimitable Prem Panicker. From these, I gained not only insight and inspiration on the art of writing but also a valued friend and mentor. Similarly, my colleague and friend Desh Gaurav Sekhri was the best sounding board I could have hoped for, reading every word as I wrote, and providing sharp perspective and moral support.

Ramachandra Guha, Sharda Ugra, Joy Bhattacharjya and Rahul Dravid were generous with their time, providing valuable feedback and sharing thoughtful blurbs. Their warmth and candour are reflections of their life's work.

If you need proof that close friends can be bullied into just about anything, Clinton Free, Jiti Nichani, Abishek Laxminarayan and Janak Nabar stand as fine examples, all of them subjected, as they were, to my first draft.

My partner Sandhya and our two young children have always been the source of love, encouragement and forbearance. Our dog provided a golden warmth as she sat at my feet as I wrote, going from puppy to full-grown retriever between my first draft and final manuscript. Family makes everything worth it.

My work has relied on the support, contributions and resources of many people, and I am destined to fail at any attempt to credit them all. My parents, teachers, coaches, referees, teammates, opponents, classmates, authors, researchers, colleagues, clients, athletes and others have added to the richness of my experiences, feeding my curiosity and my interests. Indeed, no dream is ever chased alone, and mine is no exception.

Finally, I would like to send thanks—in advance—to everyone who reads this book and engages with its ideas. I am grateful for the gift of your interest and attention.

Table of Cases

- *Anamika v. State of Kerala and Ors.*—2022 SCC OnLine Ker 3882
- *Anwar Ali v. All India Football Federation and Anr.*—W.P.(C) 7359/2020 (Delhi High Court)
- *Amit Chaudhary v. State of Uttar Pradesh*—1999 All LJ 2617
- *Board of Control for Cricket in India v. Cricket Association of Bihar and Ors.*—(2016) 8 SCC 535
- *Board of Control for Cricket in India v. Yash Sehrawat and Anr.*—(2014) 2 AIR Del R 530
- *Citizen, Consumer and Civic Action Group and Anr. v. Prasar Bharati and Ors.*—(2006) 5 CompLJ 74 Mad
- *Department of Sports v. Athletics Federation of India (AFI)*—Case 1/2015, CCI (order dated 12 July 2018)/[2016] CCI 18
- *Dhanraj Pillay v. Hockey India*—Case 73/2011, CCI (order dated 31 May 2013)/[2013] CCI 35
- *Dr. K.R. Lakshmanan v. State of Tamil Nadu*—(1996) 2 SCC 226
- *Dr. Subramanian Swamy v. Board of Control for Cricket in India*—W.P. (Civil) No.645/2017 in the Hon'ble Supreme Court of India
- *Dutee Chand v. AFI & IAAF*—CAS/ 2014/A/3759
- *ESPN Star Sports v. Global Broadcast News Ltd.*—(2008) 38 PTC 47 (DB)

- *Geeta Rani v. Union of India*–(2019) 2 CWC 6
- *Gundel v. FEI*–CAS 92/A/63
- *Gundel v. FEI*, Arrêt du tribunal fédéral suisse 4P_217/1992
- *Hemant Sharma and others v. All India Chess Federation (AICF)*–Case 79/2011, CCI (order dated 12 July 2018)
- *Henriques et al. v. IOC and IAAF*–CAS 2019/A/6225
- *ICC Development (International) and Anr. v. New Delhi Television Ltd.*–2012 (193) DLT 279
- *Indian Olympic Association v. Veeresh Malik*–ILR (2010) 4 Del 1
- *Infinity Optimal Solutions Pvt. Ltd. v. Vijender Singh*–IA No. 12369 of 2009 in CS(OS) 1807/2009 (Delhi HC)
- *Institute for Inner Studies v. Charlotte Anderson*–(2014) 57 PTC 228
- *Justice K.S. Puttaswamy (Retd.) and Anr. v. Union of India & Ors.*–AIR 2017 SC 4161
- *Justice K.S. Puttaswamy and Anr. vs. Union of India (UOI) and Ors.*–(2019) 1 SCC 1
- *K. Balaji Iyengar v. State of Kerala*–Crl.M.C. No. 2726 of 2009 (Kerala HC)
- *Lokniti Foundation v. Union of India*–(2017) 7 SCC 155
- *Media Works NZ Ltd. and Anr v. Sky Television Network Ltd.*–HC Auckland CIV 2007-404-5674
- *Mohammed Azharuddin v. The Board of Control for Cricket in India*–2004 AIHC 1276
- *Mutu and Pechstein v. Switzerland*–ECtHR, Applications nos. 400575/10 and 67474/10, judgment of 2 October 2018
- *N. Chandrasekar v. The Tamil Nadu Cricket Association and Ors.*–(2006) 3 Mad LJ 846
- *Narinder Batra v. Union of India*–ILR (2009) 4 Del 280
- *Naz Foundation v. Government of NCT*–160 DLT 277
- *NBA v. Motorola, Inc.*–105 F.3d 841 (2d Cir. 1997)

- *New Delhi Television Ltd. v. ICC Development (International) Ltd.*—FAO (OS) 460/2012
- *Nike India Pvt. Ltd. v. Virat Kohli*—Miscellaneous First Appeal 7088/2013 (CPC) (Karnataka HC)
- *Pan India Infraprojects Private Limited v. Board of Control for Cricket in India*—Case 91/2013, CCI (order dated 1 June 2018)/ [2014] CCI 15
- *Percept D'Mark (India) Pvt. Ltd v. Zaheer Khan*—(2006) 4 SCC 227
- *Percept Talent Management Pvt. Ltd. v. Yuvraj Singh and Globosport India Pvt. Ltd.*—(2008) 2 Bom CR 654
- *Prasar Bharati v. Sahara TV Network Pvt. Ltd. and Ors.*—2006 (32) PTC 235 (Del)
- *Rahul Mehra and Anr. v. Union of India and Ors.*—(2004) 114 DLT 323 (DB)
- *Rahul Mehra v. Union of India and Ors.*—W.P.(C) 195/2010 (Delhi High Court)
- *S. Nithya v. The Secretary to the Union of India The Ministry of Youth Affairs and Sports*, Writ Petition No. 3447 of 2019 and WMP No. 3745 of 2019
- *Semenya v. Switzerland*—Application no. 10934/21 (ECtHR)
- *Shravan Yadav and Other Informants. v. Volleyball Federation of India (VFI)*—Case 1/2019, CCI (order dated 7 August 2019)
- *State of Andhra Pradesh v. K. Satyanarayana and Ors.*—1968 AIR 825
- *Surinder Singh Barmi v. The Board of Control for Cricket in India (BCCI)*—Case 61/2010, CCI (order dated 29 November 2017)
- *Sushil Kumar v. Union of India*—2016 SCC OnLine Del 3660
- *The Animal Welfare Board of India v. Union of India*—Writ Petition (Civil) No. 23 of 2016 in the Hon'ble Supreme Court of India
- *The Secretary, Ministry of Information and Broadcasting v. Cricket Association of Bengal*—1995 AIR 1236

- *Tony Greig v. Insole*–[1978] 1 WLR 302
- *Varun Gumber v. Union Territory of Chandigarh*–2017 Cri LJ 3827
- *Zee Telefilms Ltd. and Anr. v. Union Of India and Ors.*–(2005) 4 SCC 649

www.boundarylab.plus

Visit this website if you'd like to read deeper on the themes of this book, keep up with the latest developments, ask a question or two, provide your feedback or just say hello.

Notes

Chapter 1: On Meaning

1 *Amit Chaudhary v. State of Uttar Pradesh*, 1999 All LJ 2617.
2 A timeline of Pickleball's history is available here: https://usapickleball.org/what-is-pickleball/history-of-the-game/, last accessed 13 May 2023.
3 Aishwarya Kumar, 'The Grandmaster Diet: How to Lose Weight While Barely Moving', https://www.espn.in/espn/story/_/id/27593253/why-grandmasters-magnus-carlsen-fabiano-caruana-lose-weight-playing-chess, last accessed May 13, 2023.
4 'Sport Accord', https://wikichiro.org/en/index.php/Sport_Accord, last accessed 13 May 2023.
5 'The Olympic Programme Evolution', https://library.olympics.com/Default/doc/SYRACUSE/174657/the-olympic-programme-evolution-the-olympic-studies-centre, last accessed 13 May 2023.
6 1999 All LJ 2617.

Chapter 2: On Change

1 Lawrence Lessig, *Code: And Other Laws of Cyberspace*, Basic Books, 1999.
2 *See*: 'Pathetic Dot Theory', https://en.wikipedia.org/wiki/Pathetic_dot_theory, last accessed 20 May 2023.
3 Andrew Jordan, 'National Playing Styles', https://sites.duke.edu/wcwp/tournament-guides/olympic-football-2016-guide/team-playing-styles-in-soccer/, last accessed 18 May 2023.

4 'Classification Table for Types of Goods', https://www.econport.org/content/handbook/commonpool/cprtable.html, last accessed 20 May 2023.

Chapter 3: On Autonomy

1 Anil Kumar, 'Denied Free IPL Passes, Bangalore's Civic Body Refuses to Clear Stadium Garbage', https://timesofindia.indiatimes.com/city/bengaluru/denied-free-ipl-passes-bangalores-civic-body-refuses-to-clear-stadium-garbage/articleshow/12605616.cms, last accessed 29 May 2023.

2 '47% Presidents in Indian Sports Federations Are Politicians', https://thebridge.in/law-in-sports/indian-politicians-presidents/, last accessed 25 May 2023.

3 *See*: 'Olympic and Sports Movement Discuss "Basic Universal Principles of Good Governance"', https://olympics.com/ioc/news/olympic-and-sports-movement-discuss-basic-universal-principles-of-good-governance, last accessed 25 May 2023.

4 ILR (2009) 4 Del 280.

5 W.P.(C) 195/2010 (Delhi High Court).

6 'Final Executive Board Meeting of 2012 Gets under Way in Lausanne', https://olympics.com/ioc/news/final-executive-board-meeting-of-2012-gets-under-way-in-lausanne, last accessed 25 May 2023.

7 'IOC Executive Board Lifts Suspension of NOC of India', https://olympics.com/ioc/news/ioc-executive-board-lifts-suspension-of-noc-of-india, last accessed 25 May 2023.

8 *See*: '"Abused His Position", CoA Moves SC Seeking Contempt against Praful Patel in AIFF Case', https://economictimes.indiatimes.com/news/india/abused-his-position-coa-moves-sc-seeking-contempt-against-praful-patel-in-aiff-case/articleshow/93470589.cms, last accessed 25 May 2023; *also see*: Contempt Petition in Special Leave Petition No. 30748-30749/ 2017, https://www.the-aiff.com/media/uploads/2022/08/220810-FINAL-FILED-contempt-petition_compressed-1.pdf, last accessed 25 May 2023.

9 'FIFA Suspends All India Football Federation', https://www.fifa.com/about-fifa/associations/media-releases/fifa-suspends-all-india-football-federation, last accessed 25 May 2023.

10 'FIFA Lifts Suspension; U-17 Women's World Cup as Scheduled', https://www.the-aiff.com/article/fifa-lifts-suspension-under-17-womens-world-cup-as-scheduled, last accessed 25 May 2023.

11 'Gokulam Kerala out of AFC Women's Club Championship due to FIFA ban', https://olympics.com/en/news/gokulam-kerala-afc-women-club-championship-2022-indian-football-ban, last accessed 25 May 2023.

12 'Politicians + Sport = Power, Patronage, Perks', https://www.hindustantimes.com/india/politicians-sport-power-patronage-perks/story-YFINksHji3pAioA77q5x8N.html, last accessed 25 May 2023.

13 Shivnarayan Rajpurohit, 'Fair Game? What Political Control of India's Sports Federations Tells Us', https://www.newslaundry.com/2023/02/09/fair-game-what-political-control-of-indias-sports-federations-tells-us, last accessed 25 May 2023.

Chapter 4: On Balance

1 Annexure XIII, National Sports Development Code of India, 2011.

2 Article 14.5 of the Memorandum and Rules and Regulation of the Indian Olympic Association (as amended up to 2 November 2022).

3 'Nine FIFA Officials and Five Corporate Executives Indicted for Racketeering Conspiracy and Corruption', https://www.justice.gov/opa/pr/nine-fifa-officials-and-five-corporate-executives-indicted-racketeering-conspiracy-and, last accessed 30 May 2023.

4 Crl. M.C. No. 2726 of 2009 (Kerala HC).

Chapter 5: On Reform

1 (2004) 114 DLT 323 (DB).

2 *See*, for instance, *Zee Telefilms Ltd. and Anr. v. Union Of India and Ors.*, (2005) 4 SCC 649.

3 'Ministers Resist; Sports Bill Denied Cabinet Nod', https://www.moneylife.in/article/ministers-resist-sports-bill-denied-cabinet-nod/19366.html, last accessed 10 May 2023; 'All Smoke and No Fire as Cabinet Rejects National Sports Bill', https://bangaloremirror.indiatimes.com/sports/all-smoke-and-no-fire-as-cabinet-rejects-national-sports-bill/articleshow/21526098.cms, last accessed 10 May 2023.

4 'Full Text of Delhi Police Statement on the Arrests', https://www.espncricinfo.com/story/full-text-of-delhi-police-statement-on-the-arrests-636279, last accessed 15 May 2023.

5 'Gurunath Meiyappan Arrested in Mumbai', https://www.espncricinfo.com/story/gurunath-meiyappan-arrested-in-mumbai-637612, last accessed 15 May 2023; 'Gurunath Named in Betting Chargesheet', https://www.espncricinfo.com/story/gurunath-meiyappan-named-in-betting-chargesheet-673261, last accessed 15 May 2023.

6 'Raj Kundra Has Admitted to Betting on Rajasthan Royals: Delhi Police', https://economictimes.indiatimes.com/raj-kundra-has-admitted-to-betting-on-rajasthan-royals-delhi-police/articleshow/20468054.cms, last accessed 15 May 2023.

7 'BCCI Probe Finds Four Players Guilty of Match-Fixing', https://www.espncricinfo.com/story/bcci-probe-finds-four-players-guilty-of-match-fixing-670975, last accessed 15 May 2023.

8 Nagraj Gollapudi, 'Supreme Court Sets Aside Life Ban on Sreesanth in IPL Spot-Fixing Case', https://www.espncricinfo.com/story/supreme-court-sets-aside-life-ban-on-sreesanth-in-ipl-spot-fixing-case-1178181, last accessed 15 May 2023.

9 Nagraj Gollapudi, 'Sreesanth's Ban Reduced to Seven Years, to End in September 2020', https://www.espncricinfo.com/ story/sreesanth-s-ban-reduced-to-seven-years-to-end-in-september-2020-1198130, last accessed 15 May 2023.

10 'IPL Spot-Fixing Scandal: Meiyappan, Kundra Get Clean Chit; Srinivasan May Return as BCCI Chief', https://economictimes.

indiatimes.com/news/politics-and-nation/ipl-spot-fixing-scandal-meiyappan-kundra-get-clean-chit-srinivasan-may-return-as-bcci-chief/articleshow/21425875.cms, last accessed 15 May 2023; Mudgal Committee Report—full text: https://static.espncricinfo.com/db/DOWNLOAD/100/0127/JUSTICE_MUDGAL_IPL_PROBE_COMMITTEE_REPORT_final_feb_9.pdf, last accessed 15 May 2023.

11 'BCCI's Probe Panel "Illegal", Says Bombay High Court', https://www.espncricinfo.com/story/bcci-s-probe-panel-illegal-rules-bombay-high-court-656499, last accessed 15 May 2023.

12 'Court Strikes Down Controversial BCCI Clause', https://www.espncricinfo.com/story/court-strikes-down-controversial-bcci-clause-823061, last accessed 15 May 2023.

13 Civil Appeal No. 4235 of 2014 in the Hon'ble Supreme Court of India.

14 'Charges against Gurunath Proved—IPL Probe Report', https://www.espncricinfo.com/story/charges-against-gurunath-proved-ipl-probe-report-717807, last accessed 15 May 2023.

15 'New Panel to Take Call On Kundra, Meiyappan', https://www.espncricinfo.com/story/new-panel-to-take-call-on-kundra-meiyappan-823067, last accessed 15 May 2023.

16 Order of the Hon'ble Supreme Court of India dated 22 January 2015 in, inter alia, *Board of Control for Cricket in India v. Cricket Association of Bihar*, Civil Appeal No. 4235 of 2014.

17 Order dated 14 July 2015, https://lodhacommittee.files.wordpress.com/2015/12/final-bcci-opinion-final-14-07-2015.doc, last accessed 15 May 2023.

18 Nagraj Gollapudi, 'Board Panel Has 82 Questions for BCCI Bosses', https://www.espncricinfo.com/story/board-panel-has-82-questions-for-bcci-bosses-861321, last accessed 15 May 2023.

19 Nagraj Gollapudi, 'BCCI Counter-Affidavit Details Reservations on Lodha Report', https://www.espncricinfo.com/india/content/story/977909.html, last accessed 15 May 2023.

20 Order of the Hon'ble Supreme Court of India dated 18 July 2016 in *Board of Control for Cricket in India v. Cricket Association of Bihar*, Civil Appeal No. 4235 of 2014.

21 'Where the BCCI Stands on Major Lodha Reforms', https://www.espncricinfo.com/story/where-the-bcci-stands-on-key-lodha-reforms-1111712, last accessed 15 May 2023.

22 'Supreme Court Removes Thakur, Shirke from Top BCCI Posts', https://www.espncricinfo.com/story/supreme-court-removes-anurag-thakur-ajay-shirke-from-top-bcci-posts-1075059, last accessed 15 May 2023.

23 Nagraj Gollapudi, 'Supreme Court Names Administrators to Supervise BCCI', https://www.espncricinfo.com/story/supreme-court-names-administrators-to-supervise-bcci-1080252, last accessed 15 May 2023.

24 Nagraj Gollapudi, 'Supreme Court Aims to Get to the Bottom of Thakur-ICC Letter Issue', https://www.espncricinfo.com/story/supreme-court-aims-to-get-to-the-bottom-of-thakur-icc-letter-issue-1062708, last accessed 15 May 2023.

25 (2005) 4 SCC 649.

26 Eleventh Status Report dated 14 October 2019 submitted by the Supreme Court-Appointed Committee of Administrators, available at https://documents.bcci.tv, last accessed 15 May 2023.

27 It is noteworthy that, in August 2023, this process appears to have commenced in the Hyderabad Cricket Association under the supervision of (Retd.) Justice L. Nageswara Rao, who was one of the members of the Justice Mudgal Probe Panel—*see*, Qaisar Mohammad Ali, 'Shakeup at Hyderabad Cricket Association: Justice Rao Bars Officials of 57 Clubs from Contesting, Voting in Upcoming Elections', https://thesouthfirst.com/telangana/shakeup-at-hyderabad-cricket-association-justice-rao-bars-officials-of-57-clubs-from-contesting-voting-in-upcoming-elections/, last accessed 15 August 2023.

28 G. Viswanath, 'BCCI Election Not Held in Spirit of Reforms and Legal Structure We Suggested: Justice Lodha', https://www.thehindu.com/sport/cricket/bcci-election-not-held-in-spirit-of-reforms-and-legal-structure-we-suggested-justice-lodha/article61976125.ece, last accessed 15 May 2023.

29 Nagraj Gollapudi, 'BCCI Plans Sweeping Changes, Lodha Reforms under Threat', https://www.espncricinfo.com/story/bcci-plans-sweeping-changes-lodha-reforms-under-threat-1206246, last accessed 15 May 2023.

30 Nagraj Gollapudi, 'Sourav Ganguly, Jay Shah Term Extension: BCCI Moves Supreme Court Again', https://www.espncricinfo.com/story/sourav-ganguly-jay-shah-term-extension-bcci-moves-supreme-court-again-1223579, last accessed 15 May 2023.

31 Order of the Hon'ble Supreme Court of India dated 14 September 2022 in *Board of Control for Cricket in India v. Cricket Association of Bihar*, Civil Appeal No. 4235 of 2014.

32 Nagraj Gollapudi, 'Reform Rollback—What the Supreme Court Judgment Means for the BCCI', https://www.espncricinfo.com/story/indian-cricket-what-the-supreme-court-judgment-means-for-the-bcci-sourav-ganguly-and-jay-shah-1335253, last accessed 15 May 2023.

33 Vijay Tagore, 'Delhi Excise Scam Accused Sarath Chandra Reddy Re-Elected Andhra Cricket President', https://www.cricbuzz.com/cricket-news/124561/delhi-excise-scam-accused-sarath-chandra-reddy-elected-andhra-cricket-president-cricbuzzcom, last accessed 15 May 2023.

34 Sandeep Dwivedi, 'BCCI Was Waiting for Weather to Change, Says Reform Panel Head Lodha', https://indianexpress.com/article/sports/cricket/bcci-was-waiting-for-weather-to-change-says-reform-panel-head-lodha-8151745/, last accessed 1 June 2023.

Chapter 6: On Difference

1 Anne Maass, et al., 'Checkmate? The Role of Gender Stereotypes in the Ultimate Intellectual Sport', *European Journal of Social Psychology*, Vol. 38 (2), March/April 2008, 231–245.

2 Ibid.

3 *Dutee Chand v. AFI & IAAF*, CAS/2014/A/3759.

4 S. Bermon and P-Y. Garnier, 'Serum Androgen Levels and Their Relation to Performance in Track and Field: Mass Spectrometry Results from 2127 Observations in Male and Female Elite Athletes', *Br J Sports Med* 2017; 51:1309–14.

5 'Correction: Serum Androgen Levels and Their Relation to Performance in Track and Field: Mass Spectrometry Results from 2127 Observations in Male and Female Elite Athletes', http://dx.doi.org/10.1136/bjsports-2017-097792corr1; Jere Longman, 'Scientists Correct Study That Limited Some Female Runners', https://www.nytimes.com/2021/08/18/sports/olympics/intersex-athletes-olympics.html, last accessed 20 May 2023.
6 Application no. 10934/21.
7 2022 SCC OnLine Ker 3882.
8 'World Aquatics to Debut "Open Category" Races for Transgender Swimmers in Berlin', https://abcnews.go.com/Sports/wireStory/world-aquatics-debut-open-category-races-transgender-swimmers-102304357, last accessed 17 August 2023.
9 'FIDE Regulations on Transgender Chess Players' Registration on FIDE Directory', https://doc.fide.com/docs/DOC/2FC2023/CM2_2023_45.pdf, last accessed 20 August 2023.

Chapter 7: On Integrity

1 'London 2012: Four Pairs Disqualified', https://olympics.bwfbadminton.com/news-single/2012/08/01/london-2012-four-pairs-have-been-disqualified, last accessed 3 June 2023.
2 'Badminton-Disgraced Korean Shuttlers Have Domestic Bans Lifted', https://www.reuters.com/article/badminton-korea-bans-idUSL4E8K61CX20120906, last accessed 3 June 2023.
3 (2014) 2 AIR Del R 530.
4 (2017) 7 SCC 155.
5 'U-19 World Cup Hero Manjot Kalra Suspended for 1 Year from Ranji Trophy for "Age-Fraud"', http://timesofindia.indiatimes.com/articleshow/73060584.cms, last accessed 15 May 2023.
6 Ava Wallace and Emily Giambalvo, 'A Timeline of Russia's State-Sponsored Olympic Doping Scandal', https://www.washingtonpost.com/sports/olympics/2022/02/11/russia-olympics-doping-scandal/, last accessed 5 June 2023.
7 Siddarth Ravindran, 'A Decade's Worth of Scandal', https://www.espncricinfo.com/story/10-years-after-cronje-a-timeline-of-match-fixing-in-the-2000s-464111, last accessed 20 May 2023.

8 Dhananjay Mahapatra, 'Lack of a Law Saved Mohd Azharuddin, Ajay Jadeja', http://timesofindia.indiatimes.com/articleshow/20269079.cms, last accessed 20 May 2023.

9 Pradeep Magazine, 'Azharuddin and 4 Others Are Punished for Cricket Match Fixing: Former India Captain Banned', https://www.nytimes.com/2000/12/06/sports/IHT-azharuddin-and-4-others-are-punished-for-cricket-match-fixing.html, last accessed 20 May 2023.

10 'Sreesanth Gets Life Ban for IPL Fixing', https://www.espncricinfo.com/story/sreesanth-gets-life-ban-for-ipl-fixing-671043, last accessed 20 May 2023.

11 'IPL Spot-Fixing: MCOCA Made Out against Some Accused, Says Court', https://economictimes.indiatimes.com/news/politics-and-nation/ipl-spot-fixing-mcoca-made-out-against-some-accused-says-court/articleshow/22441069.cms, last accessed 20 May 2023.

12 *See*: 276th report of the Law Commission of India on Gambling and Sports Betting Including in Cricket in India.

Chapter 8: On Skill

1 See: *Dr. K.R. Lakshmanan v. State of Tamil Nadu*, (1996) 2 SCC 226.

2 1968 AIR 825.

3 (1996) 2 SCC 226.

4 2017 Cri LJ 3827.

5 (2019) 2 CWC 6.

6 *Dr. K.R. Lakshmanan v. State of Tamil Nadu*, (1996) 2 SCC 226.

Chapter 9: On Innovation

1 Robert M. Kunstadt,, 'Are Sports Moves Next in IP Law?', NAT'L L. J., 20 May 1996, at C1.

2 105 F.3d 841 (2d Cir. 1997).

3 (2014) 57 PTC 228.

4 Section 2(qq) of The Copyright Act, 1957.

Chapter 10: On Value

1 'More than Half the World Watched Record-Breaking 2018 World Cup', https://www.fifa.com/tournaments/mens/worldcup/2018russia/media-releases/more-than-half-the-world-watched-record-breaking-2018-world-cup, last accessed 25 May 2023.

Chapter 11: On Agreement

1 (2006) 4 SCC 227.
2 (2008) 2 Bom CR 654.
3 IA No. 12369 of 2009 in CS(OS) 1807/2009 (Delhi HC).
4 Miscellaneous First Appeal 7088/2013 (CPC) (Karnataka HC).
5 (2006) 3 Mad LJ 846.
6 'Ticket Term', https://www.iplt20.com/about/ticket-term?id=9, last accessed 10 June 2023.
7 'Major Match Ticket Refund Scheme', https://www.ecb.co.uk/news/117295, last accessed 10 June 2023.
8 'Cricket Australia Refund Policy', https://www.cricket.com.au/tickets, last accessed 10 June 2023.
9 'Windies Tickets Refund Policy', https://www.windiescricket.com/cwi-refund-policy/, last accessed 10 June 2023.

Chapter 12: On Competition

1 *Dhanraj Pillay v. Hockey India*, Case 73/2011, CCI (order dated 31 May 2013)/ [2013] CCI 35.
2 [1978] 1 WLR 302.
3 Case 73/2011, CCI (order dated 31 May 2013)/ [2013] CCI 35.
4 Case 61/2010, CCI (order dated 29 November 2017).
5 Case 91/2013.
6 Case 1/2019, CCI (order dated 7 August 2019).
7 Case 79/2011, CCI (order dated 12 July 2018).
8 Case 1/2015, CCI (order dated 12 July 2018)/ [2016] CCI 18.

Chapter 13: On Community

1 1995 AIR 1236.
2 *Dr. Subramanian Swamy v. Board of Control for Cricket in India*, W.P. (Civil) No.645/2017 in the Hon'ble Supreme Court of India.
3 (2006) 5 CompLJ 74 Mad.
4 2006 (32) PTC 235 (Del).
5 (2008) 38 PTC 47 (DB).
6 2012 (193) DLT 279.
7 FAO (OS) 460/2012.
8 HC Auckland CIV 2007-404-5674.
9 David Rowe, 'Watching Brief: Cultural Citizenship and Viewing Rights', *Sport in Society*, Vol. 7, No. 3, pp. 385–402; Jay Scherer and David Rowe (eds), *Sport, Public Service Media, and Cultural Citizenship*, Routledge, 2013.

Chapter 14: On Influence

1 Clause 2(a) of the BCCI Memorandum of Association registered in 2018.
2 ILR (2010) 4 Del 1.

Chapter 15: On Rights

1 *Henriques et al. v. IOC and IAAF*, CAS 2019/A/6225.
2 Article 3.6 and Article 11.1.1 of the Memorandum and Rules and Regulation of the Indian Olympic Association (as amended up to 2 November 2022).
3 Article 3.7 and Article 11.1.1 of the Memorandum and Rules and Regulation of the Indian Olympic Association (as amended up to 2 November 2022).
4 *S. Nithya v. The Secretary to the Union of India The Ministry of Youth Affairs and Sports*, Writ Petition No. 3447 of 2019 and WMP No. 3745 of 2019.
5 W.P.(C) 7359/2020 (Delhi High Court).

Chapter 16: On Individuality

1 160 DLT 277.
2 AIR 2017 SC 4161.
3 Wu Youyou, et al., 'Computer-Based Personality Judgments Are More Accurate than Those Made by Humans', https://doi.org/10.1073/pnas.1418680112.
4 (2019) 1 SCC 1.

Chapter 17: On Risk

1 Bryan Alary, 'Mixed Martial Arts Bloodier but Less Dangerous than Boxing', https://www.ualberta.ca/folio/2015/11/mixed-martial-arts-bloodier-but-less-dangerous-than-boxing.html, last accessed 15 May 2023.
2 *See*, for instance, *The Animal Welfare Board of India v. Union of India*, Writ Petition (Civil) No. 23 of 2016. In this case, a Constitution Bench of the Hon'ble Supreme Court of India upheld the validity of Tamil Nadu law permitting *jallikattu*, thereby overturning the Supreme Court's own decision in 2014 that had imposed a ban on the practice.
3 Association for Democratic Reforms, *Lok Sabha Elections 2019, Analysis of Criminal Background, Financial, Education, Gender and other details of Winners*, https://adrindia.org/download/file/fid/7994, last accessed 15 June 2023.

Chapter 18: On Justice

1 Mihir Bose, 'Azharuddin Confesses All', https://www.telegraph.co.uk/sport/cricket/4774886/Azharuddin-confesses-all.html, last accessed 15 May 2023.
2 2004 AIHC 1276.
3 *Gundel v. FEI*, CAS 92/A/63.
4 *Gundel v. FEI*, Arrêt du Tribunal Fédéral Suisse 4P_217/1992.
5 ECtHR, Applications Nos. 400575/10 and 67474/10, Judgment, 2 October 2018.

6 Grit Hartmann, 'Tipping the Scales of Justice—The Sport and Its "Supreme Court"', https://www.playthegame.org/publications/tipping-the-scales-of-justice-the-sport-and-its-supreme-court/, last accessed 26 June 2023.
7 2016 SCC OnLine Del 3660.
8 2004 AIHC 1276.
9 Nagraj Gollapudi, 'Mohammad Azharuddin Rings Eden Gardens Bell, Gautam Gambhir Calls It "Shocking"', https://www.espncricinfo.com/story/mohammad-azharuddin-rings-eden-gardens-bell-gautam-gambhir-calls-it-shocking-1164192, last accessed 15 June 2023.
10 'Stand to Be Named after Azhar', https://www.thehindu.com/sport/cricket/stand-to-be-named-after-azhar/article30108458.ece, last accessed 15 June 2023.
11 Paul Oommen, 'The Mess in Hyderabad Cricket Association: How Azharuddin Lost the Game', https://www.thenewsminute.com/article/mess-hyderbad-cricket-association-how-azharuddin-lost-game-173302, last accessed 15 June 2023.

Chapter 19: On Collaboration

1 VOCASPORT, 'Vocational Education and Training in the Field of Sport in the European Union: Situation, Trends and Outlook', https://educamp.coni.it/images/documenti/mercatolavoro/vocasport_en.pdf, last accessed 30 June 2023.
2 *See*, for instance, *Rahul Mehra v. Union of India and Ors.*, W.P.(C) 195/2010 (Delhi High Court).

Chapter 20: On Legacy

1 B. Flyvbjerg, et al., 'Regression to the Tail: Why the Olympics Blow Up', *Environment and Planning A: Economy and Space*, Volume 52, Issue 2, https://journals.sagepub.com/doi/10.1177/0308518X20958724, last accessed 5 July 2023, Alberto Cervantes, 'The Tokyo Olympics' Staggering Price Tag and Where It Stands in History', https://www.wsj.com/articles/

the-tokyo-olympics-staggering-price-tag-and-where-it-stands-in-history-11627049612, last accessed 5 July 2023.

2 J. Chappelet and T. Junod, 'A Tale of 3 Olympic Cities: What Can Turin Learn from the Olympic Legacy of Other Alpine Cities?' in D. Torres, (ed.), *Proceedings of Workshop on Major Sport Events as Opportunity for Development*, 14–16 June 2006, Valencia, Spain, pp. 83–90.

3 T. Kokolakakis, et al., 'Did London 2012 Deliver a Sports Participation Legacy?' https://shura.shu.ac.uk/20934/, last accessed 5 July 2023.

4 L.R. Potwarka and S. Leatherdale, 'The Vancouver 2010 Olympics and Leisure-Time Physical Activity Rates among Youth in Canada: Any Evidence of a Trickle-down Effect?' *Leisure Studies*, 35(3), pp. 241–57, http://doi.org/10.1080/02614367.2015.1040826, last accessed 5 July 2023.

5 World Health Organization, 'Physical Activity India 2022 Country Profile', https://www.who.int/publications/m/item/physical-activity-ind-2022-country-profile, last accessed 5 July 2023.

6 Avishek Roy, 'Fear Keeping the Next Sakshi, Vinesh off the Mat', *Hindustan Times*, 25 May 2023; Pritish Raj, 'Fear Creeps into Haryana's Akhadas as Wrestlers' Protest Drags On', https://thebridge.in/wrestling/haryana-akhadas-fear-wrestlers-protest-drags-42413, last accessed 5 July 2023; Sushil Manav, '"Girls Don't Come to Train Anymore"—in Haryana Hinterland, Anger Brews over Treatment of Wrestlers', https://theprint.in/india/girls-dont-come-to-train-anymore-in-haryana-hinterland-anger-brews-over-treatment-of-wrestlers/1616756/, last accessed 5 July 2023.

7 Vinayak Uppal, 'The Impact of the Commonwealth Games 2010 On Urban Development of Delhi— An Analysis with a Historical Perspective from Worldwide Experiences & 1982 Asian Games', https://ccs.in/sites/default/files/2022-10/Impact%20of%20Commonwealth%20Games%20on%20urban%20planning%20in%20Delhi.pdf, last accessed 10 July 2023.

Index

Scan QR code to access the Penguin Random House India website